Nelson A. Dunning

The Philosophy of Price

and its relation to domestic currency - Vol. 1

Nelson A. Dunning

The Philosophy of Price
and its relation to domestic currency - Vol. 1

ISBN/EAN: 9783337239220

Printed in Europe, USA, Canada, Australia, Japan

Cover: Foto ©Suzi / pixelio.de

More available books at **www.hansebooks.com**

THE

PHILOSOPHY OF PRICE,

AND ITS

RELATION TO DOMESTIC CURRENCY,

SECOND EDITION.

———

By N. A. DUNNING.

———

"Ill fares the land to hastening ills a prey,
Where wealth accumulates and men decay."—*Goldsmith.*

———

WASHINGTON, D. C.:
The National Economist Publishing Co.
1890.

CONTENTS.

CHAPTER I.

Price—What it Is, and how established; The theory of price; Value in use and value in exchange; Commercial value; Supply and demand; Overproduction; Ability to purchase; Conditions compared; Labor the sole producer of wealth; Visible and invisible capital; Products purchases money; How wages are reduced; Products of labor the ruling factor; Relations in exchange of money.

CHAPTER II.

Price and its Dependence upon Currency—The discovery of money; More money higher prices, less money lower prices; Money during the Dark Ages; Contrast between an abundance and want of currency; Effects of a decreasing currency; Worst effect upon labor; Conflict between labor and capital; The quantity of currency governs price; Unjust money system; Loss to the country

CHAPTER VII.

CONCLUSIONS.

APPENDIX.

PREFACE.

——o——

In attempting to place this volume before the public, an apology would perhaps be in order. While this may be true I am led to believe my excuse will sufficiently justify the act. At an early age I began the business of merchandising, which I have recently given up. From 1862 to 1885 I was continually engaged in selling dry goods, groceries, etc., over the counter to my fellow townspeople and farmers from the adjoining country. Upon going out of business I was surprised to find myself, though comparatively young, the oldest business man in our city—my business sign being the oldest in town. I have since had leisure to examine into the changes of the past twenty-three years, and am astonished at the result. But eight men, out of more than one hundred and eighty who had tried to accumulate property by going into mercantile and mechanical business, had made a success. And not a single manufacturing establishment had weathered the storm. In fact, the business ventures in our town of 2,000 inhabitants resulted about as follows: Every person who had engaged in the business of loaning money, no matter how small his beginnings, had made a success, while about ninety-five per cent. of all other business ventures had proved a failure. Beginning with this revelation I have carefully and diligently sought for the cause, and to my own satisfaction at least, I have succeeded in finding it. My experience is simply that of all others engaged in similar vocations. I used to buy large bills of goods, bring them home, sell them to my customers and have a margin of profit. I would give credit to those asking it, to a more or less extent. The loss from this source was but trifling. After a time, buy goods as cheap as I could, the decline in price during the year consumed my profits. Besides this, men whom I had for years trusted with goods, and had paid promptly, either asked for more time or failed to pay altogether. This continued until self-protection compelled me to curtail my business—buy much less goods and give but little credit. A general distrust took the place of confidence, so much so, that everyone asking credit was an object of suspicion. A sort of forced economy seemed to take possession of the people, which upon close inspection proved only an inability to purchase what they actually needed. A struggle for cheap goods, to sell cheap in order to meet the wants of the people, who for some unknown cause were not prospering in their business, took the place of regular trade, and with it legitimate merchandising ceased. Now, bankrupt stocks, auction stores and brokers' offices reign supreme in all branches of trade. During all these years, when values of all other forms of wealth have shrunk to such an alarming extent, *money* has continued steadily to increase in value, and now holds high carnival over all others. That this one branch out of all our vast and varied enterprises should thrive and all others wither and go down, is in my judgment a subject of profound importance. It calls for the most careful examination and the highest order of statesmanship. Labor, which is the architect of wealth in all its forms, calls loudly for justice and fair play. The innumerable business ventures of our people demand recognition of their right to survive. In fact, the continued preservation of our civilization, our high standard of morals, and our social and political equality, all conspire to direct attention to this ever increasing separation of values.

This volume, which I venture to place before the public, contains my ideas of the cause and its remedy. However much they may be at variance with others, I have endeavored to have them represent independence of thought and honesty of purpose.

I have received many suggestions of value, and many kind expressions predicting success, for which I am truly grateful.

To my esteemed friend, Milton Ryan Esq., I desire to acknowledge a debt of gratitude not easily repaid. He has, with characteristic unselfishness, aided me in every manner possible in the prosecution of this work. He has given me many valuable ideas and assisted in the development and completion of many intricate arguments and propositions, which

in a work of this kind must of necessity be thoroughly investigated.

A careful perusal of this volume will enable the reader, if
not convinced of the correctness of the propositions put forth,
to at least become conversant with the arguments in their favor.

N. A. D.

THE PHILOSOPHY OF PRICE

AND

ITS RELATION TO DOMESTIC CURRENCY.

——o——

CHAPTER I.

PRICE—WHAT IT IS, AND HOW ESTABLISHED.

In all ages past, the conditions of mankind, morally, socially and intellectually have been subject to changes, sometimes for better, but often for worse. Why these varied conditions exist, has led to much thought and consideration. Men, who have built for themselves enduring monuments, are those who have sought and been successful in discovering and pointing out ways and means by which the human family could make advancement toward the consummation of life's chief end—peace, happiness and prosperity. While attempting this, many theories have been put forward; some good, others bad, many impracticable, occasionally one sound enough to stand the test of centuries. Experience has performed an important part in this connection, and, while it has not, in all cases, selected that which was best, it has retained but a small portion of that which was bad. But, as civilization progresses, new questions are continually presenting themselves for solution. Sometimes they are old ideas coming up under different circumstances in new forms, and again the same proposition may remain unsolved for many years, yet, periodically claiming the attention of statesmen and scholars.

Most men have theories for all the actions of life, and those who know the least concerning the real truth are apt to advance a theory the most promptly. For this reason, nothing but a careful study of the subject will enable any person to even approximate conclusions toward the right.

The theory of price, what it is, how made, and the factors governing it, is no exception to this general rule. The more thought I have given this subject the more profoundly I am impressed with its importance. Notwithstanding this question has been under discussion for hundreds of years, it has assumed gigantic proportions in our own nation within a recent period. Without further remarks I will begin its consideration.

Adam Smith, the father of political economy, attempts to prove, in his great work, "The Cause of the Wealth of Nations," the idea of a double value, or, as he expresses it, "a value in use and a value in exchange." This proposition has been assailed by some of the ablest writers since that time, such as Mill, Senior and others. It has likewise been defended by some of the greatest minds the world has ever known. It is therefore now, as it has been in the past, a debatable question, and calls for careful, candid consideration before opinions with any degree of honesty or intelligence can be given.

Value is, without doubt, an essential element used in exchange, but I do not believe that exchange is an essential element in value. In my judgment there is a manifest difference between value in use and in exchange which should be fully examined. Value in use is the holder's value; value in exchange is the seller's value. A person may hold a thing, not in order to sell or exchange it, but in order to use it. Many things may possess value that are not exchangeable at all. If we limit value to things that are wholly exchangeable we shall exclude a large and very important class of commodities. A man may own an article which has no exchangeable value and at the same time place a very high value upon it himself, because he understands its use and can turn it to a profitable account. Many instances showing the truth of this proposition might be given. Prof. Syme says: "Value in use is the basis of all industrial activity. Without it there would be no production, and without production there could be no exchange. To limit value to exchange then, is to deprive economic science of the very foundation on which the whole superstructure rests." Mill and others say: "There are two elements to value —utility, and scarcity or difficulty of attainment." This can not be true, as these two elements cannot of themselves constitute value. There are many things, such as water, that may be useful, but at the same time have no value. Also an article may be exceedingly scarce and yet be valueless, neither difficulty of possession nor attainment, though combined with utility, will confer value. Water, however useful, and ever so scarce, as in the case of a traveler in a desert, does not have any value conferred upon it on that account, if the traveler does not want it. But if he wanted it,—if he was suffering for it—and if he believed it would satisfy his thirst, water would then be immediately invested with a value in his estimation which neither its acknowledged utility nor its inaccessibility or scarcity previously conferred.

Value in use is an absolute term. Value in exchange, commercial value, or price, is a relative term. The intrinsic value of a thing is what it is worth to me, if I keep it.

The price, or commercial value of a thing, on the other hand, is what some one else will give me for it. The price of a thing is what it will bring in the market; and while there is only one price, there are always several values. A price can only be arrived at when two or more values coincide, or when the estimate put upon an article by a seller agrees with the estimate put upon it by a buyer. Not only do individuals differ in their ideas of commercial value (as I shall call it), but they have different methods of arriving at them. The commercial value of an article is always ascertained by a comparison of individual values. Each party to an exchange demands a certain amount. If the demands are equal, the price will be made and the exchange will be effected. If the demands are unequal, no price will be established and consequently no exchange will take place, unless the demands of the one rise or fall to the demands of the other. The price of any article, therefore, is simply its commercial value. Almost everything, at the present time, and, as the arts and sciences are advanced, everything, no doubt, will have two values—commercial value or price, intrinsic value or worth. The first always fluctuates, the latter never. The first depends entirely upon the conditions surrounding it; the latter remains the same under all circumstances. The iron girders which span the stream are not changed in their intrinsic value by their use, no matter if their commercial value varies from five to fifty cents per pound. This being true, price, then, is the result of commerce, trade or business. It is purely a commercial phrase, and obtains recognition in the language of the world by its connection with traffic or exchange. We inquire the price of wheat to-day, and are informed it is worth one dollar per bushel. This is the commercial value placed upon that product from the present understanding of the situation it occupies. To-morrow it may be higher or lower, according to a better knowledge of all the facts relating to it; but during this fluctuation it requires only the same quantity to relieve hunger or sustain animal life.

That price is commercial value, and that commercial values are always changing, I conclude are facts beyond question. But when we enter upon an investigation of the causes for this difference in price, why it is less or more at some times than at others, we pass into a field almost limitless in extent, which shows signs of constant travel by the most profound thinkers of all ages past. For this reason we are met at the commencement with innumerable theories and speculations. Some writers have treated the subject as a matter of but trifling importance, while others have written volumes upon it. Political economists have sought to make it plain, but, in my judgment, have utterly failed. There seems to be no advancement beyond the old ideas of one hundred years ago.

While the world is making rapid strides in all other arts and sciences, why should it not in that art or science—no matter which it is called—that treats of the desired end of all labor, the accumulation and enjoyment of wealth?

When people come to understand that political economy treats of the most common and ordinary affairs of life—the business relations of men to each other—that these relations are viewed from different standpoints, they will learn to look upon that science with less awe, and believe writers upon that subject less infallible.

In the early ages of our race there were no commercial relations, no exchanges, and consequently no commercial value or price. The intrinsic value of food and raiment was alone considered. Soon, however, trade, barter or exchange came into use among the different families and tribes. The products of one tribe were exchanged for those of another. Then the idea of a price, or commercial value, began to obtain and has continued to the present time.

To ascertain what makes that price, what constitutes the commercial value of the products of labor, is the subject of this chapter.

Many writers have settled down to the theory that supply and demand wholly establish the price; that with a surplus of products prices always decline, and with a scarcity always advance. This theory has come to be almost the only recognized explanation of this question. It has been adopted by many able writers, and quoted as true by both statesmen and scholars. This is a dangerous doctrine, and from it emanates many destructive theories. This dogma of supply and demand can, with propriety, be placed beside Ricardo's theory of rent or the Malthusian theory of the population of the earth. Each has some foundation in fact, but when arguments are brought to bear upon them, the superstructure is quickly ascertained to be much larger than the foundation, and other theories must be manufactured and put forward to make up the necessary supports. The theory of supply and demand will not admit of want and hunger amidst plenty and low prices. It cannot explain the stubborn fact of pauperism and distress during an era of great abundance and cheap commercial values. The signs of the times and the hard experiences of daily life are a direct refutation of its soundness.

It is claimed that overproduction is the prime cause of all this difficulty, or in other words, that the people are suffering from the effects of a surplus of success, or from the evils of a reckless and persistent industry. For, if the term "overproduction" means anything, it is that our business enterprises have been too successful; that the economic laws governing our people are too perfect and our inventive genius too prolific of good results; that the nation has been so prosperous and so fortunate in its undertakings that the present hard times have been brought upon us in consequence. Here is an argument where too great a victory brings defeat, too much happiness brings distress and misery. Let us examine the subject in that light. Does an overproduction of wheat and beef cause my neighbor to go hungry? Is an abundant supply of clothing the cause of his being ragged; or of boots and shoes the cause of his going barefoot? Is yonder supply of wood and coal a reason for his being half frozen with wintry winds? Certainly not. In all these cases the supply is abundant, and the demand most urgent, yet the supply is not lessened nor the demand satisfied. Why? Because there is a want of ability to purchase. It is plain that there can be no real overproduction unless a large surplus remains after all the people have been fully supplied with the necessaries and comforts of life. The public cannot overtrade by distributing each year's productions among those who really need them to use. Too high prices cannot be paid for labor, unless the laborers in general actually gain more than their equitable share of the year's productions. Neither can there be an overstock of laborers so long as thousands are suffering for want of the very articles these laborers would gladly produce, if they could be employed. There cannot be too many houses, when they would be filled with tenants able to pay the rent if work could be obtained. We must look, therefore, for the real cause of these calamities, not in overproduction, but in the power that governs the distribution of the products. It does not matter how urgent the demand or abundant the supply, there must be some ability to purchase, or the demand is not satisfied. How, then, can it be truthfully said that supply and demand are the sole arbiters of price?

John Stuart Mill discusses the question at greater length, but with the same conclusion. He says:

"The argument against the possibility of general overproduction is quite conclusive, so far as it applies to the doctrine that a country may accumulate capital too fast; that produce in general may be increasing faster than the demand for it, reducing all persons to distress. This proposition, strange to say, was almost a received doctrine so late as thirty years ago."

There can be no price without a purchaser; no purchaser without the necessary ability to purchase. Therefore it must follow that the ability to purchase, in all cases, absolutely establishes the commercial value or price. There may be isolated instances of an unexpected demand, or an unlooked for scarcity, which will initiate a competition among buyers, yet the wealth of the purchasers determines the limit beyond which prices cannot be driven. On the other hand, an abundant supply

may tend to lower the price of a commodity; but the wealth of
the people, the ability to hold and not sell, or to buy and hold,
determines completely and finally how low the price shall go—
acting at all times as a check and safeguard. Let me illustrate
this point—that supply and demand do not make the price.
Mr. A has a good dinner to sell. Mr. B is hungry. Mr. A
has the supply, and Mr. B has the demand. In this case what
establishes the price of the dinner; its original cost to Mr. A,
or Mr. B's hungry stomach? Neither. The commercial value
is finally and fully fixed by the contents of Mr. B's pocket-
book. It should always be remembered that price knows no
original cost. No matter how much a bushel of wheat costs in
production, its commercial value is made without any regard to
it. The idea that cost of production enters into price is all
wrong. Price is what it will sell for and nothing else. A
man may consume a lifetime in making a machine, or something else, perhaps of value to mankind, and when completed
cannot dispose of it for a single dollar. Mr. A may want fifty
cents for his dinner—it may have cost that much or more—but
if Mr. B has but twenty-five cents, the dinner must be sold for
that or remain unsold, and consequently without price, because
a thing that cannot be exchanged has no commercial value or
price. If supply and demand were the only factors in price,
legislation might, to a large extent, regulate not only the price
of the products of labor, but of labor itself. It could say to
the farmer: You shall raise but a certain amount of grain;
and to the laborer: You shall do but so many days' work. No
greater calamity could befall a civilized nation. It would put
an end to all progress or advancement, and destroy all intelligence and just emulation. But fortunately this is not the case,
as the laws governing this question are of a social nature, and
seem to rest on the prosperity and happiness of the whole people, and point with the finger of prophecy to one universal
republic governed and controlled by wise and generous regula-

tions, which aim at making the people equal in all respects before just laws.

No nation is, or can be, happy or prosperous with low prices. They operate as a gradually increasing weight in the great race of life; and those who are the most in want usually carry the heaviest burdens.

The condition of every nation is gauged, as regards advancement and social privileges, not by the *cheapness* of its products, but by their higher commercial values. The people who place the highest value on their labor and its products are the most enlightened, prosperous, and consequently the happiest. To prove this, I refer to the cheap wheat of Russia and India; the cheap rice of China and Japan; the cheap cotton of India and Egypt, and the cheaper wools of the South American states. Compare the countries named with our own, or with France, England and Germany. These comparisons will prove my assertions true. This proposition is a strong argument against unrestricted commerce, as the poorest and most degraded nations can and do sell their products the cheapest, thereby compelling other nations, in their industrial pursuits, to sink down to a common level or not sell their products. For it is a well established fact that the products of each nation represent its civilization, and its social, intellectual and religious standing. And, as the products of labor constitute the germ and extend the growth of national prosperity, they necessarily pay for all things beneficial to mankind in the form of direct and indirect taxation. Therefore it follows that the products of nations differ in cost of production in proportion to their different degrees of intelligence and social position. In commercial transactions, men buy where they can buy cheapest; consequently the products of the half savage are taken in preference to those put upon the market by more civilized nations, thereby forcing civilization out of the markets of the world and leaving its products unsold and without price.

With this view of the question, price assumes a more prominent position than many have supposed—a position that makes it the arbiter of our joys and our woes, our intelligence or degradation. How important, therefore, is a careful and candid consideration of the subject, to the end that we may all be benefited, by ascertaining, if possible, the different factors that enter into its composition.

Since *ability* to purchase makes the price, and that commercial values are an important factor in the success or failure of this life, let us inquire:

1. What this ability to purchase is.
2. From what causes or sources it originates.
3. How it is obtained.

In answer to the first inquiry: Ability to purchase or possess is ability to labor and accumulate the products of labor, called wealth.

In answer to the second inquiry: It comes from the brain and brawn of the toiling millions, and is that part of invisible capital called labor, the architect of all wealth.

In answer to the third inquiry: The ability to purchase or possess is obtained by physical and mental labor alone.

No matter how much political economists differ on other subjects, they all agree that labor is the sole producer of wealth. This one fact alone ought to place labor in a position where it would receive the recognition and respect which it so justly deserves. Instead of this it stands on the lowest round of the social ladder with every social advantage above it, seeking to prevent its climbing higher. While this is an admitted wrong to labor which calls loudly for justice and fair play, its condition is not bettered nor are its wrongs righted.

We see, all about us, evidences of wealth, such as houses, farms, factories, railroads, shops, etc., etc. These were not stolen; neither are they the spoils of war, nor the result of fraud and knavery. We find by tracing back the history of each that at the ultimate stands bare-handed labor ; that labor and that alone was the prime first cause—the fiat of it all.   Then I ask: Why should the created dictate to the creator?   Why should the accumulated products of labor be placed at all times and under all circumstances above and before labor itself?

Wealth is divided into two classes—visible and invisible. The former consists of money, houses, merchandise, etc.   The latter, of physical or mental exertion, stored up by nature in the human body as a means of self-preservation.   The last being the creator of the first, as all visible wealth is the production of the invisible.

Some may ask how this is accomplished—how these, almost, self-evident truths could remain undiscovered all these years under the light of modern civilization—why have we not thought of them before?   I answer : Because as a people, characteristically, we are not inclined to search for causes, but are constantly looking for results or effects.   Men gather riches; nations become wealthy.   These facts are plain, yet but very few ever take the trouble to examine into the cause.   We see a new country to-day, almost an unbroken forest, perhaps, with here and there scattered through it a few hardy pioneers. Years afterwards the wilderness has disappeared.   In its place we find great cities, pleasant villages, splendid farms, costly churches, schools, and all the numerous adjuncts of civilization. Where did they come from?   How came they here?   The change seems impossible, miraculous; yet all this is the rich, ripe fruit of labor, of honest toil.

We might, perhaps with profit, notice how this change was brought about.   It should be well understood as it has been man's chief employment from the days of Adam.

Mr. A comes to this locality with his family, and, as is the usual custom, builds a log house and goes to work, clearing up his land.   He clears off a small piece of land and plants it to crops.   While they are growing he makes more improvements. His products the first year perhaps feed and clothe himself and family. Those of the second year leave him a surplus. At this time Mr. B makes his appearance with neither shelter nor food, but is able and willing to work. Mr. A contracts with Mr. B at once to exchange some of his visible capital, such as corn, wheat, and a shelter, for some of Mr. B's invisible capital called labor. Then there are two at work. Soon Mr. B has exchanged more of his invisible capital than he has consumed of visible, and finds himself the possessor of visible capital. With this he starts out for himself; and in like manner others come, and make a start in life, the result being that soon the once dense forest is made to blossom with evidences of visible wealth in every direction—all brought about by that one agency—labor.

Again, we find Mr. A with ten dollars in money, Mr. B with ten bushels of wheat, Mr. C with neither money nor wheat and a family to support. Mr. C wants bread to supply his family. How is he to obtain it? Let us examine. Mr. A wants some wood cut for market. Mr. C engages to prepare the wood, that is, he sells Mr. A ten dollars' worth of his invisible capital. When the labor is performed, or when Mr. A has received ten dollars' worth of invisible capital from Mr. C in the shape of a certain number of cords of wood, he remunerates Mr. C with ten dollars in cash. This ten dollars Mr. C pays to Mr. B for his ten bushels of wheat which Mr. C's family at once begin to consume. Mr. A, by this transaction, is wealthier by the profit on his wood, and Mr. B by the profit on his wheat; and the nation at large is wealthier by the aggregate of both. This process of accumulating wealth has been going on during the history of the world, and yet, but comparatively few persons either care about, or know, the conditions and circumstances surrounding these ever present and every day proceedings.

From the above conclusions we can clearly draw the inference that the more Mr. A pays Mr. C for his labor, the more Mr. C can pay Mr. B for his wheat; and the more Mr. B receives for his wheat, the more he can expend for clothing, groceries, farming tools, etc., etc. Here again we are reminded of the prominent position that price occupies in all the commercial transactions of life. We notice that the price of one article—labor—governs all other prices, in the normal condition of trade, that the products of that labor come in direct contact with. It determines the price of B's wheat, and the price of his wheat determines the price of all his purchases. The necessity of having a fair price, and to begin in the right place, is not only just, but important to the general welfare of mankind. That place is with labor. When labor brings a good price, everything else does. But when labor is poorly and grudgingly paid, dull times overtake us and all business drags. Upon this point rest several propositions of vital importance to every individual and nation:

1. The degradation of every nation is measured accurately by the amount of the products of its labor given in exchange for a dollar, or unit of their currency. The poorest, meanest, most servile and abject nation and people, always have, and always will, barter the greatest amount of their products for a dollar.

2. The civilization, grandeur, position and social status of every nation is gauged absolutely by the amount of the necessities and comforts of life that a day's labor will purchase for its people.

I bring as proof of these assertions the wages received and position occupied by the people of every nation on earth. These propositions are too plain to be disputed. Compare the low wages of India, Egypt, China and many other countries that might be mentioned, with the wages paid for labor in the United States, England, France, Germany and other like countries, and then note the difference of their standing among the nations of the world. The proof is absolute and positive. Here, again, we find that labor is the prime factor in bringing about the best interests of the human family. Its only terms for such service is being well paid—that is, justly compensated.

In my judgment, the greatest error into which the commercial world has fallen—and that error seems to have made way for many others—is, that money buys or purchases products. This cannot be true. A little candid consideration of the question will demonstrate at once that products always buy or purchase money. The child who sold his pennies for candy was much nearer the truth in his ideas than his father who bought his coat with cash. This point is of the utmost importance in the discussion of the question of price. There may be those who will not admit the correctness of this proposition because it is an innovation and somewhat novel; besides it demolishes at once many oft quoted and long cherished theories.

Let us take the example of the farmer, and inquire why he raises wheat. His object is, first to feed his own family, and then with the surplus he purchases money. Bear in mind we are not discussing barter, but commercial transactions where money is a factor. Now, if he uses some of this money to pay his debts, he is simply making a delivery of what he had sold and agreed to deliver some time previous. If he wishes to "purchase" a wagon, for instance, as the phrase goes (wrong nevertheless), what factors enter into that transaction?

The wagon-maker has made (produced) a wagon to purchase some money with, and he buys as much money of the farmer as he can for the wagon. A bargain, bear in mind, is the result of a mutual understanding between two or more persons.

The farmer goes into the market with his money to sell for a wagon. The person who will pay him the most for his money, that is, sell him a wagon "the cheapest," as the term is used, will purchase his money. The wagon-maker pays, or sells this same money to his workmen who had already paid for it with labor by manufacturing the wagon. Here we have traced money from one producer to another, and find it does not purchase at all, and in its legitimate use has no purchasing power, as it is a creation of law, and not in the true sense a product of labor. Money never goes in advance. Labor takes the lead, money follows. It is the incentive for all production. Destroy the fact that production will buy money, and to a large extent all surplus production will cease.

There is always an obligation preceding the payment of money. That obligation is either labor or its products, or the stipulated payment at some future time of one or both. As before stated, money has no purchasing power ; its one function is to pay debts. It only levels up the difference in bargains. Neither can money be bartered for money, because it has only the one function. But products can be, and often are, bartered for each other, both parties to the transaction being benefited. Here we see products exercising purchasing functions independent and exclusive of money. But on the other hand, money cannot perform its functions without the aid of products. Nor does capital employ labor. Labor employs capital always, but does not employ money. It only employs some previous product of labor. Money can be utilized only by the laborer, in his vocation, as a medium to obtain some product of labor that he desires to use. Can a man cut down a tree with a five dollar bill? He will first sell enough of his money to obtain an axe, and with that product of labor cut down the tree. Capital employs labor? Never. Capital is only sold for labor. That is the true and only sense in which it can be used. This explains why so much money is idle in dull times. Men who have money part with it for labor. In time they buy money with the products of that labor. When such products will not purchase more money than was sold to purchase the labor in the first place, there is a loss. When they will bring more, there is a gain.

Wages are reduced by men going into the market to sell money for labor. Those who will pay the highest price for the money, that is, give the greatest amount of labor for it, are sure to get it. Hence, the strife among laborers to buy money brings down the price of their own efforts.

If it were true that money employs labor, then, with all the money hoarded, labor would of necessity cease.

The fact is, a desire to possess money in order to gratify some other desire in its disposal is the main incentive to labor. This incentive includes the natural disposition of mankind to use all his faculties to sustain life.

We are accustomed to say that money is invested in property, but this is not true. Money is no more invested in property than the yard-stick is invested in the cloth that it measures. When money has passed from one person to another, either as a loan or in payment of property, it is ready to be lent again or to be paid for another piece of property. The money is no more used up by passing from one person to another than the yard-stick is used up by measuring a single piece of cloth. We are often told, in the money articles of daily newspapers, that the money of the country has been used up in railroads; but upon traveling over these roads we see evidences that a great deal of *labor* has been expended in grading them, furnishing the iron and timber and so forth, but we do not see any money. If the money has been invested in these roads, it has now gone somewhere else; and it is still going to and fro in the earth, and up and down it.

How true this is, and yet how few ever think of it in this light. In one breath we hear men say: "Times are hard because the money has been sunk in speculation," and "there is just as much money as ever in the country if it could be found."

This places the products of labor as the ruling factor or

sole purchaser. And when products are cheap it means that money is dear, and when products are dear, that money is cheap. Money is inert matter. Men gather it together and there it remains until some one wants it, and then it is bought, either with an obligation or with labor and its products. When we take this view of commercial relations, many of the most intricate phases of business are made plain. We can then discover the hidden sources from which financial depression, low prices, and labor strikes emanate; and can also catch a glimpse of those fountains from which streams of plenty and prosperity flow.

This proposition clearly shows us where and how to look for the true solution of price. It enables us to examine intelligently one of the most intricate subjects of economic science. That products purchase money I believe is a sound doctrine, and one that will be accepted by all writers and thinkers in the near future.

In looking in upon our social and business relations, we cannot fail to see the prominent position occupied by price. It is brought to our attention from almost every direction, and by the careful study of almost every subject pertaining to economic science; in fact, upon it depends, to a more or less degree, our social, religious and commercial standing. One of old said : "Price is the dictator of civilization."

Price, then, is the value put upon labor by the accumulated products of labor—the recompense given to invisible capital by visible capital. It is the war cry that gathers the army of capital on one side and labor on the other, keeping them in almost perpetual strife. Without it the world would relapse into barbarism, and the nations of the earth would vanish. Intelligence, civilization and human progress would cease forever. Price always should be the cost of well-paid labor in production, with reasonable profits for commercial exchange. But that is not the case; it is established by conditions entirely foreign and in no wise related to the cost of production.

A recent writer sums it all up in the following:

"The existing financial policy of the world is the same as that which in all ages has given the power of distributing the products of industry to non-producers; so that while the great bulk of all burdens, of all miscarriages, of all follies and (fiscal) crimes by government and non-producing classes fall upon the industrious producers, no just share of the distribution has ever been made to them; on the contrary, the greater the profits from the distribution of productions the greater is the contrast in the division between non-producing distributors and the producing industries; the non-producers take to themselves so inordinate a proportion that the gap or contrast between the condition of distributors and producers in times of prosperity, or seeming prosperity, continually widens; the prodigious and augmenting wealth of the non-producers and the everlasting subjection of the producers to the most moderate and often precarious supplies of necessaries.

The producing classes, the authors and architects of all wealth, have never in any age been allowed the distribution of their own earnings, of the productions of their industry; nor in its distribution by non-producers have they been allowed a just share.

It has been this "creature" money which has controlled the world; this creature of the law is the sinew of war; it upraises and oversets kingdoms, empires and republics, as in time of peace it dominates despotically over productive industries; whosoever commands a man's purse, generally commands him. That such is the power of money, of fiscal legislation, is a truth, known to all men."

But again, it is also true that the ability to purchase depends entirely upon price. They are dependent upon each other. When prices are high it shows that the ability to purchase is increasing. When the ability to purchase is impaired, it indicates lower prices; while the measure of ability to purchase makes prices higher or lower, the high or low price clearly shows the degree of ability to purchase. We see from this the sources from which come this ability to purchase. This denominator of prices, this motive power of all industrial.

action, upon which the hopes and fears of all nations are placed, should be sought out, carefully nourished and con- stantly strengthened. While the accumulation of wealth enters into this question, the distribution of wealth is the overshad- owing factor. The proper distribution of wealth will solve this great problem of price. Nothing else will. When labor and capital each has its just due—when one cannot dictate to the other—then will the idea of price be fairly and fully appreciated. Further; price, in other words, is the expression in money terms of the relation which the unit of money bears to a specified quantity, or to the unit of each and every other thing in exchange. It is also the expression in units of prop- erty and services of the value of the unit of money, and with- out having any influence on the relations, is the sure indicator of the exchange relations which the units of all other things bear to each other. Market-price is the expression in the units of money of an equilibrium between the correlative demands of buyer and seller. It is, in fact, generally established through a competition between sellers, rather than buyers; the market- price of any article being the smallest quantity of money for which the unit of such an article is offered for sale in open market. By the word unit, when applied to money, is intended that denomination in which accounts are kept, and in which judgments are rendered for money, as the dollar in this country and the pound sterling in England. By the same word, as applied to commodities, is intended that specific portion or quantity by multiples or fractions of which all quantities are accustomed to be described, as a ton for coal, or a yard for cloth. The relations in exchange of all other things than money are not at all affected by the volume of money, or by its increase or decrease. Nor do changes in the volume of money practically affect a transaction wherein a seller of prop- erty makes immediate purchase of other property with the pro- ceeds of such sale. Exchange by barter can be as equitably effected under one volume of money, and under one range of prices, as another. But under a credit system, where contracts aggregating a vast amount, to pay money at future periods, have been made, steadiness in prices becomes the all-important consideration, and that steadiness depends on the steadiness in the quantitative relation between money and all other things. The performance of contracts to deliver commodities or render services is not made either less or more difficult by an increase or decrease in the volume of money. But nearly all contracts in the commercial world are for the future delivery of money, and the consideration received and the promise made in such contracts are based on existing prices. The command, therefore, which commodities and services may have over money in the future, and which will find its expression in price, becomes a matter of vital importance.

Whenever under any firmly-established government a system of money has been generally accepted, the value of each unit of such money becomes a general mental conception, which, if it be what is called a value, or metallic money, is not based on the past or probable future cost of producing the material of which it is composed, nor on the average cost of its production, nor on the cost of its production in either the most or least prolific mine. Nor, if it be what is called credit-money, having full legal-tender functions, is that portion of it which is unhoarded and in circulation and performing the functions of money, based upon the present value of the promise of the issuer to redeem it, nor upon the proximity or remoteness of such redemption.

Under firmly-established systems the value of each unit of either metallic or paper money depends absolutely upon the number of such units and the relation they bear to the services they are required to perform.

It is the limitation of the quantity of money without reference to its cost of production that regulates the value of each unit of money, whether it be paper or meta..ic. In the instance of paper money, limitation is imposed by law; in that of metallic money it is imposed by nature. The effect in each case is precisely the same. In the one this limitation is regulated by the wisdom and judgment of men; in the other by the numerous obstacles which nature throws in the way of production. The value of money, of whatever kind, is measured by the cost of obtaining it *after* it has been produced, and not by the expense of its production; and this value is correctly indicated by the general range of prices. Hence the truth of this proposition: Price is commercial value and is fully established by the ability of the people to purchase, and that ability is greater or less as the volume of currency is increased or decreased.

CHAPTER II.

PRICE AND ITS DEPENDENCE UPON CURRENCY.

The proposition sought to be made plain and substantiated beyond contradiction in this chapter is, that price, or commercial value, depends entirely—excepting in cases of a sudden demand or an unexpected deficiency—upon the amount of circulating medium in the country where the price is established; this circulating medium always controlling the ability to purchase. That with an increase of currency prices advance, while with a decrease they fall. That this has been true in ages past I will call economic history to verify. That it is proving true at the present time I will bring our own condition as a nation to testify.

The volume of currency indicates the purchasable quantity which can be distributed for labor and its products. The greater that amount, the more can be distributed; the less that amount, the less can be distributed. Money, or currency, is a medium of exchange, and also a measure of value for the purpose of exchange. These were the original and primitive functions of money; and anything that by common consent performs these functions was and is money. The age has passed when kings rule by divine right; also the time has gone by when any particular creation of Deity is recognized as the only material out of which money can be made. Money has come to be known as purely a creation of law; that the fiat or command which clothes it with these functions is simply the recognized sovereignty of government; that the material out of which it is made is commodity, and only valued as such. In tracing this back we find *barter*, an exchange between individuals and tribes. As barter increased, the necessity for something to make up the difference in labor value between articles exchanged became apparent. Necessity compelled it, and, as has been the custom of mankind, it was found. Various expedients were resorted to—skins of beasts, shells, cattle, iron, porcelain, copper, brass, silver and gold, all have had their turn; but in each and every case the commercial value of all products was given as a certain multiple or division of the unit of whatever was used as money. For example, in this country the commercial value of articles is reckoned either as multiples or divisions of the dollar; in England, the same with the pound sterling; in France, with the franc. But, in all these the business or barter had been conducted, as regards buying and selling, by common consent. But human progress ascertained in the course of time that this money should have another function, a debt paying power. This was given it by law.

Now we consider money in our business transactions as a legal tender for the payment of debts. This legal tender function is given it by law; consequently money, as used to-day, is simply and only the creation of law, as I stated before.

Money has no purchasing power, but when once the bargain is consummated money steps in and liquidates the debt.

If money had purchasing power it would be simply confiscation, as it would then have the functions both to possess and remunerate. This has been wisely withheld. Legal tender money being the creation of law, it therefore follows that the same power giving it its legal tender properties can designate its shape, form, and consistency.

Here we meet with various theories, some wild, others reasonable, all honest. Some would confine the unit of currency to a certain quantity of gold and silver. Others would use copper, iron, or brass; again, others would use the faith and integrity of the nation stamped upon paper. There may be objections to all these, but in my judgment the last is by far the most preferable.

No matter what this medium of exchange is, no matter what the fiat or authority of law determines is money, the great question after all is its quantity.

The truth is, the most enormous power known to man, or that ever can be his, lies in money—in the increase and decrease of its quantity. It is the tide of human affairs upon which all things must rise or sink. It is inevitable and cannot be resisted. This power has been obtained through the carelessness of the people, who have been and are now held in ignorance for that very purpose. So early as 1557 we find the keen and piercing intellect of Bodin saying the following:

"For men have so well obscured the *facts* about money that the great part of the people do not see them *at all*. The money-ers do as the doctors do, who talk Latin before women, and use Greek characters, Arab words, and Latin abbreviations, *fearing* that if the *people* understood their receipts they would not have much opinion of them."

What was true then is practised now. Take the financial reports of Congress; there is not one person in a hundred who can read them understandingly. They are written so purposely; that the people may become disgusted and disheartened trying to decipher them, conclude the subject is too deep for their intellect, and leave it for others to interpret. This is exactly the end sought and will continually bring distress upon the nation. If the plain people of the country could have these questions fully and simply explained, there would be many vacant seats soon among our present law-makers.

Whenever prices have become adjusted to a given amount of currency, an increase of that amount, other things remaining unchanged, will cause a rise, and decrease will cause a fall, in prices. But under such conditions other things never do remain unchanged. There are powerful causes, moral and material, which invariably operate, when money is increasing in volume, to moderate the rise in prices, and to intensify their fall when it is decreasing. Hence, the fall in prices caused by a decreasing volume of money would be much greater in degree than would be the rise caused by a proportionately increasing volume.

Whenever it becomes apparent that prices are rising and money falling in value in consequence of an increase of its volume, the greatest activity takes place in exchanges and productive enterprises. Everyone becomes anxious to share in the advantages of rising markets. The inducement to hoard money is taken away, and consequently the disposition to hoard it ceases. Its circulation becomes exceedingly active, and for the very plain reason that there could be no motive for holding or hoarding money when it is falling in value, while there would be the strongest possible motive for exchanging it for property, or the labor which creates property, when prices are rising. Under these circumstances labor comes into great demand and at remunerative wages. This results in not only increased production, but increased consumption, as the wants and expenditures of laborers increase with their earnings.

I quote the following from the report of the silver commission appointed in 1876:

"At the Christian era the metallic money of the Roman Empire amounted to $1,800,000,000. By the end of the fifteenth century it had shrunk to less than $200,000,000. During this period a most extraordinary and baleful change took place in the condition of the world.

Population dwindled and commerce, arts, wealth, and freedom, all disappeared. The people were reduced by poverty and misery to the most degraded conditions of serfdom and slavery. The disintegration of society was almost complete. The conditions of life were so hard that individual selfishness was the only thing consistent with the instinct of self-preservation. All public spirit, all generous emotions, all the noble aspirations of man, shriveled and disappeared as the volume of money shrunk and prices fell.

History records no such disastrous transition as that from the Roman Empire to the Dark Ages. Various explanations have been given of this entire breaking down of the framework of society, but it was certainly coincident with a shrinkage in the volume of money, which was also without historical parallel. The crumbling of institutions kept even step and pace with the shrinkage in the stock of money and the falling of prices. All other attendant circumstances than these last have occurred in other historical periods unaccompanied and unfollowed by any such mighty disasters. It is a suggestive coincidence that the first glimmer of light only came with the invention of bills of exchange and paper substitutes, through which the scanty stock of the precious metals was increased in efficiency. But not less than the energizing influence of Potosi and all the argosies of treasure from the New World were needed to arouse the Old World from its comatose sleep, to quicken the torpid limbs of industry, and to plume the leaden wings of commerce. It needed the heroic treatment of rising prices to enable society to reunite its shattered links, to shake off the shackles of feudalism, to relight and uplift the almost extinguished torch of civilization. That the disasters of the Dark Ages were caused by decreasing money and falling prices, and that the recovery therefrom and the comparative prosperity which followed the discovery of America were due to an increasing supply of the precious metals and rising prices, will not seem surprising or unreasonable when the noble functions of money are considered.

Money is the great instrument of association, the very fiber of social organism, the vitalizing force of industry, the protoplasm of civilization, and as essential to its existence as oxygen is to animal life. Without money civilization could not have had a beginning; with a diminishing supply it must languish, and, unless relieved, finally perish.

Symptoms of disasters similar to those which befell society during the Dark Ages were observable on every hand during the first half of the century. In 1809 the revolutionary troubles between Spain and her American colonies broke out. These troubles resulted in a great diminution in the production of the precious metals, which was quickly indicated by a fall in general prices. As already stated in this report, it is estimated that the purchasing power of the precious metals increased between 1809 and 1848 fully 145 per cent., or, in other words, that the general range of prices was 60 per cent. lower in 1848 than it was in 1809. During this period there was no general demonetization of either metal and no important fluctuation in the relative value of the metals, and the supply was sufficient to keep their stock good against losses by accident and abrasion. But it was insufficient to keep the stock up to the proper correspondence with the increasing demand of advancing populations. The world has rarely passed through a more gloomy period than this one. Again do we find falling prices and misery and destitution inseparable companions. The poverty and distress of the industrial masses were intense and universal, and since the discovery of the mines of America, without a parallel. In England the sufferings of the people found expression in demand upon Parliament for relief, in bread-riots and in immense Chartist demonstrations. The military arm of the nation had to be strengthened to prevent the all-prevading discontent from ripening into open revolt. On the Continent the fires of revolution smoldered everywhere and blazed out at many points, threatening the overthrow of States and the subversion of social institutions. Whenever and wherever the mutterings of discontent were hushed by the fear of increased standing armies, the foundations of society were honey-combed by powerful secret political associations. The cause at work to produce this state of things was so subtle, and its advance so silent, that the masses were entirely ignorant of its nature. They had come to regard money as an institution fixed and immovable in value, and when the price of property and the wages of labor fell, they charged the fault, not to the money, but to the property and the employer. They were taught that the mischief was the result of overproduction. Never having observed that overproduction was complained of only when the money stock was decreasing their prejudices were aroused against labor-saving machinery. They were angered at capital, because it either declined altogether to embark in industrial enterprises or would only embark in them upon the condition of employing labor at the most scanty remuneration. They forgot that falling prices compelled capital to avoid such enterprises on any other condition, and for the most part to avoid them entirely. They did not comprehend that money in shrinking volume was the prolific parent of enforced idleness and poverty, and that falling prices divorced money, capital, and labor, but they none the less felt the paralyzing pressure of the shrinking metallic shroud that was closing around industry.

The increased yield of the Russian gold-fields in 1846 gave some relief, and served as a parachute to the fall in prices, which might otherwise have resulted in a great catastrophe. But the enormous supplies of gold from California and Australia were all needed to give substantial and adequate relief. Great as these supplies were, their influence in raising prices was moderated and soon entirely arrested by the increasing populations and commerce which followed them. In the twenty-five years between 1850 and 1876 the money stock of the world was more than doubled, and yet, at no time during this period was the general level of prices raised more than 18 per cent. above the general level in 1848. A comparison of this effect of an increasing volume of money after 1848 with the effect of a decreasing volume between 1809 and 1848 strikingly illustrates how largely different in degree is the influence upon prices of an increasing or decreasing volume of money. The decrease of the yield of the mines since about 1865, while population and commerce have been advancing, has already produced unmistakable symptoms of the same general distrust, non-employment of labor, and political and social disgust which have characterized all former periods of shrinking money."

"It is in a volume of money keeping even pace with advancing population and commerce, and in the resulting steadiness of prices, that the wholesome nutriment of a healthy vitality is to be found. The highest moral, intellectual, and material development of nations is promoted by the use of money unchanging in its value. That kind of money, instead of being the oppressor, is one of the great instrumentalities of commerce and industry. It is as profitless as idle machinery when it is idle; differing from all other agencies, it cannot benefit its owner except when he parts with it. It is only under steady prices that the production of wealth can reach its permanent maximum, and that its equitable distribution is possible. Steadiness in prices insures labor to all and exacts labor from all. It gives security to credit and stability and prosperity to business. It encourages large enterprises, requiring time for their development, and crowns with success well matured and carefully executed plans. It discourages purely speculative ventures, and especially those based upon disaster. It encourages actual transactions rather than gambling on future prices. It metes out justice to both debtor and creditor, and secures credit to those who deserve it. It prevents capital from oppressing labor and labor from oppressing capital, and secures to each the just share of the fruits of industry and enterprise. It secures a reasonable interest for its use to the lenders of money, and a just share in the profits of production to the borrower. It keeps up the distinction between a mortgage and a deed. It insures a moderate competence to the many rather than colossal fortunes to the few at the expense of the many."

It may be impossible to devise any system through which the volume of money shall always increase or decrease in corresponding ratio to the increase or decrease of all those things to measure which is its function. If it be admitted that the volume of money should increase in proportion with either wealth, commerce, or population, the least measure of increase would be that based on population, as in commercial countries both wealth and exchanges are multiplied more rapidly than population. The narrower measure of increase would probably be the more accurate one, as the thing to be measured and which it is important should have an unvarying value is human effort, and as that can neither be increased nor diminished except through an increase or diminution of the population, it would seem that the volume of money should only vary with population.

As steadiness in prices, which depends on steadiness in the relation between money and all other things, is essential to prosperity, it follows that in any change in money-systems the volume of the new money, that is to say, the number of units of the new money issued, should if possible be neither greater nor less than the number of units in circulation at the time of the change. A strict observance of this rule, whatever may be the material of money, will prevent any general rise or fall in prices.

The quantity of metallic money, or of paper money constantly convertible into metallic money, which can be main-

tained in circulation of any particular country cannot be controlled arbitrarily. It cannot be greater than such an amount
as may be requisite to maintain the prices of such country at a
substantial parity with the prices of all other countries using
the same kind of money. Any change from this amount must
be temporary, and will be soon automatically corrected by the
course of exchange.

The volume of inconvertible paper money, on the contrary,
is local to, and subject to the control of, the country issuing it,
and should be regulated solely with reference to existing prices,
and consequently should be neither increased nor diminished,
except in correspondence with changes in population and commerce.

The rates of interest for money are not lowered by increasing its quantity. It is prices, and not interest, which depend
upon the volume of money. The rates for the use of
loanable capital depend upon entirely different factors—such
as the current rates of business profits, productiveness of the
soil, the security of property, the stability of government, pressure of taxation, and the fiscal policies of governments such
as the maintenance of public debts, which necessarily increase
the rate of interest. In truth, increasing the amount of money
tends indirectly to increase the rate of interest by stimulating
business activity, while decreasing the amount of money
reduces the rate of interest by checking enterprises and thereby
curtailing the demand for loans. This is signally illustrated
by the present condition of things in every part of the commercial world. The rate of interest should be, and under a correct
money system would be, merely an expression of the rate
of profit which could be made through the use of borrowed
capital.

While the volume of money is decreasing, even although
very slowly, the value of each unit of money is increasing
in corresponding ratio, and property is falling in price. Those

who have contracted to pay money find that it is constantly becoming more difficult to meet their engagements. The margins of securities melt rapidly away, and the confiscation by the creditor of the property on which they are based becomes only a question of time. All productive enterprises are discouraged and stagnate because the cost of producing commodities to-day will not be covered by the prices obtained for them to-morrow. Exchanges become sluggish, because those who have money will not part with it for either property or services, beyond the requirements of actual current necessities, for the obvious reason that money alone is increasing in value, while everything else is declining in price. This results in the withdrawal of money from the channels of circulation, and its deposit in great hoards. This hoarding of money, from the nature of things must continue and increase, not only until the shrinkage of its volume has actually ceased, but until capitalists are entirely satisfied that money lying idle on special deposit will no longer afford them revenue, and that the lowest level of prices has been reached. It is this hoarding of money, when its volume shrinks, which causes a fall in prices greater than would be caused by the direct effect of a decrease in the stock of money. Money in shrinking volume becomes the paramount object of commerce instead of its beneficent instrument. Instead of mobilizing industry, it poisons and dries up its life-currents. It is the fruitful source of political and social disturbance. It foments strife between labor and other forms of capital, while itself hidden away in security gorges on both. It rewards close-fisted lenders and filches from and bankrupts enterprising borrowers. It circulates freely in the stock exchange but avoids the labor exchange. It has in all ages been the worst enemy with which society has had to contend, while its legitimate function is to benefit society.

The great and still continuing fall in prices in the United States has proved most disastrous to nearly every industrial enterprise. The bitter experience of the last few years has been an expensive but most thorough teacher. It has taught capitalists neither to invest in nor loan money on such enterprises, and just as thoroughly has it taught business men not to borrow for the purpose of inaugurating or prosecuting them. Of the few business enterprises now being successfully prosecuted, the larger part are based on a monopoly secured either by patents or exceptional conditions. The business man has discovered that the less active and enterprising he is the better he is off. The manufacturer avoids loss by damping down furnace-fires and slowing down machinery.

The mining companies would find profit in inactivity, and would probably suspend operations, were it not for the great loss they would sustain in doing so. Mines can be properly opened only through a great outlay of capital, which would be practically lost if they were closed down for any considerable period of time. The filling up with water, the caving in of galleries, the crushing in of shafts, the rusting of machinery, and the general disarrangement of their interior workings would require for their repair a not much less expenditure than was necessary for their original opening. Hoping for better times, they therefore struggle on against an adverse current, without profit and generally only without loss by reducing their miscellaneous expenditures to the lowest possible point and wages to a starvation level. The miners ascend from the dark and gloomy depths of the mine with their scanty pittance, called wages, to find in a famishing household a gloom that is more profound.

The stockholders of railroads have suffered a vast shrinkage in the value of their property and in the volume of their traffic and in rates of transportation, while their debts have remained nominally the same but really increasing. In order to make their decreased receipts meet the interest on their bonds, they are forced to reduce their operating expenses to the lowest possible point. Their struggles seem to be in vain, and unless that system can be changed which is making each dollar which they owe more valuable, and at the same time causing a shrinkage in their business, and which is chaining labor and all other forms of capital to the chariot-wheels of money-capital, they will, one after another, be swallowed by the bondholders. In the end the stockholders will be entirely out of the account, and the contest will be between different classes of bondholders, if that can be called a contest where victory is assured in advance to the liens which have priority.

Farmers whose lands are not mortgaged, and their employes who at least are insured against absolute want, best escape the evils of the times, but the prices of agricultural products must finally decline with the reduction in the number and means of the consumers. The tendency of falling prices is to break down the vast diversified interests of the country, and to force a constantly increasing proportion of the population into the one single primitive industry of cultivating the soil. The United States, instead of containing a highly commercial and manufacturing nation, will, until falling prices are checked, become more and more exclusively agricultural and pastoral.

Securities have already become so impaired through falling prices that loanable capital has fled affrighted from the newer and more sparsely settled sections of the country and accumulated in large amounts in the great financial centers where securities are more ample. The personal and property securities of individuals have generally ceased to be available, except at the highest rates of interest, or at ruinously low valuations. Money can be borrowed readily only upon such securities as bonds which are *based on the unlimited tax-levying power of the government*, or upon the bonds and stocks of first-class trunk-lines of railroad corporations, whose freight and fare rates are practically a tax upon the entire population and resources of the regions which they traverse and supply. The competition

among capitalists to loan money on these more ample securities
has become very keen, and such securities command money at
unprecedentedly low rates. These low and lowering rates of interest, instead of denoting financial strength and industrial prosperity, are a gauge of increasing *prostration*. Large accumulations
of money in financial centers, instead of being caused by
the overflow of a healthful circulation, or even being proof of
a sufficient circulation, are unmistakable evidence of a congested
condition, caused by a decreasing and insufficient circulation.
The readiness with which government bonds bearing a very low
rate of interest are taken, instead of showing that the credit of
the government has improved, is melancholy evidence of the
*prostrated condition to which industry and trade have been
reduced.*

When the money stock is diminishing and prices are falling, the lender not only receives interest but finds a profit in
the greatly increased value of the principal, when it is returned
to him. A loan of money made in 1809 if repaid in 1848
would have been repaid with an addition of 145 per cent.
in the purchasing power of principal and interest besides
all the interest paid. Those who have loaned money to this
government since 1861 have already received nearly or quite
as much in the increased value of their principal as
in interest, and all the probabilities are, in respect to the
four per cent. thirty year national bonds, if they are redeemed
in gold, that more profit will be made by the augmentation
in the value of principal than through interest. Indeed,
the signs of the times are that the bonds of a country possessing
the unbounded resources and stable institutions of the United
States, payable in gold at the end of thirty years without any
interest whatever, would, through the increase of the value of
that metal, prove a most profitable investment.

The worst effect, however, economically considered, of
falling prices, is not upon existing property nor upon debtors,

evil as it is, but upon laborers whom it deprives of employment and consigns to poverty, and upon society, which it deprives of that vast sum of wealth which resides potentially in the vigorous arms of the idle workman. A shrinking volume of money transfers existing property unjustly, and causes a concentration and diminution of wealth. It also impairs the value of existing property by eliminating from it that important element of value conferred upon it by the skill, energy and care of the debtors from whom it is wrested. But it does not destroy any existing property, while it does absolutely annihilate all the values producible by the labor which it condemns to idleness. The estimate is not an extravagant one that there are now in the United States four million persons willing to work, but who are idle because they cannot obtain employment. This vast poverty-stricken army is increasing and will continue to increase as long as falling prices shall continue to separate money-capital, the fund out of which wages are paid, from labor, and to discourage its investment in other forms of property.

Money capital, labor, and other forms of capital are the warp and woof of the economical system. Labor, co-operating with the forces of nature, is the source of all wealth, and to reach the highest degree of effectiveness it must be classified through the aid of capital and supported by capital during the process of production and be measured and paid in money, each unit of which is a sight-draft on all other forms of property, bearing a value in proportion to the number of such drafts. In order that any country may reach the maximum of material prosperity, certain conditions are indispensable. All its labor, assisted by the most approved machinery and appliances, must be employed, and the fruits of industry must be justly distributed. These conditions are only possible when capital is absolutely protected against violence and free from illegitimate and legislative interference, and when the laborer is protected in his natural right to dispose of his labor in such manner as he may prefer. They are utterly impossible when the money-stock is shrinking and the money-value of property and services is declining. Howsoever great the natural resources of a country may be, however genial its climate, fertile its soil, ingenious, enterprising and industrious its inhabitants, or free its institutions, if the volume of money is shrinking and prices are falling its inhabitants will be overwhelmed with bankruptcy, its industries will be paralyzed, and destitution and distress will prevail.

The instinct of self-interest is the mainspring of industrial and commercial activity. It is the animating motive alike of the capitalist and of the laborer. Without it no labor would be performed, nor would capital have an existence. If money-capital is withdrawn from productive enterprises, it is from the apprehension of loss, and from the same instinct of thrift through which it was acquired. It is natural that the money-capitalist should exact from labor all he can, in exchange for his money, and that the laborer should exact all the money he can in exchange for his labor.

What is known as the conflict between capital and labor is not so much a conflict between other forms of capital and labor as it is between money and labor. Indeed, the conflict between money and other forms of capital is as distinctly marked and quite as severe as the conflict between money and labor, and in that conflict other forms of capital suffer fully as much as labor, the only difference being that they are better able to endure losses. Other forms of capital must be constantly converted into money in order to pay wages and to meet other demands incident to industrial enterprises. When the stock of money is shrinking and prices are falling, this conversion can only be made at rates continually growing more unfavorable, while at the same time the products of the laborer for whose wages sacrifices have been made are also undergoing a shrinking of money-value. Thus loss and sacrifice are encountered at every turn, and the owners of other capital than money shrink from the friction of exchange, withdraw from productive enterprises, and only exchange as much of their property for money as will suffice to meet the necessary expenditures of living, which are reduced to the most economical level, as it is principal and not income that is being consumed. Little more labor will be employed under these circumstances than is sufficient to support the owners of capital on this parsimonious basis, and as a consequence the labor market will be overstocked, and the competition between laborers will reduce wages to a starvation level. But during this period, when property is being sacrificed to meet current necessities, and laborers are being remitted to idleness and destitution, money fattens on the general disaster. Under any money system whatever, labor, money and other forms of capital confront each other as opposing forces, each seeking, through a natural instinct, to secure as much as possible of the others in exchange. These forces, although always operating against, are not necessarily inimical to or destructive of each other. On the contrary, under a just money system, they are not even harmful to each other. The conflict between them is essential to the proper adjustment and harmonious working of all parts of the economical machinery. They are the centripetal and centrifugal forces of the industrial system.

The equilibrium of all things is maintained through counter-balances. It is out of the action and counteraction of antagonistic forces that the harmonies of the universe are evolved. But under an unjust money-system which through law or accident fails to regulate the *quantity* of money so as to preserve the equilibrium between money and the other factors of production, the conflict between money and labor and other forms of capital becomes destructive and ruinous. It is in the shadow of a shrinking volume of money that disorders, social and political, gender and fester, that communism organizes, that riots threaten and destroy, that labor starves, that capitalists conspire and workmen combine, and that the revenues of governments are dissipated in the employment of laborers, or in the maintenance of increased standing armies to overawe them.

The peaceful conflict which under a just money system is continually waged between money-capital and labor, and which tends only to secure the rights of each, and is essential to the progress of society, is changed under a shrinking volume of money to an unrelenting war, threatening the destruction of both. Money, in either shrinking or unduly increasing volume, like a dissolving chemical, separates capital from labor. It is not against capital, but against the false financial system that permits the volume of money to either shrink or unduly increase, that the hostility of society should be aroused. Let labor and capital be put on equal terms, so that idle capital will be as unfruitful as idle labor, and the conflict between them will cease to be destructive.

An unjust money-system produces an unnatural relation between labor, capital and money, and the resulting evils cannot be remedied by special legislation on particular cases, nor by general legislation abridging the natural rights of either. Such legislation would be futile and impertinent, destructive of that freedom of individual action so essential to progress, and subversive of the true interests of all classes of society, and would powerfully tend to the overthrow of free institutions.

The equitable adjustment of the correlative demands of capital and labor cannot be made through violence, and is utterly impossible through any legal, or other contrivance, under any system that permits contraction or undue expansion of that great instrument which measures alike the property of the capitalist and the labor of the workman. It is only through the action and counteraction of the antagonistic forces of capital and labor, automatically operating under a just money-system, that equity and harmony can be evolved.

The very same reasons which make capitalists refuse to exchange money, whose command over property is increasing, for property whose command over money is decreasing, also makes them refuse to exchange it for labor for the production of property. In a commercial sense industrial enterprises are never undertaken nor carried on, except with the hope and expectation of gain. This expectation, unless under exceptional conditions, falling markets destroy. While capitalists for these reasons cannot afford to invest money in productive enterprises, still less can anybody afford to borrow money for such investments at any rate of interest, however low, and but little money is being now borrowed, except for purely speculative ventures, or to supply personal and family wants, or to renew old obligations. Money withdrawn from circulation and hoarded in consequence of falling prices, although neither paying wages nor serving to exchange the fruits of industry, nor performing any of the true functions of money, is nevertheless not unproductive. It may not be earning interest, but it is enriching its owner through an increase of its own value, and that, too, without risk, and at the expense of society. If this were not the case, and if money were, while idle, losing a little in value instead of gaining, or if it simply held its own, it would be constantly diminished to the extent of the necessary expenditures of its owners who, under such conditions, would be impelled by every instinct of thrift to seek for revenues through its employment in productive enterprises. The peculiar effect of a contraction in the volume of money is to give profit to the owners of unemployed money, through the appreciation of its relative purchasing power—or rather its comparative value with products—by the mere lapse of time. It is falling prices that robs labor of employment and precipitates a conflict between it and money-capital, and it is the appreciating effect which a shrinkage in the volume of money has on the value of money that renders the contest an unequal one, and gives to money-capital the decisive advantage over other forms of capital invested in industrial enterprises. Idle machinery and industrial appliances of all kinds, instead of being productive of profit, are a source of loss. They constantly deteriorate through rust and waste. They cannot escape the assessor and tax-gatherer, as the bulk of money does, and must pay extra insurance when idle.

Labor, unlike money, cannot be hoarded. The day's labor unperformed is so much capital lost forever to the laborer, and to society. It being his only capital, his only means of existence, the laborer cannot wait on better times for better wages. Absolute necessity forces him to dispose of it on any terms which the owners of money dictate.

These are the conditions which surround the laborer throughout the commercial world to-day. The labor of the past is enslaving the labor of the present. At least that portion of the labor of the past which has been crystallized into money is enabled through a shrinkage of its volume and while lying idle in the hands of its owners to increase its command over present labor and over all forms of property and to transform vast numbers of honest and industrious workmen into tramps and beggars. These laborers must make their wants conform to their diminished earnings. They must content themselves with such things as are absolutely essential to their existence. Consumption is therefore constantly shrinking toward such limits as urgent necessity requires. Production, which must be confined to the limits indicated by consumption, is constantly tending towards its minimum, whereas its appliances, built up under more favorable conditions, are sufficient to supply the maximum of consumption. Thus idle labor, idle money, idle machinery, and idle capital stand facing each other, and the stagnation spreads wider and wider. The future affords no hope or prospect of improvement, except through a change in financial policies.

Prices have been persistently falling throughout the world since 1873, and as fast and as far in specie-paying countries as elsewhere. If the policy of chaining the industry and commerce of the world to a single metal be persisted in by the United States, Germany, and other European countries acting in concert with them, money must still rise in value, and prices must continue to fall. The depression in productive industry will become more deathly, and the number of idle laborers will indefinitely multiply.

The loss which this country sustains by reason of the enforced idleness of four millions of persons who, although idle, must still in some scanty way be supplied with food, clothing, and shelter, is in the aggregate very great. If it be estimated at one dollar per day for each laborer it would amount in two years to a sum sufficient to discharge the national debt. It would pay the interest, at five per cent per .annum, on $1,800,-000,000. It would be a sum more than sufficent to supply anew each year the circulating medium of the country. It would amount, in four years, to a greater sum than the world's entire gold product has amounted to in the last fifty prolific years. It would aggregate in ten years a value far greater than the value of the world's entire product of both gold and silver for the last hundred years. It would amount in four years to a sum more than sufficient to duplicate and stock every mile of railroad now in the United States.

Contrasted with the startling sum thus annually lost through the shrinkage of money and falling prices, the amount which could, by any possibility be lost in a generation through fluctuations in the relative values of gold, silver, and paper, would weigh as mere dust in the balance. If to this loss be added that caused by the non-employment of productive machinery and appliances, the aggregate becomes appalling.

The average stocks of nearly all commodities are at no time sufficient for more than a few months' consumption. Without constant reproduction mankind would soon be stripped of all their movable possessions. No more fatal blow, therefore, could be directed against the economical machinery of civilized life than one against labor; and that blow can be most effectively delivered through a policy which strikes down prices. If all debts in this country had been doubled by an act of legislation, it would have been a far less calamity to the debtor and to the country than the increase in the real burden already caused by a contraction in the volume of money. And infinitely more disastrous in every sense than an unjust increase in the burden of debt is the universal stagnation of industry and commerce resulting from the same cause. The doubling of debts would have left the productive forces unimpaired, while falling prices are sapping them insidiously and fatally. Nations have often exhibited an astonishing capacity for sustaining and repairing the destruction of great and protracted wars. The explanation of this will be found in the fact that their productive forces have at such times continued vigorous and active. Armies in barracks and on parade are as essentially non-producers as when actively engaged, and a considerable proportion of the additions made to armies in times of war are recruited from the ranks of non-producers. England was never more prosperous than during the Napoleonic wars. The Northern and Western states of the Union were never more prosperous than during the civil war, and for some time afterward. So long as all the productive forces are active almost any burden can be borne. The debts of the country, great as they are, would scarcely weigh as a feather if all its labor were employed. Indeed, this country could better afford, in an economical view, to support one million soldiers in the field, than to support its present army of four millions that falling prices have conscripted into the ranks of non-producers.

At this point I purpose to let authority emphasize what is taught by experience, and make liberal quotations from the soundest thinkers upon this subject, from authors, writers, statesmen, and scholars, to the end that their testimony may substantiate the position taken in this chapter. I have no apology to offer for their number or length except an earnest desire to make clear the proposition, that price depends upon the volume of currency. The earliest in point of time is the following, from David Hume's Essay on money:

"It is certain that since the discovery of the mines in America industry has increased in all the nations of Europe. * * We find that in every kingdom into which money begins to flow in greater abundance than formerly, everthing takes a new face; labor and industry gain life; the merchant becomes more enterprising, the manufacturer more diligent and skillful, and even the farmer follows his plow with greater alacrity and attention. * * * It is of no manner of consequence with regard to the domestic happiness of a state whether money be in a greater or less quantity. The good policy of the magistrate consists only in keeping it, if possible, still increasing; because by that means he keeps alive a spirit of industry in the nation and increases the stock of labor, in which consists all real power and riches. A nation whose money decreases is actually at that time weaker and more miserable than another nation which possesses no more money, but is on the increasing hand."

William H. Crawford, Secretary of the Treasury, in a report (February 12, 1820) to Congress, says:

"All intelligent writers on currency agree that when it is decreasing in amount, poverty and misery must prevail."

Mr. R. M. T. Hunter, in a report (1852) to the United States Senate, says:

"Of all the great effects produced upon human society by the discovery of America, there were probably none so marked as those brought about by the great influx of the precious metals from the New World to the Old. European industry had been declining under the decreasing stock of the precious metals, and an appreciating standard of values; human inge-

nnity grew dull under the paralyzing influences of declining
profits, and capital absorbed nearly all that should have been
divided between it and labor.   But an increase in the precious
metals, in such quantity as to check this tendency, operated as a
new motive-power to the machinery of commerce.   Production was stimulated by finding the advantages of a change in
the standard on its side.   Instead of being repressed by having
to pay more than it had stipulated for the use of capital, it was
stimulated by paying less.   Capital, too, was benefited, for new
demands were created for it by the new uses which a general
movement in industrial pursuits had developed ; so that if it lost a
little by a change in the standard, it gained much more in the
greater demand for its use, which added to its capacity for reproduction, and to its real value."

The Encyclopedia Britannica, 1859, (article Precious
Metals, by J. R. McCulloch,) says:

"A fall in the value of the precious metals, caused by the
greater facility of their production, or by the discovery of new
sources of supply, depends in no degree on the theories of
philosophers, or the decisions of statesmen or legislators, but
is the result of circumstances beyond human control; and although, like a fall of rain after a long course of dry weather,
it may be prejudicial to certain classes, it is beneficial to an in-
comparably greater number, including all who are engaged in
industrial pursuits, and is, speaking generally, of great public
or national advantage."

Ernest Seyd, 1868, (Bullion, page 613,) says:

"Upon this one point all authorities on the subject are
agreed, to-wit, that the large increase in the supply of gold has
given a universal impetus to trade, commerce, and industry,
and to general social development and progress."

The American Review (1876) says:

"Diminishing money and falling prices are not only oppressive upon debtors, of whom, in modern times, states are the
greatest, but they cause stagnation in business, reduced production, and enforced idleness.   Falling markets annihilate profits,
and as it is only the expectation of gain which stimulates the
investment of capital in operations, inadequate employment is
found for labor, and those who are employed can only be so
upon the condition of diminished wages.   An increasing
amount of money, and consequently augmenting prices, are at-
tended by results precisely the contrary.   Production is stimu-

lated by the profits resulting from advancing prices; labor is consequently in demand and better paid, and the general activity and buoyancy insure to capital a wider demand and higher remuneration."

Leon Fauchet, (1843,) in Researches upon Gold and Silver, says:

"If all the nations of Europe adopted the system of Great Britain, the price of gold would be raised beyond measure, and we should see produced in Europe a result lamentable enough."

Before a French monetary convention in 1869 testimony was given by the late M. Wolowski, by Baron Rothschild, and by M. Rouland, governor of the Bank of France.

M. Wolowski said:

"The sum total of the precious metals is reckoned at fifty milliards, one-half gold and one-half silver. If, by a stroke of the pen, they suppress one of these metals in the monetary service, they double the demand for the other metal, to the ruin of all debtors."

Baron Rothschild said:

"The siumltaneous employment of the two precious metals is satisfactory and gives rise to no complaint. Whether gold or silver dominates for the time being, it is always true that the two metals concur together in forming the monetary circulation of the world, and it is the general mass of the two metals combined which serves as the measure of the value of things. The suppression of silver would amount to a veritable destruction of values without any compensation."

At the session (October 30, 1873) of the Belgian Monetary Commission, Professor Laveleye said:

"Debtors, and among them the state, have the right to pay in gold or silver, and this right cannot be taken away without disturbing the relation of debtors and creditors, to the prejudice of debtors, to the extent of perhaps one-half, certainly of one-third. To increase all debts at a blow, (*brusquement*), is a measure so violent, so revolutionary, that I cannot believe that the government will propose it, or that the Chambers will vote it."

The contrast presented by these authorities between the effects of an increasing and decreasing volume of money, shows that if a change in the one direction or the other is unavoidable, a change in the direction of an increase is the most desirable. Because the enlargement of commercial exchanges which results from an increase of money speedily restores the equilibrium, the real danger of an unduly increasing money is theoretical and fanciful. The trouble which practically threatens the world and which has been the most prolific cause of all the social, political, and industrial ills which have afflicted it, is that of a decreasing and deficient amount of money. It is from such a deficiency that mankind are now suffering, and is the actual and present evil with which we are now confronted.

I quote further:

Adam Smith, the father of political economy, says, page 205:

"From the high or low money price either of goods in general, or of corn in particular, we can infer only that the mines which at that time happened to supply the commercial world with gold and silver were fertile or barren."

"Any rise in the money price of goods which proceeded altogether from the degradation of the value of silver, would affect all sorts of goods equally, and raise their price universally a third, or a fourth, or a fifth part higher, according as silver happened to lose a third, or a fourth, or a fifth part of its former value."

John Stuart Mill, in Principles of Political Economy, says, page 301:

"The proposition which we have laid down respecting the dependence of general prices upon the quantity of money in circulation, must be understood as applying only to a state of things in which money, that is gold or silver, is the exclusive instrument of exchange, and actually passes from hand to hand at every purchase, credit in any of its shapes being unknown. When credit comes into play as a means of purchasing, distinct from money in hand, we shall hereafter find that the connection between prices and the amount of the circulating medium is much less direct and intimate, and that such connection as does exist, no longer admits of so simple a mode of expression. But on a subject so full of complexity as that of currency and prices, it is necessary to lay the foundation of our theory in a thorough understanding of the most simple cases, which we shall always find lying as a groundwork or substratum under those which arise in practice. That an increase of the quantity of money raises prices, and a diminution lowers them, is the most elementary proposition in the theory of currency, and without it we should have no key to any other."

Again he says:

"If the whole money in circulation was doubled, *prices* would double. If it was only increased one-fourth, *prices* would rise one-fourth. The very *same* effect would be produced on *prices* if we suppose the *goods* (the uses for money) diminished instead of the money increased; and the contrary effect if the *goods* were increased or the *money* diminished. So that the value of money—*all other things remaining the same*—varies *inversely* as its quantity; every increase in quantity lowering its value, and every diminution raising it in a ratio exactly equivalent."

Ricardo plainly says in regard to this question:

"That commodities would *rise* and *fall* in *price* in *proportion* to the increase or diminution of money, I assume as a fact that is *incontrovertible*. That such would be the case, the most celebrated writers on political economy are agreed. * * The value of money does not *wholly* depend upon its absolute quantity, but on its quantity *relative* to the payments it has to accomplish; and the *same* effect would follow either of *two* causes—from increasing the *uses* for money one-tenth, or from diminishing its quantity one-tenth; for, in either case, its value would rise one-tenth."

William Stanley Jevons, Professor of Political Economy and Logic in Owen University, England, says:

"I *cannot* but agree with Mr. Macculoch, that putting out of sight *individual* cases of hardship, if such exist, a fall in the value of gold (increasing the quantity of money) must have, and, as I should say, has already, a most *powerful* beneficial effect. It loosens the country from the old bonds of debt and habit, as *nothing* else could. *It throws increased rewards before all who are making and acquiring wealth*, somewhat at the expense of those who are enjoying acquired wealth. It excites the active and skillful classes of the community to new exertions, and is, to some extent, like a discharge of his debts is to the bankrupt and insolvent long struggling against his burdens. All this is effected without the break of national good faith which nothing could compensate."

The Professor proves by methods too lengthy to quote here, that the money already (in 1862) issued from the gold and silver mines of California and Australia had in effect reduced the burden of the debt of England 40 per cent. by increasing the price of labor and all forms of wealth.

He further says (Money and the Mechanism of Exchange, page 338):

"Considerable changes, it is true, are taking place in the mode of conducting business in some parts of the Continent. Professor Cliffe Leslie, who is well known to be intimately acquainted with the economical systems of the continental countries, attributes the rise of prices in Germany in a great degree to the quicker circulation of the money, and the freer use of instruments of credit. In the *Fortnightly Review* for November, 1870 (pages 568-9), he says: 'The improvements in locomotion and in commercial activity which have so largely augmented the money-making power of the Germans, have also quickened prodigiously the circulation of money, and the development of credit, likewise following industrial progress, has added to the volume of the circulating medium a mass of substitutes for money which move with greater velocity. A much smaller amount of money than formerly now suffices to do a given amount of business, or to raise prices to a given range, and to the increased amount of actual money now current in Germany we must add a brisk circulation of instruments of credit. Were the circulating medium composed of coin alone, whatever the amount of the precious metals issuing from the mines, or circulating in other countries, and whatever the price of German commodities in markets abroad, no rise in the price of German commodities could take place without additional coin to sustain it.'"

Page 335:

"To decide how much money is needed by a nation, we must, firstly, determine the quantity of work which money has to do. This will be proportional, *ceteris paribus*, to the number of the population. Twice the number of people, if equally active in trade and performing it in the same way, will clearly want twice as much money. It will be proportional, again, to the activity of industry, and to the complexity of its organization. The more goods are bought and sold, and the more often they pass from hand to hand, the more currency will be needed to move them. It will be proportional, again, to the price of goods, and if gold falls in value and prices are raised, more money will be needed to pay the debts increased in nominal amount."

Prof. Francis Wayland, in his work, "Elements of Political Economy," which is taught in our schools and colleges, page 296, says:

"The opening of new and richer mines, or the use of improved means for extracting the metals, may cheapen money. The value of money, like that of any other commodity, is also affected in short periods by fluctuations of supply and demand."

Page 297:

"If there is more money in a country than is needed for its exchanges, the price of goods is raised and it is sent abroad for new purchases. If there is a scarcity of money in a country, the price of goods declines, and money comes in from other hands to be exchanged for them."

Page 298:

"So if one million of dollars serves all the purposes of exchange in a city, to double the amount of money will bring no benefit. If it is a city isolated from the rest of the world, such an increase will merely double prices, that is, twice as much money will be used in every exchange."

"If money is abundant because business is stagnant and exchanges are few, it is a sign of adversity rather than of prosperity. If a scarcity of money is caused by an increase of products and great activity of trade, it indicates a prosperous condition. In countries containing rich mines of the precious metals, money, or the material for money, becomes a product of regular industry, and its abundance is a favorable sign."

Prof. Francis Bowen in his work, "American Political Economy," page 280, says:

"The power of money thus to determine its own amount arises from the reciprocal action of the quantity of money *in active circulation* and the price of commodities. All exchange, as I have said, is a barter of merchandise for money; and the quantity of money which an article of merchandise will command in the market is termed its *price*. Increase that quantity,.

and the price of all articles inevitably rises; diminish it, and the price as certainly falls. The whole process of exchange may be compared to the operation of weighing a well-poised balance; the money and the merchandise being placed on the opposite arms of the lever, increase the weight on the money side and the merchandise is sure to rise. We can easily see, therefore, why the amount of currency for the whole world distributes itself, by its own laws, among all nations, in exact proportion to their respective wants. If by any means one nation should obtain a larger portion than belongs to it by the regular course of trade, all articles of merchandise belonging to that nation must rise in price; they must be exchanged for a larger quantity of money. Articles of foreign growth and manufacture would be irresistibly attracted thither by this alteration of values. A single article might possibly be excluded by prohibitory legislation. But no arbitrary enactments can so clip the wings of commerce as to prevent it from seeking a market in a country where the price of all commodities has risen above their average value all the world over. Foreign goods must necessarily be imported in such a case, whether by open trading or by smuggling; and, being imported, they must be paid for. Money is the only redundant article in such a community, the only one which can be offered in payment, for all other goods are, by the hypothesis, of a higher price with them than in any other country, and cannot be sent abroad but at a sacrifice. Money then would be exported in spite of all coast guards, and the currency would thus be reduced to its natural level."

Page 281:

"In the other case, if the currency of any nation should fall below the average proportion to its wants, the price of all merchandise there would fall, they being exchanged against a smaller amount of money."

"The equalization of money is but another name for the equalization of prices."

Prof. Thompson, Political Economy, while not exactly in accord with this theory as a whole, quotes from many eminent authors as follows:

Page 22:

"Mr. Ricardo (following Say and Torrens) also elaborated the theory of international exchanges, in connection with the notion that money is a purely passive instrument of exchanges, changing its purchasing power according to the amount of it that a country possesses. From this it was an easy inference that a drain of money from a country would either have no effect, or would correct itself by so increasing the purchasing power of money in comparison with commodities, as to make the country a bad place to sell in, but a good place to buy in."

Page 149:

"On the principles generally accepted by the English school, and first enunciated by David Hume in 1752, the rate of decrease in value should have been exactly proportional to the increase in amount. He says that 'the only influence which a greater abundance of coin has in the kingdom' is 'by heightening the price of commodities and obliging every one to pay a greater number of these little yellow or white pieces for everything he purchases.' He admits indeed a *temporary* effect of quite another kind. 'In every kingdom into which money begins to flow in greater abundance than formerly, everything takes a new face; labor and industry gain life, the merchant becomes more enterprising, the manufacturer more diligent and skillful, and the farmer follows his plow with greater alacrity and attention."

Page 150, quotes J. S. Mill:

"If the whole money in circulation was doubled, prices would be doubled; if it was only increased one-fourth, prices would rise one-fourth."

Page 208, quotes Thomas Tooke:

"Hence new uses will be found for it when it is abundant, new avenues of commerce will be opened, new branches of industries will be essayed, until increased production finds employment for the increase of money. If money has increased, industry and trade are increased; and thus the tendency to depreciation is met and strongly counteracted."

Page 208:

"The drain of precious metals from a country, though its effects are alleviated by the creation of the credit-fund for domestic payments, is therefore decidedly injurious to its general interests. It is not exactly true to say, as has too often been said over and over again, since Turgot first said it, that money is a commodity like any other. That proposition is untrue,

except as it regards the metal of which money is made, but in so
far as it is the means of exchange, it has peculiarities of its own,
which clearly distinguish it from other commodities.   If iron
and cotton are scarce, those who need them suffer by the
scarcity, but it has no effect upon the prices of other materials.
If, on the other hand, money is scarce, the price of everything
else is affected. Every one must make exchanges, must buy and
sell; if, therefore, there is a tendency to a deficiency or a
scarcity of the means of exchange, everyone is straitened, and
all transactions become difficult.   Just as when the water falls
in its rivers, traffic is interrupted because the vessels are
aground, so, when money is diminished or disappears from the
channels of circulation, articles pass from one owner to another
with great difficulty.   We have got to the point of dispensing,
in the commercial transactions of advanced countries, with a
great quantity of money by replacing with credit in all its forms;
but, given the quantity of money that is still necessary, its
rarity produces an embarrassment, and sometimes even a general
crisis."

Professor Perry says:

"The fact that such a medium is in universal circulation,
and that the holders are ready and willing to exchange it
against any sort of service adopted to gratify their desires, ex-
ercises a kind of *creative* power, and brings a thousand productions to market which would *otherwise* never have come into
existence.   Since money will buy anything, men are on the
alert to bring forward something which will buy money; and
since money is divisible into small pieces, an incredible number and variety of small services are brought forward to be exchanged against these pieces, which service we have no reason
to suppose would ever be brought forward at all, were it not
for the strong attraction of money.   *Money is a form of capital which stimulates and facilitates all the processes of production without exception.*"

Professor Chevalier, of France, than whom no greater
authority on money has ever lived, in speaking of the increase
of money, says:

"Such a change will benefit those who live by current labor and enterprise; it will injure those who live upon the fruits
of past labor.   In this repsect it will work in the same direction
with most of the developments which are brought about by
that great law of cizilization to which we give the noble name

of progress.   *   *   *   It has been wisely said that there is no machine which *economizes* labor like money, and its adoption has been likened to the discovery of letters."

In his work (1831) on the so-called precious metals, hereinbefore quoted from, Mr. Jacob says:

"The following sheets owe their composition to the friendship with which, during more than twenty-five years, I had the honor of the late Mr. Huskisson (Member of Parliament).   *   *   *   I had made some progress in the collection of facts from the sacred and profane writers of antiquity, when the dreadful accident occurred by which his country and the world were deprived of the services of that eminent and estimable man.   *   *   *   It will readily be believed that his *penetrating* and assiduous habits would lead him to accurate views of the *influence* of the precious metals on the industry of mankind.   He saw that an increase in the production of the mines might act as a stimulus to excite industry, invention, and energy (consider the march of civilization since the issue of money by the mines of California and Australia, and the issue of paper money during the war of the rebellion) ; while a *decline* in their produce might have a contrary tendency.   He looked with *attention* to *other* consequences which might arise from the *failure* or *defalcation* of the mines, and considered the effect of gold and silver (of money) on the *production* of wealth to be of *less* importance than the influence it would exercise in the *distribution* of it, in the *complex* situation of the several classes of which modern society in Europe is composed."

Francis A. Walker, of Yale College, Professor of Political Economy and History, says:

"Perhaps we shall get a better view of this subject by confining ourselves to the claims made in favor of a *progressive* increase of the money.   It does not need to be said that Mr. Hume had in view an increase of money *not* so great as to bewilder the producer and the trader through a fiercely rapid rise in prices, or to render sober business calculations impossible.   *   *   *   The public indebtedness of the civilized world to-day probably stands between twenty-five and thirty thousand millions of dollars of American money.   The volume of *private* debts, including the capitalized value of fixed charges—loans, annuities, etc.,—is vastly greater.

"Nearly the whole of this vast body of obligations is payable, principal and interest, in money. The question whether the supply of money shall *increase* or *decrease* is, then, the question whether the *burden* of these more or less *permanent* charges shall be *diminished* or *enhanced*. It is the *fact* of a large body of indebtedness (some *hundreds* of thousands of millions) which gives its chief importance to the current production of the precious metals. * * * That gold or silver should be yielded in exactly the amount, from time to time, from generation to generation, which will serve to keep the *value* of money uniform, *is not to* be expected. We are not to expect, therefore, that the value of money will *remain* constant through any long period. One of the two parties to long contracts (no matter how short they are, provided they are *renewed* instead of being paid, and public debts, as well as those of merchants, generally speaking, grow larger and larger) will, in *all* probability, *lose*, while the other will *gain* by the change in values. The losses thus sustained may be slight, or they may be serious and even ruinous. * * * Certainly, I think, no one could refuse to admit that, if it were an issue between having the pressure of the whole body of indebtedness *diminished* by natural causes, or *increased*, the former result would be preferable. If it were a question of *sacrificing* the *Present* to the *Past*, or the Past *to* the Present, all would agree in saying, *Let the dead bury its dead*."

"The *weight* of opinion among economical writers of *reputation* seems to be in the affirmative. Mr. J. R. McCulloch, the English economist, has perhaps taken the strongest grounds in favor of the desirableness of a gradual reduction in the burden of debts, through the natural increase in the volume of the precious metals. * * * *It promotes industry, and diminishes the weight of obligations which press upon the producing classes, whether employer or employed*."

Mr. Horton, after advocating the gradual increase of money, says:

"I know the danger of giving the support of science to that spirit. On the other hand, I have confidence in truth and in the honesty and acuteness of my countrymen; and I think the *safe* course for the advocates of sound currency is to grasp this mettle firmly. The *truth* will bear to be seen; the greatest danger is in misrepresenting it."

Regarding the observation of Professor Horton, Professor Walker says:

"On this point Mr. Horton's remark seems to me thoroughly just and manly."

Such are the opinions of men who occupy the world's honored seats of learning, and who are familiar with every page of the history of mankind, and are profoundly acquainted with all the facts and principles which have been established by the last three thousand years of man's experience.

Prof. A. L. Perry, Political Economy, page 66, says:

"Price is indeed only a case under the class values, but practically it becomes a very important thing in Political Economy, because the value of almost all exchangeable things is determined through price. So far as commodities, personal services, and claims are exchanged against each other directly, without the intervention of money or the use of the denominations of money price plays no part though value does, but these cases are few and insignificant as compared with the whole. It is hardly necessary to add, that price, though relative, is specific and not general, and consequently that there may be a general rise or fall of prices. If the money of a country becomes relatively more abundant than before, general prices will rise in that country for reasons already made apparent; and when money becomes less abundant prices will fall for corresponding reasons."

Mason and Lailor, Primer of Political Economy, page 50:

"One thing may rise in value, but in order that it may do so, other things (Prop. twenty-six) must fall. If money rises in value, it will take less of it to buy other commodities. Therefore, general prices will fall. If money falls in value, it will take more of it to buy other commodities. Therefore, general prices will rise. If tea has been selling for ninety cts., coffee for thirty, and sugar for twenty-two and one-half, a pound, and a scanty supply (Prop. six) forces their prices up to one dollar, eighty, sixty, and forty-five cents, a pound, the value of money so far as they are concerned will have fallen. A dollar will not exchange for as much of them as it used to. There has been a general rise of their prices, but there has been neither rise nor fall in their values, compared with each other. For a pound of tea, before the rise in price, would have bought three pounds of coffee or four of sugar, and it will buy precisely the same amount now. Therefore, there may be a general rise or fall in prices."

Prof. Syme, Industrial Science, page 151:

"The price of money, or the rate of interest, does not depend on its quantity, as even Mill acknowledges, although somewhat inconsistently, as I consider, for why should not the price of money be regulated in the same manner as the price of any other commodity? Money is subject to the same fluctuations as ordinary commodities, and its price ought to be regulated in the same way, namely, by demand; and demand, again, is influenced, as in the case of ordinary commodities, by profits. If profits are small, the demand will be small, and the rate of interest will be low; if profits are large the demand will be large, and the rate of interest will be high. Money in the United States is more plentiful than it is in England (as proved by the higher prices of commodities and wages in the former than in the latter country), and it is more plentiful in Australia than it is in the United States."

Linderman, in his Money and Legal Tender, page 118 says:

"If a nation may not depart from its metallic money standard, except as a last resort for its own preservation, it surely should not undertake to return too rapidly to the metallic standard, especially when there has been a wide departure from it. Years of frugality on the part of the people, as well as a wise and economical administration of public affairs, are necessary to bring a country from a depreciated paper money to the metallic standard previously existing, however great may be its natural resources. This is shown in the United States, where a credit-money standard, which has prevailed since eighteen hundred and sixty-two (1862), has not yet been brought to a parity with the metallic standard."

Fawcett, in Handbook of Finance, pages 146 to 148, says:

"The decline of prices since 1872-3 is explained by the increased value of gold. The first effect was to cause a collapse in 'speculative securities' viz: bonds of railroads, etc., which were based on the expectations of a continuance of high prices for commodities, or in other words, a low value for gold. The losses which followed caused panic and a decrease in manufacturing industry and improvement enterprises. This diminished employment for labor and necessarily decreased the consumptive demand for all commodities. Theorists have been jangling for three years about the cause of the reaction which began in 1872-3, and the decline of prices which has continued almost without interruption since.   These causes are, however, not obscure.   The progress of the physical sciences and of labor-saving inventions has undoubtedly had an important tendency to reduce the prices of nearly all manufactured articles and, to a small extent also, the value of raw materials.   But the increased burden of debt, the increase of traffic (thus requiring a larger volume of the circulating medium), and the demonetization of silver, have all contributed to increase the value of gold beyond its equitable value as a measure for values of commodities.   The era of golden debt, like the era of gold, has had its culmination, and the causes at work are now preparing the way for some new era in financial affairs which will, in all probability, be as unique as either of the two which have preceded it.   No man can yet foresee what it is to be.   It is, however, not difficult to distinguish a few tendencies, that must operate toward the new development.   The first of these is the decline in the rates of interest for money in order to reduce the burden of funded and mortgage debt everywhere.   This will be accomplished partly by the repudiation and complete loss of a very large portion of the existing volume of funded debts, and partly by the concentration of capital (seeking safety rather than high rates of interest) on a smaller amount of the debt. Another tendency that must continue, is the necessity for supplementing the stock of gold in the world with the stock of silver, and a universal recognition of both metals as money at about the same relative values they maintained prior to the era of gold.   Until these things are accomplished, "prices" will continue to decline, and the commercial world will be in distress."

Sir. E. Sulleran, in his work, Protection to Native Industry, page 7, says:

"Nearly twenty years have elapsed since the discovery of gold in California and Australia, and the spread of steam communication by land and sea over the whole face of the globe, increased to an inconceivable extent the trade of the world, and equalized the trading conditions of the different nations of the globe and people that inhabit it.   Every nation, every industry, received an influence and enormously increased its commercial forces."

A modern writer says:

"That contraction of the currency (the *money* of a community) must contract values and derange industry, is a proposition as simple and as true as that two added to two will make four; that, so long, therefore, as contraction shall continue, shrinkage must progress and enterprise halt, because no one can buy anything under a continuing contraction without certain loss on any purchase. With an increase of money, a material rise in all values is not invariable. It may be that the increase will give rise to new enterprises, which give employment to the idle, so that legitimate demand for money may keep pace with the increase, and relatively the demand and supply may continue on a par."

The following extract from Alison's History of Europe shows that this ruinous policy of contraction has obtained in other countries besides our own, and that the effect was then as now to fill the coffers of the rich money-lenders at the expense of all other classes:

"The evils complained of arose from the unavoidable result of a stationary currency, co-existing with a rapid increase in the numbers and transactions of mankind, and these were only aggravated by every addition made to the energies and productive powers of society. * * * But if an increase in the numbers and industry of men co-exists with a diminution in the circulating medium by which their transactions are carried on, the most serious evils await society, and the whole relations of its different classes to each other will be speedily changed; and it is in that state of things that the saying proves true, that "the rich are every day growing richer and the poor poorer."

Henry C. Carey, one of our soundest thinkers, says in his work, Harmony of Interests, page 186:

"The introduction of a third commodity, itself liable to variation in the supply, as is the case with money, tends to produce additional variations in the quantity of one commodity that must be given for another. Thus, if the supply of money be large among one set of wheat raisers, and small among another, the raiser of sugar will sell in the first, and buy in the last, obtaining much money from the one and giving little to the other. Were all arrangements for the production, purchase, or sale of commodities or property executed on the instant, this cause of disturbance would scarcely exist, because the prices of all would be similarly affected, being high when money was plenty and low when it was scarce, and the quantity of sugar to be given for wheat or wheat for sugar, would depend upon the size of the crops almost as completely as if no intermediate commodity were used. Such, however, is not the case. The merchant buys coffee in January, and contracts to deliver its equivalent in money in July, at which time money may be so scarce that six pounds of coffee will command no more than would have been done in January by four pounds. The merchant commences to build a ship in July, when money is scarce, and the price of labor is low, and he finishes it when money is plenty and wages are high, and it costs him ten, fifteen, or twenty per cent. more than he had calculated upon. The little trader, on the contrary, who buys and sell from day to day, loses nothing. If he buys high, he sells high, and if prices are low to buy, he makes them low to sell, and the measure of his business is the measure of his profits. The great suffers by such variations are those the nature of whose property, or the character of whose business, requires them to make arrangements far ahead, and to take the risks incident to changes in the currency for the whole period that elapses between the commencement and the conclusion of an undertaking. Such are all the persons the products of whose labor are not intended for immediate consumption. the owners of houses, farms, factories, furnaces, railroads—all, in fact, connected with the improvement of land. In a time of pressure for money in one place, flour, cotton, cloth, and other articles intended for daily consumption, may be transferred to other places where money is plenty, and the changes in their prices are therefore small when compared with those which are experienced by the possessors of property that cannot be transferred, and are therefore obliged to bear the whole burden of the change. In such cases land becomes entirely unsalable except at an enormous reduction of price, to which its owners must submit if they are placed in a position to render sales necessary; and thus it is that so many persons connected with land and its improvement are ruined by revulsions that affect but in a small degree the operations of the retail grocer. Such, likewise, is the case with labor. The man who has a family and finds no demand for his labor cannot change his locality. He and his family must suffer together. Food may be at a *low money-price,* but if he can obtain no employment, *the labor-price* is so high he cannot purchase it. Land and labor, then, are especially interested in the maintenance of uniformity in the standard by which the products of both are measured, because they are the great sufferers by the changes which occur in the progress of time."

W. G. Sumner, American Currency, page 329:

"We have seen that prices alone govern the flow of the precious metals, or, more strictly stated, that the movement of the metals and the prices of commodities in different countries act and react upon one another in such a way as to keep up the exact natural relation of prices between different countries, and give to each country in the world's market its full relative advantage in production. If, therefore, a nation has a specie currency, a drain upon it by an adverse balance of trade, a foreign payment, or any other similar cause, would immediately produce a lowering of prices and a return of current specie until the natural level was once more restored."

Nothing more certain than this. Henry Clay, during the debates on the sub-treasury in 1840, made the following eloquent, truthful and logical speech. It shows clearly that his great mind had grasped the idea, that price, not only of products, but of labor, depended upon the quantity of money in circulation:

"The proposed substitution of an exclusive metallic currency to the mixed medium with which we have been so long familiar, is forbidden by the principles of eternal justice. Assuming the currency of the country to consist of two-thirds of paper and one of specie; and assuming, also, that the money of a country, whatever may be its component parts, regulates all values, and expresses the true amount which the debtor has to pay his creditor, the effect of the change upon that relation, and upon the property of the country, would be most ruinous. All property would be reduced in value to one-third of its present nominal amount, and every debtor would, in effect, have to pay three times as much as he had contracted for. The pressure of our foreign debt would be three times as great as it is, while the six hundred millions, which is about the sum now probably due to the banks from the people, would be multiplied into eighteen hundred millions!   *   *   *   Have gentlemen reflected upon the consequences of their system of depletion? I have already stated that the country is borne down by a weight of debt. If the currency be greatly diminished, as beyond all example it has been, how is this debt to be extinguished? Property, the resource on which the debtor relied for his payment, will decline in value, and it may happen that a man, who honestly contracted debt, on the faith of property which had a value at the time fully adequate to warrant the debt, will find himself stripped of all his property, and his debt remain unextinguished. The gentleman from Pennsylvania (Mr. Buchanan) has put the case of two nations, in one of which the amount of its currency shall be double what it is in the other, and, as he contends, the prices of all property will be double in the former nation of what they are in the latter. If this be true of two nations, it must be equally true of one, whose circulating medium is at one period double what it is at another. Now, as the friends of the bill argue, we have been, and yet are in this inflated state; our currency has been double, or, in something like that proportion, of what was necessary, and we must come down to the lowest standard. Do they not perceive that inevitable ruin to thousands must be the inevitable consequence? A man, for example, owning property to the value of five thousand dollars, contracts a debt for five thousand dollars. By the reduction of one-half of the currency of the country, his property in effect becomes reduced to the value of two thousand five hundred dollars. But his debt undergoes no corresponding reduction. He gives up all his property, and remains still in debt two thousand five hundred dollars. Thus this measure will operate on the debtor class of the nation, always the weaker class, and that which, for that reason, most needs the protection of government.

But if the effect of this hard-money policy upon the debtor class be injurious, it is still more disastrous, if possible, on the laboring classes. Enterprise will be checked or stopped, employment will become difficult, and the poorer classes will be subject to the greatest privations and distresses. Heretofore it has been one of the pretensions and boasts of the dominant party, that they sought to elevate the poor by depriving the rich of undue advantages. Now their policy is, to reduce the wages of labor, and this is openly avowed; and it is argued by them, that it is necessary to reduce the wages of American labor to the low standard of European labor, in order to enable the American manufacturer to enter into a successful competition with the European manufacturer in the sale of their respective fabrics. Thus is this dominant party perpetually changing; one day cajoling the poor, and fulminating against the rich, and the next, cajoling the rich, and fulminating against the poor. It was but yesterday that we heard that all who were trading on borrowed capital, ought to break. It was but yesterday we heard denounced the long-established policy of the country, by which, it was alleged, the poor were made poorer, and the rich were made richer.

Mr. President, of all the subjects of national policy, not one ought to be touched with so much delicacy as that of the wages, in other words, the bread, of the poor man. In dwelling, as I have often done, with inexpressible satisfaction upon the many advantages of our country, there is not one that has given me more delight than the high price of manual labor. There is not one which indicates more clearly the prosperity of the mass of the community. In all the features of human society, there are none, I think, which more decisively display the general welfare, than a *permanent* high rate of wages, and a *permanent* high rate of interest. Of course, I do not mean those excessively high rates, of temporary existence, which result from sudden and unexpected demands for labor or capital, and which may, and generally do, evince some unnatural and extraordinary state of things; but I mean a settled, steady and durable high rate of wages of labor, and interest upon money. Such a state demonstrates activity and profits in all the departments of business. It proves that the employer can afford to give high wages to the laborer, in consequence of the profits of his business, and the borrower high interest to the lender, in consequence of the gain which he makes by the use of capital. On the contrary, in countries where business is dull and languishing, and all the walks of society are full, the small profits that are made will not justify high interest or high wages."

In another speech later upon the same subject he spoke as follows:

"And what is the remedy to be provided for this most unhappy state of the country? I have conversed freely with the members of the Philadelphia committee. They are real, practical, working men—intelligent, well-acquainted with the general condition, and with the sufferings of their particular community. No one, who has not a heart of steel, can listen to them, without feeling the deepest sympathy for the privations and sufferings unnecessarily brought upon the laboring classes. Both the committee and the memorial declare that their reliance is, exclusively, on the *legislative* branch of the government. Mr. President, it is with subdued feelings of the profoundest humility and mortification that I am compelled to say that, constituted as Congress now is, no relief will be afforded

by it, unless its members shall be enlightened and instructed by
the people themselves. A large portion of the body, whatever
may be their private judgment upon the course of the president, believe it to be their duty, at all events safest for themselves, *to sustain him*, without regard to the consequences of
his measures upon the public interests. And nothing but clear,
decided, and unequivocal demonstrations of the popular disap-
probation of what has been done, will divert them from their
present purpose.

But there is another quarter which possesses sufficient
power and influence to relieve the public distresses. In twenty-four hours the executive branch could adopt a measure which
would afford an efficacious and substantial remedy, and re-
establish confidence. And those who, in this chamber, support
the administration, could not render a better service than to repair to the executive mansion, and, placing before the chief
magistrate the naked and undisguised truth, prevail upon him
to retrace his steps and abandon his fatal experiment. No one,
sir, can perform that duty with more propriety than yourself.
You can, if you will, induce him to change his course. To you,
then, sir, in no unfriendly spirit, but with feelings softened
and subdued by the deep distress which pervades every class of
our countrymen, I make the appeal. By your official and personal relations with the president, you maintain with him an
intercourse which I neither enjoy nor covet. Go to him and
tell him, without exaggeration, but in the language of truth
and sincerity, the actual condition of his bleeding country. Tell
him it is nearly ruined and undone, by the measures which he
has been induced to put in operation. Tell him that *his* experiment is operating on the nation like the philosopher's experiment upon a convulsed animal in an exhausted receiver, and
that it must expire in agony, if he does not pause, give it free
and sound circulation, and suffer the energies of the people to
be revived and restored. Tell him that, in a single city, more
than sixty bankruptcies, involving a loss of upward of fifteen
millions of dollars, have occurred. Tell him of the alarming
decline in the value of all property, of the depreciation of all
the products of industry, of the stagnation in every branch of
business, and of the close of numerous manufacturing estab-
lishments, which, a few short months ago, were in active and
flourishing operation. Depict to him, if you can find language
to portray, the heart-rending wretchedness of thousands of the
working-classes cast out of employment. Tell him of the tears
of helpless widows, no longer able to earn their bread; and of

unclad and unfed orphans, who have been driven, by his policy, out of the busy pursuits in which but yesterday they were
gaining an honest livelihood."

Was eloquence ever more logical? Could language portray
our present situation more completely? This whole magnificent plea was for more currency. That through this medium
the distress in the land might disappear and bring relief to the
toiling millions.

Henry C. Carey, in his treatise on Wealth:

"The money price of labor would have fallen with the
increased difficulty of procuring the precious metals, but for
the substitution therefor of credits in the form of drafts, bank
notes, etc., in most of the operations of the world."

From a speech in Congress on the currency:

"Undue contraction, on the other hand, is fraught with
like evil to the same classes. I cannot better illustrate this than
by quoting from Sir Archibald Alison, in his 'England in 1815
and 1845; or, a Sufficient and Contracted Currency,' wherein
he says:

'The period of a contraction of the currency and consequent fall in the money prices of all the articles of human consumption is one in which great profits are sure to be realized
by the larger capitalists, and great losses sustained by the smaller. The former prosper because the magnitude of their transactions enables them to realize a handsome income upon the
whole from a declining and at length almost inconceivably
small amount of profit from each transaction; and they gradually get the monopoly of the market in their own line of business by the extinction of the lesser capitalists whom the fall in
the price of commodities has ruined, or the diminished profits
have repelled from entering into competition with them.
*   *   * Small traders, therefore, and farmers without
capital are speedily ruined in such a state of things, and the
laboring or destitute condition is only rendered the more distressing by the contrast which it affords to the wealth and splendor with which the holders of large capital in the same line of
business are surrounded. *   *   * A period of contracted currency is one of embarrassment, difficulty, and generally,
in the end, of insolvency to the small farmer and moderate
land-holder.
*   *   * If a supply proportioned to the increase

of men and the wants of their commercial intercourse is not afforded, the circulating medium will become scarce; it will rise in price from that scarcity, and become accessible only to the more rich and affluent classes. The industrious poor or those engaged in business but possessed of small capital will be the first to suffer."

· The following short extract from Doubleday's Financial History of England will give an idea of some of the consequences of that act of folly:

"As the memorable 1st of May, 1823, drew near, the country bankers as well as the bank of England, naturally prepared themselves, by a gradual narrowing of their circulation, for the dreaded hour of gold and silver payments 'on demand,' and the withdrawal of the small notes. We have already seen the fall in prices produced by this universal narrowing of the paper circulation. The effects of the distress produced all over the country, the consequence of this fall, we have yet to see.

The distress, ruin and bankruptcy which now took place were universal, affecting both the great interests of land and trade; but among the landlords whose estates were burdened by mortgages, jointures, settlements, legacies, etc., the effects were most marked and out of the ordinary course. In hundreds of cases, from the tremendous reduction in the price of land which now took place, the estates barely sold for as much as would pay off the mortgages; and hence the owners were stripped of all and made beggars. I was myself personally acquainted with one of the victims of this terrible measure. He was a school-fellow, and inherited a good fortune, made principally in the West Indies. On coming of age and settling with his guardians, he found himself possessed of fully £40,000; and with this he resolved to purchase an estate, to marry, and settle for life. He was a young man addicted to no vice, of a fair understanding and most excellent heart, and was connected with friends high in rank and likely to afford him every proper assistance and advice. The estate was purchased, I believe, about the year 1812 or 1813, for £80,000, one moiety of the purchase money being borrowed on mortgage of the land bought. In 1822–23 he was compelled to part with the estate in order to pay off his mortgage and some arrears of interest; and when this was done he was left without a shilling, the estate bringing only half of its cost in 1812! Thus, without imprudence or fault of any kind, was this amiable man, together with his family, plunged in irretrievable and inevitable ruin, by the act of a legislature which ought to have protected both, and which was fully warned of the consequences of what it was about to do; but which, in requital, chose to laugh those who warned to utter scorn. My readers must not suppose that this was either an exaggerated or uncommon case. On the contrary, the country teemed with similar examples, and on the commencement of the session of 1823 the tables of both houses were loaded with petitions, detailing scenes of hardship and destitution appalling in the extreme."

That great man, the astronomer Copernicus, whose amazing genius penetrated and discovered a truth that all the ages and millions of men who had gone before him failed to perceive or to comprehend—the proper movements of the planets of the solar system—in his treatise "*Monete Cudende Ratio*," addressed to the king of Poland in the first part of the 16th century, said :

"Numberless as are the evils by which kingdoms, principalities and republics are wont to decline, these four are, in my judgment, most baleful: civil strife, pestilence, sterility of the soil, and corruption of the coin. The first three are so manifest that no one fails to apprehend them; *but the fourth, which concerns money, is considered by few, and those the most reflective, since it is not by a blow, but little by little, and through a secret and obscure approach, that it destroys the State.*"

Mr. William Jacob, F. R. S., of England, in his profound examination into the quantity of money in use by man at various periods of history, states the quantity probably in use at the time of the Roman Augustus, and gives a table showing its decrease from that time forward—through the exhaustion of the gold and silver mines known to man prior to the discovery of the American continent. I can only spare space for a part of his table. I begin with the time of Augustus, and close with that of the Saxon heptarchy, giving a few intervening sums to show the rate of diminution:

A. D.		
14,	£358,000,000	About $1790,000,000
230,	181,943,000	" 909,000,000
410,	107,435,924	" 537,000,000

| 662, | 51,324,889 | " | 256,000,000 |
| 806, | 33,674,256 | " | 168,000,000 |

Mr. Jacobs says:

"If we take a view of Europe during the existence of the Saxon heptarchy in England, we shall probably find the scarcity of money and the depression of prices to have reached their lowest point. The Romans, in abandoning Britain, Gaul, and the other western portions of the dominions over which their power had once extended, had carried with them all that was portable and valuable. We select a few facts to show how very small must have been the quantity of the money at that period in Britain, and how very low was the metallic valuation of every description of property."

I can only give room to the following quotation of prices made by Mr. Jacob:

	£	s.	d.
Price of a slave or man,	2	16	3
" horse,	1	15	2
" mule, or ass,	0	14	1
" ox,	0	7	2
" cow,	0	6	2
" swine,	0	1	10
" sheep,	0	1	2
" goat,	0	0	4

And such was the power of the Nobles over the *money-less* people, many of whom were held in slavery, while others were reduced to a condition of servitude little, if any, preferable to actual slavery, that the price of a hawk or a greyhound was the same as that of a man, and the robbing of a hawk's nest was as great a crime in the eye of the law, as was the murder of a human being.

Numerous laws prohibited the farmers from weeding and hoeing, so that the young partridges should not be disturbed; steeping seeds lest it should harm the game, and manuring with night soil for fear of injuring the flavor of the partridges.

Regarding this, and a later period of time, Sir Archibald Allison, in his history of Europe, says:

"*The two greatest events in the history of mankind have*

been brought about by a successive contraction and expansion in the circulating medium of society. The fall of the Roman Empire, so long ascribed in ignorance to slavery, to heathenism, and moral corruption, was in reality brought about by a decline in the silver and gold mines of Spain and Greece. . . . . And as if Providence had intended to reveal in the clearest manner possible the influence of this mighty agent on human affairs, the resurrection of mankind from the ruin this cause had produced was owing to the directly opposite set of agencies being put in operation. Columbus led the way in the career of renovation; when he spread his sails across the Atlantic, he bore mankind and its fortunes in his bark. . . . *The annual supply of the precious metals—of money—for the use of the globe was tripled; before a century had elapsed the price of every species of produce was quadrupled. The weight of debt and taxation insensibly wore off under the influence of that prodigious increase; in the renovation of industry the relations of society were changed, the weight of feudalism cast off, the rights of man established.* Among the many concurring causes which conspired to bring about this mighty consummation, the *most* important, though hitherto the least observed, was the discovery of Mexico and Peru"—(their gold and silver mines).

Bryant, in his work on Money, says:

"*Any reduction in the price which the producer or the artisan is able to obtain for his labor, or the product of his labor, is an injury, misfortune and loss to every single member of society, excepting solely those who live upon the interest of loaned money.* If the reduction is temporary, then the loss is temporary; if it is permanent, then the loss is permanent."

Albert Gallatin, ex-Secretary of the United States Treasury, in his work on Money, published in 1831, says:

"It is well known that the discovery of America was followed by a great and permanent fall in the price of the precious metals, which reduced it to one-fourth of their previous relative value to all other commodities."

Humboldt says that the gold and silver money in circulation in the eighteenth century is—at the time he wrote—thirty times greater than in the fifteenth century, and that its value or purchasing power was only one-twelfth of what it then was

—that is, 8 1-3 cents would then buy as much as 100 would at the time he wrote.

Professor Bonamy Price says that the purchasing power of the so-called precious metals has fallen fourteen times since the reign of the Henrys—that is, 7 1-7 cents would then buy as much as 100 will now.

The Boston Daily Advertiser of March 11, 1875, says:

"The prime element in determining the value of money, whether gold or paper, is quantity, and it is subject to the same laws as other commodities. Increase the quantity, it will buy less. In other words, it produces a rise in prices, but no increase in values."

Dr. Soetbeer, the great German authority, says:

"The value of money has fallen through the issue of paper money, as well as through the increased productions of gold and silver."

Judge John Barnard Byles, one of England's greatest jurists, in his work, Popular Political Economy, page 154, says:

"Men talk glibly of variations in the currency. Few reflect on the awful extent to which such changes affect the prosperity of all ranks. The laborer, the pauper, and the beggar are as much interested in the currency question as the manufacturer, the shopkeeper, or the great proprietor of land or funds, and even more.

Sudden and great alterations in the amount of value of the circulating medium are at best transfers of property—gigantic robberies; they are often much worse; they involve wanton destruction of immense property, and stoppage of industry.

The cure provided by the Act of 1844, for an adverse balance of trade, and for every export, or tendency to an export of the precious metals, is a sudden and great diminution in the quantity of the currency—a rise in its value—next, a great and sudden rise in the rate of interest—a fall in the price of all things—a fearful injury to all the industrious classes.

What you expected always eventually happened; the balance of trade brought the bullion back. The issue of notes was then, in easier times, contracted to its safe and ordinary amount. You passed through the crisis with little or no alteration in the value of money, or rate of interest. When the bullion went away, notes, by supplying its place, broke the shock to credit; when bullion returned, the withdrawal of those notes still preserved the equilibrium. The paper portion of the currency, over and above its other advantages, was then an ingenious contrivance in the nature of a spring or elastic band, which, enabling you safely to expand the currency in times of distress, and to contract it again in times of prosperity thus equalized and averaged the tension. Lord Ashburton has shown how the currency often was relaxed in periods of severe pressure with perfect safety. And this occasional relaxation in times of difficulty was the ordinary course of proceeding long before the Bank Restriction Act. Its advantage was well understood even as early as the beginning of the last century. Addison, writing in the time of Queen Anne, says: 'When the bullion leaves us, we make credit supply its place.' There was in the paper currency a union of convertibility with elasticity. There was a compensatory and self-adjusting action which artificially secured uniformity of value, and made a mixed currency, partly metallic, partly paper, a much better and more invariable standard of value than a mere metallic currency could possibly have been.

You can now no longer rely on an average favorable balance of trade; there may not only be (as there will certainly be) periodical drains of the precious metals, but there may be a perennial stream running out, not as formerly less than the perennial stream running in, but much larger.

How is it now proposed to meet the drain when the misery begins to be felt?

Not as before, by supplying the void with notes. That is no longer consistent with the preservation of a metallic basis to the currency; for we are told, and truly told, that if new notes were issued as fast as gold went out, the drain of gold would be continually going on, till all the gold had left the kingdom, the banknote would be inconvertible, and another bank restriction act would be inevitable.

No, it is to be stopped violently by a diminution in the quantity, and consequent rise in the value, of the whole currency, just as if it were entirely metallic. No notes are to be issued in place of the gold that goes out. Nay, the law may even contract the notes as the gold goes out. Prices of everything are to fall. The industrious classes are to see their property thus taken from them, and their debts and incumbrances thus really augmented. Industry is to be paralyzed, trade stopped, and the pressure of the public burthens indefinitely aggravated; while the transactions of the empire are being dwarfed and stunted to fit a short allowance of the circulating medium of the civilized world.

Then it is said prices will be effectually beaten down, and so at length imports will be checked, exports promoted, and an adverse balance of trade *naturally* redressed. Never mind, though this desirable and necessary result should be produced by the diminution or cessation of the ordinary operations of industry and commerce, and the bankruptcy of otherwise solvent houses.

It will be seen at a glance how insignificant the aggregate amount of coin and notes is, compared with the aggregate amount of bankers' checks, bills of exchange, and money of account.

But then the quantity and value of these checks, bills and money of account, depend entirely on the quantity and value of the coin and notes. Diminish the quantity of coin and notes by five per cent., and you may augment the exchangeable value of the residue, even of the coin and notes, by twenty or fifty per cent; for when the quantity of money or of any other article of first necessity, but of limited supply, is diminished, its exchangeable value rises in a much higher degree than the degree of diminution. Added to all which there is the effect of uncertainty and panic. That, however, is the least part of the mischief. Touch the coin and notes, the other and greater currency shrinks at once, like the sensitive plant.

And no one can tell the proportion in which, when you curtail the lesser currency, the greater is actually curtailed; in some instances it may be in a less proportion, but in many instances a far greater proportion. The enhancement in value of the greater currency is the same, but who can tell or conjecture what the diminution in quantity is?

Lord Ashburton declared that the importations, large as they necessarily were, were not more than, under a wiser management of the currency, the country could have easily borne. Mr. Mill says: 'The crisis of 1847 was of that sort which the provisions of the Act had not the smallest tendency to avert, and when the crisis came, the mercantile difficulties were probably *doubled* by its existence.'

And why was the industry of the country subjected to this horrible torture? That an adverse balance of trade might be corrected by what is called the natural flow of the precious metals. That a theory might be carried out. In vain did men, grown gray in business, remonstrate against the measure three years before. It was carried in contemptuous defiance of their warnings.

Few subjects are so intricate as the distribution of the precious metals among the countries of the world. Many considerations are overlooked by those who prophesy that the evil will work its own cure. David Hume says that a progressive increase in the quantity of the precious metals, and their declining value in any country, is favorable to a progressive increase of industry. And no doubt that is so. A stream, therefore, of the precious metals poured into a country, produces effects exactly the converse of the effects which its dereliction produces in the country which it is leaving. This fertilizing stream, in the country to which it goes, stimulates industry, multiplies transactions, creates its own demand, and counteracts its tendency to return. Our industry is crippled—our neighbor's is augmented. We permanently need the bullion less—he permanently needs it more."

The following is from the celebrated report on the high price of gold bullion made to the English Parliament in 1810:

"An increase or diminution in the demand for gold, or what comes to the same thing, a diminution or increase in the general supply of gold, will, no doubt, have a material effect upon the money prices of all other articles. An increased demand for gold, and a consequent scarcity of that article, will make it more valuable in proportion to all other articles; the same quantity of gold will purchase a greater quantity of any other article than it did before; in other words, the real price of gold, or the quantity of commodities given in exchange for it, will rise, and the money prices of all commodities will fall; the money price of gold itself will remain unaltered, but the prices of all other commodities will fall. That this is not the present state of things is abundantly manifest; the prices of all commodities have risen, and gold appears to have risen in its price only in common with them. If this common effect is to be ascribed to one and the same cause, that cause can only be found in the state of the currency of this country.

The same rise of the market price of gold above its mint price will take place, if the local currency of this particular country, being no longer convertible into gold, should at any time be issued to excess. That excess cannot be exported to other countries, and, not being convertible into specie, it is not necessarily returned upon those who issued it; it remains in the channel of circulation, and is gradually absorbed by increasing

the prices of all commodities. An increase in the quantity of
the local currency of a particular country, will raise prices in
that country exactly in the same manner as an increase in
the general supply of precious metals raises prices all over
the world. By means of the increase of quantity, the value
of a given portion of that circulating medium, in exchange
for other commodities, is lowered; in other words, the money
prices of all other commodities are raised, and that of bullion with the rest.

The same amount of paper may at one time be less
than enough, and at another time more. The quantity of
currency required will vary in some degree with the extent
of trade; and the increase of our trade, which has taken
place since the suspension, must have occasioned some increase in the quantity of our currency. But the quantity of
currency bears no fixed proportion to the quantity of commodities; and any inferences proceeding upon such a suppo-
sition would be entirely erroneous. The effective currency of
the country depends upon the quickness of circulation, and the
number of exchanges performed in a given time, as well as
upon its numerical amount; and all the circumstances, which
have a tendency to quicken or to retard the rate of circulation,
render the same amount of currency more or less adequate to
the wants of trade. A much smaller amount is required in a
high state of public credit, than when alarms make individuals
call in their advances, and provide against accidents by hoarding; and in a period of commercial security and private confidence, than when mutual distrust discourages pecuniary
arrangements for any distant time."

The Right Hon. George I. Goschen, M. P., an eminent
English financier, in an address delivered before the Bankers'
Institute, April, 1883, said:

"If we take the $50,000,000 as the amount required for
arts and manufactures and for all purposes other than circulation, and subtract that sum from the $100,000,000 of annual
supply, it leaves for the purposes of circulation $50,000,000
only, and on this hypothesis the extraordinary demand of $1,-
000,000,000 would absorb the available yield. Economists will
accordingly ask themselves what result, if any, is such a phenomenon likely to have produced. I think there is scarcely
an economist but would answer at once: 'It is probable, it is
almost necessary, it is according to the laws and the principles

of currency, that such a phenomenon must be followed by a fall in the prices of commodities generally.' Let us now turn to the other side of the question and examine the range of the prices of commodities, and see whether or not it is a fact that there has been a great fall.

For the figures I am about to place before you I am indebted to Mr. Giffin, of the board of trade. I have examined the prices of commodities as published by the board of trade, but I have also consulted other sources. I have here a classification of articles under certain heads showing prices in the years 1873 and 1883 respectively. (Here he gives the table.) I am bound to say it appears to me that these figures reveal an extraordinary state of things. * * * It appears to me that if it be true that population continually increases, and that there is a certain increase in wealth, an additional amount of circulation will be necessary in order to meet the increased demand unless there are compensating counter economies by the extension of the check system and other methods. On the one hand you undoubtedly have increased population. You also have an increase of wealth. Then again, you require more gold for more transactions. Gold has two or three functions to perform in circulation. It has to supply what I may call pocket-money, and it has to liquidate large transactions between nations and nations, and what is almost an analagous function, it has to remain in the vaults of bankers on deposit against the notes that are issued against it; still it is more simple to treat these two latter functions as one. Such being the two functions of gold, if the population increases the necessary pocket-money must 'increase, and if the transactions increase, somewhat more is required for liquidating the balances.

Let us now consider whether the economies in the use of gold (checks and clearings) have been as great as the increase in the population and as the increase in the amount of gold required to liquidate the balance of transactions. Mr. Giffin, in an article printed in the Journal of the Statistical Society for March, 1879, expresses the opinion that the United Kingdom was thoroughly 'well banked' even twenty years ago, and that there have been no new devices invented during the last twenty years which have much economized the use of gold in the United Kingdom. We have already reduced the use of gold in this country almost to a minimum, and I am confirmed in this view by the statement that the total circulation of gold in England increased, according to the estimate of the authorities of the Bank of England, from $515,000,000 to $620,000,-000 between 1870 and 1880. This would mean, and it is a most significant fact, that in this country, which is so 'well banked,' $100,000,000 more circulation was nevertheless required in 1880 than in 1870.

As regards England, then, I do not see that there has been any economy in the use of gold to counterbalance the increasing demand of the population, nor are we aware—those of us who have been able to look into the matter—that in France or Germany, or elsewhere, the economies have been such as to counterbalance the increasing demand for gold. I am now brought to the point that if there is any truth in the theory that the amount of circulation stands in a certain relation to the question of price, then this strain upon the gold circulation must have produced an effect upon prices. We have to deal with the fact, let us look at it how we will, the sovereign goes further than it used to go. Happy, then, it is for those who have the sovereigns; on the other hand, unhappy it is for those who have commodities left on hand and produce which they have not sold.

*   *   *   *

Let us now assume that there will be a continuance of low prices; that is to say, a continuance of the increased value of gold. Two classes would be permanently affected. One is the class which is entitled to receive gold. They will be much better off. The class of debtors, on the other hand, who are bound to pay a given amount of gold for a long period to come, will be much worse off. In the same way, as the rise in prices is generally to the advantage of the debtor, so a fall in prices will be to his disadvantage. The holders of mortgages would be in a distinctly favorable position. While the mortgages would run, they will continue at a sum that will be on the constant increase in its purchasing power. Those who have borrowed the sum will be in a worse position by having their means of payment constantly diminishing in price. The influence of this circumstance on land owners will not be overlooked. Land owners who have borrowed money on their estates will be under contract to pay a sum which represents more value than when the loan was made, while the produce of the land, if it should fall in price like other commodities, would not secure the same amount of gold. It is impossible to see how farmers should be able to continue to pay the same amount of gold for rent if the prices of what they raise from the soil should permanently fall.

*   *   *   *

A distinguished French economist has said that he was not sure whether France would have been bankrupt in 1848 but for that great increase in .the production of gold, which created a degree of commercial prosperity which enabled the French to escape from their difficulties. I have heard another distinguished man suggest that the great difficulties of the old Roman Empire with regard to laws that had to be passed for the relief of debtors was due to the fact that they never had an expansive currency, but that the supply of the precious metals was stationary, at least if compared with the increasing transactions and the increasing population, and that it did not enable the Roman men of business to conduct their operations with that continuously small increase in the supply of the precious metals which are required to meet the increased demands of population and increasing wealth."

Alexander Hamilton, in his report on the Mint in 1792, said:

"To annul the use of either of the two metals as money is to abridge the quantity of circulating medium, and is liable to all the objections which arise from a comparison of the benefits of a full with the evils of a scant circulation."

I make no apology, in view of the importance of the question, for giving some quotations I find grouped in a very able and comprehensive pamphlet on this subject by Judge Robert W. Hughes, of Virginia. He quotes M. Edward Cazalet, of Milan, a distinguished and very able Italian banker, who says: •

"It is computed that the total metallic circulation of the world amounts to $7,000,000,000, of which about 3,750,000,-000 are gold, and 3,250,000,000 are silver.

The whole of this mass of metal is now doing service as currency, and to demonetize or eliminate either metal would involve a reduction of the circulation by about one-half. The half demonetized would be incalculably depreciated in value; the half which remained to do double service would be appreciated to an equal extent. Since the value of all articles of commerce is represented by the currency, the value of these articles must fall in proportion to the reduction in the volume of the currency, otherwise the moneyed currency could not possibly do the work which the two metals combined had previously performed. Thus, to settle a debt of $100 it would be necessary to sell merchandise which under the double currency had been valued at $200. The creditor would gain at the expense of the debtor. * * * As the currency of a country is the only legal tender which can be offered in payment of a debt, the debtor would have to procure that currency from a circulation which had been suddenly contracted, and in proportion to this contraction the debtor would be a loser and the creditor a gainer. When the enormous amount of international and national as well as personal indebtedness is considered, and when we bear in mind that this indebtedness would be well-nigh doubled by the demonetization of either gold or silver, it becomes clear that such an event would revolutionize the actual conditions of society, and be nothing short of a universal calamity." (See M. Cazalet's pamphlet on bimetallism, pages 14, 15.)

Speaking of a later period, the historian Allison says:

"If this circulating medium of the globe had remained stationary, or declining, as it was from 1815 to 1859, from the effects of South American revolution and English legislation, the necessary result must have been that it would have become altogether inadequate to the wants of man ; and not only would industry have been everywhere cramped, but the price of produce would have universally and constantly fallen. Money would every day have become more valuable ; all other articles measured in money less so ; debt and taxes would have been constantly increasing in burden and oppression; the fate which crushed Rome in ancient, and has all but crushed Great Britain in modern, times would have beset that of the whole family of mankind. All of these evils have been entirely obviated, and the opposite blessings introduced, by the opening of the great reserve treasures of nature in California and Australia. * * * Before half a century has elapsed the prices of every article will be tripled, enterprise proportionately encouraged, industry vivified, debts and taxes lessened."

Sir Archibald wrote before 1873, says the author.

The author then quotes from a distinguished German writer, M. Herr von Barr, who, after showing the direct loss to Germany from the depreciation of her silver coin, and the product of her silver mines, which he places at an enormous figure, from the demonetization of silver, says :

"This direct loss, important as it is, is nothing, however, compared with the indirect loss resulting from the fall of prices."

Himself a large land-owner, he first speaks of agriculture :

"It is cruelly suffering from the reduced value of all produce. The farmers are paying their rents irregularly, or not at all ; their stock in trade has often to be distrained to recover arrears of rent. The land-owners are overwhelmed by mortgages. When at last, in order to extricate themselves, they try to sell their estates, they find no purchasers, or have to be satisfied with a price one-third below former estimates. The discouragement is universal. No more agricultural improvements are being effected ; employment is, consequently, lacking ; and there is great indigence. Hence that increasing emigration, for which special trains and steamers have to be arranged. It is a veritable exodus. What remedy for so much suffering? The agriculturists, perceiving at length the real cause of the evil, demand the abandonment of the gold standard. * * * The fact is strange, yet certain, that from this intense crisis has sprung that odious and inexplicable return to the intolerance of the Middle Ages, called the anti-semitic movement, the *Judenhetze* (Jew hatred). The Jews, being large holders of the gold, whose power is unduly increased, are regarded by the populace as enriching themselves by the ruin of others. The capitalist, unhurt, even profits by the cheapness of enforced sales."

The awful disaster of 1847, falling like a thunder-clap from a clear sky,—for the promise had been that nothing of the kind could ever happen under the patent system adopted in 1844,—caused an enormous public commotion and the appointment by the House of Lords and the House of Commons of a "Secret Committee" to make a solemn investigation into the affairs and management of the Bank. From a vast mass of testimony taken before this "Secret Committee," I quote the following, confining myself to brief extracts taken from the testimony of the chief officers of the Bank ; *whose ability and knowledge to testify in the matter is beyond the pale of cavil or dispute.* The following is a portion of the testimony given by Mr. John H. Palmer, at that time a director, and soon after made Governor of the Bank of England:

"It is by *producing* a fall in the value of commodities in this country that you correct the exchanges? *Ans.* Yes; not merely in that way, but you would bring capital into the country by a high rate of interest.

It is by interference with trade that it acts, and not merely by the inconveniences of the bill-holders? *Ans.* It causes the stoppage of trade.

What would be the effect upon the manufacturers and laborers of the country during such an operation? *Ans.* It destroys the labor of the country. At the present moment, in the neighborhood of London, and in the manufacturing districts, you can hardly move in any direction without hearing universal complaint of the want of employment by the laborers of the country.

That you ascribe to the measures it was *necessary* for the Bank to adopt in order to preserve the *convertibility* (specie payment) of its notes? *Ans.* I think the present depressed state of labor is *entirely* owing to that circumstance.

And the pressure of the Bank produced forced sales? *Ans.* It stops credit, and the British merchant sells his goods for the purpose of meeting his private payments, and brings his capital to the Bank at an earlier period than it would come in the ordinary course of business. There is no means of supplying the Bank with gold, excepting only the diminution of the bank-notes, which immediately contracts the currency, and lowers prices by increasing the value of money."

The following is a portion of the testimony of James Morris and Henry J. Prescott, the Governor and Deputy Governor of the Bank of England, before the " Secret Committee":

"Is there, in your opinion, any mode by which the tendency to an efflux of the precious metals, and the *consequent* diminution of the circulating medium, can be arrested, other than that of such a reduction of prices of commodities as shall lead to export, and such a rise in the value of money as is indicated by the advance of the rate of interest? *Ans.* No, I think there is no other method.

'A diminished power of consumption on the part of the public would have been rather advantageous to the system (coin) of circulation? *Ans.* A diminished circulation would have checked importation.

Then the more deprivation the public was subjected to, the safer the system of convertible circulation? *Ans.* It is necessary sometimes . . . . in order to restore circulation to a proper state.

Was it the intention of the act of 1844 (reorganization of the bank) to check importations, so as to correct the unfavorable balance of trade? *Ans.* I consider the act of 1844 was to cause the circulation of the country to be acted upon, by the exports and imports, in the same way as the currency would have been acted upon had it been entirely a metallic one.

Then there having been an export of gold in the spring of 1847, the tendency of the system was to check imports? *Ans.* Inasmuch as the export of a certain amount of bullion would contract the circulation of the country, and cause a fall of prices, it would tend to check importation.

Then, in 1847, when there was a great deficiency of food, the tendency was to check an importation of food? *Ans.* The export of the precious metals, by reducing the circulation, tended to keep down the prices of grain, and also kept down the price of manufactures which might be exported in payment.

Do you think this system of circulation should be preserved at any cost to the employment of the people? *Ans.* I think it desirable that the circulation should be placed on such a footing that it should expand and contract in the same way that a metallic currency would do. I cannot vary from that."

Mr. Sealy, of England, in his work on "Coins and Currency," published at London in 1853, holds the following opinion of the Bank of England. And I might quote an entire volume of the like opinions uttered by eminent and competent men. Mr. Sealy says:

"The commerce of the country is now *in the power* of the Bank of England, as it was before in the legislature. For legislative enactment we have substituted the decision of the Bank Parlor; for a responsible government, composed of King, Queen, Lords and Commons, we have substituted an irresponsible body composed of twenty-four directors, and a governor and deputy governor. To these we have confided the commerce of this mighty empire. Instead of a mercantile system supported by merchants and manufacturers and agricultural in-

terests, we have now the monetary system endangering the
welfare of merchants, manufacturers and agricultural interests—for the benefit of the fund-holding classes."

Stephen Williamson, a prominent Liverpool merchant, in
his pamphlet, "Bad Trade and its Causes," proves beyond
question it is caused by a want of currency. He says:

"England has now entered upon the sixth year of commercial and manufacturing distress and decadence. There is
as yet not a single ray of light shooting up through the dark
mercantile horizon. A crisis without parallel in the experience
of the present generation not only rests upon us, but intensi-
fies as time rolls on. When a condition of affairs baffling all
experience acquired in previous times of prostration exists, it
is surely our paramount duty to investigate and to inquire
whether this prolonged distress may not be traced in large
measure to some special or peculiar cause.

My object in writing this paper is to call attention to the
serious injury inflicted on our commerce by the discrediting of
silver; and my contention is, that the practical cutting off of
silver from the world's money has been at the root of much of
our distress during late years, and is now one of the chief hindrances to the return of prosperity. Undoubtedly, our declen-
sion in 1873, 1874, and part of 1875, was the natural revulsion
from undue extension, and from the unduly high prices paid
for labor and the products of our industry. Since 1875 these
causes, however, have ceased to operate. It is undoubtedly
true that hostile tariffs and the competition of several nations
(particularly the United States) have greatly curtailed the demand for our manufactured goods which previously existed
within their borders; but we have a large and open field almost
to ourselves in many quarters of the globe; and the lamentable
fact is, that in these regions, peculiarly our own, trade continues to languish as it does elsewhere, and the demand for our
goods is greatly restricted and diminished.

It will not be questioned that the large increase of the
world's money, due to the Australian and Californian gold discoveries, led to a great extension of the world's commerce.
The interchange of commodities was marvelously stimulated;
labor had for many years a greatly augmented recompense; the
material comfort and welfare of mankind were greatly promoted; real and personal property increased enormously in value
all over the civilized world; the foreign commerce of England

alone rose from £250,000,000 in 1852 to £650,000,000 in 1875; the foreign commerce of many other nations rose in like proportion. From the surplus gains of our commerce in those years, we invested many hundreds of millions of pounds sterling in state and corporation bonds, railways and industrial enterprises, and in property and mortgages in foreign countries—leaving us immeasurably wealthier as a nation, notwithstanding many foolish investments, such as Turkish, Peruvian and Paraguayan bonds. It is difficult to believe that so great prosperity and increase of national wealth had proceeded from a cause apparently so inadequate to produce results so fabulous. Such, however, was in large measure the result of the enlarged reservoir of the world's money created by the accession of gold from the Australian and Californian mines. It acted as a stream of warm blood impelled through all the arteries of the world's commerce, vitally and powerfully stimulating the vast organisms of trade and industry.

We have in this, our late national experience, a direct contradiction to the theories of some political economists who assert that, after all, international commerce is only barter, and that money has little or nothing to do with its extent or volume. The very small measure of truth underlying this assertion has led many intelligent minds astray. It is because the largely increased supply of money had guaranteed to men and nations the payment of large international balances, that the volume of the world's trade, prior to 1874, had augmented with such marvelous rapidity. And now it is in great measure because the world has of late greatly restricted and diminished the capacity of its money reservoir, that distress and calamity augment and intensify around us. A large portion of the life-blood of commerce has been artificially congealed. The whole organism has felt the shock; but the financial intellect has become so beclouded and benumbed as not to have fully realized, even yet, the cause of the deadening paralysis which has overtaken it.

Let us present for consideration the diagnosis: The world, of late years, traded on an effective metallic capital estimated at £1,400,000,000. Of this, we have good evidence for believing that about

£750,000,000 were gold coins and bullion,
and   £650,000,000   "   silver coins and bullion.

Now, we assert that the world, of late, has been committing the suicidal act of discarding, discrediting and cutting off from performing its wonted functions one of the two agents or solvents for the liquidation of balances of international indebtedness. In other words, the world, acting under the legal injunctions of the leading monetary powers, has divorced from its monetary system that silver which, from time immemorial, has, conjointly with gold, formed its 'money.' Widespread suffering has been the inevitable result of its folly.

Our unwise legislation of 1816, which made gold sole legal tender in England, has been the underlying cause of all this evil. For years we played upon the currencies of Europe, and often swept away large quantities of silver for transmission to India, where, with an admirable contradiction in our monetary legislation, we have enforced a silver currency. While availing ourselves of the stores of silver belonging to our continental neighbors, we constantly vaunted about the superiority of our gold currency, and stimulated them to follow our short-sighted example. Even a Liberal Chancellor of the Exchequer (Mr. Lowe) boasted in full Parliament, in the year 1869, that he had made a convert of France. Germany, however, stole a march on France in the insane career which we had pointed out to them as the high road to success, and in 1874 decreed the demonetization of silver and its substitution by gold. France, which had, in conjunction with the states of the Latin Union, provided for the world an equilibrium or par of exchange between the two metals, by means of her free-mintage system and making both metals full legal tender on the ratio of 15 1-2 of silver to 1 of gold, thereupon suspended the free coinage of silver. France was driven to this act by the unwise monetary legislation of powerful neighbors. The par of exchange provided betwixt gold and silver money was thereby lost to the world. Silver was dethroned. War to the knife was declared against that metal. Gold now reigns supreme and omnipotent.

The results have been disastrous in the extreme. The hard money capital of the world has been practically reduced from £1,400,000,000 to £800,000,000, and yet men are at a loss to account for the greatly reduced interchange of commodities, and the greatly reduced prices now paid for property, for goods and for labor!"

Let us turn to the words of wisdom uttered by the late Mr. Ernest Seyd, one of the most able and reliable statisticians and financiers of Great Britain. He was the author of a very able and exhaustive book, advocating the restoration of the double standard to Great Britain, and his efforts are said to have produced a profound impression on his conservative countrymen. But financial disasters or events have done more in this direction than the able arguments of Mr. Seyd. In 1867, this far-sighted and clear-headed financier, in discussing this question, that was then exciting considerable interest, expressed himself very freely on the evils that would probably fall on the world, in an attempt to discard silver as a full legal tender money metal. He said:

"Throughout the world a fall in prices will take place, injurious alike to the owners of solid property and to the laboring classes, and advantageous only, and unjustifiably so, to the holders of state debts and other contracts of that kind."

He also said, that when these results followed the discarding of silver, all sorts of reasons would be brought forward to account for the distress, and thus the real cause would be neglected until this distress compelled thinking men to refer it to the legitimate cause.

Blake, in his report on the precious metals, page 235. said:

"With this continued decrease in the annual production, it seems probable that gold will soon begin to sensibly appreciate in value, unless some new and unlooked for discovery of placers shall be made, of which, however, there does not appear to be much probability.

It was argued by Chevalier and others soon after the great discoveries in Australia and California, that gold would necessarily depreciate in value; that its purchasing power was destined to be much lessened by the great influx of the metal from these new sources. But the relative value of gold has not changed as much as was expected, and it would now seem that the supply did not more than keep pace with the ever increasing demands of commerce and industry, stimulated as they have been by an increasing supply of gold. The wonderful increase of the industrial activity of the world, resulting chiefly from the varied developments and application of the physical sciences, has been sufficient to appropriate all the excessive production of the past twenty years."

North American Review:

"A glut of loanable capital and low rates of interest are the inevitable final accompaniments of a shrinking money volume and the consequent decline in market values."

Sir Robert Peel in his great speech of May 6 and 20, 1844, on the British act regulating the issue of currency, said:

"There is no contract, public or private; no engagement, national or individual, which is unaffected by it. The enterprises of commerce, the profits of trade, the arrangements made in all the domestic relations of society, the wages of labor, pecuniary transactions of the highest amount and of the lowest, the payment of the national debt, the provision for the national expenditure, the command which the coin of the smallest denomination has over the necessaries of life, are all affected by the decision to which we may come on that great question which I am about to submit to the consideration of the committee."

A contraction of the money volume changes the relations between money and other things, and necessarily affects prices. John Locke long ago laid down the true law relating to the value of money, as follows:

"Money, while the same quantity of it is passing up and down the kingdom in trade, is really a standing measure of the falling and rising value of other things in reference to one another, and the alteration in price is truly in them only. But if you increase or lessen the quantity of money current in traffic in any place, then the alteration of value is in the money."

That is, with a stable volume of money for a given population with given wealth, which determines the volume of business, variation in the price of commodities is a variation in the goods themselves as compared one thing with another; but when the volume of money is changed, then the measure itself is changed, and we have what is taking place now, a double effect—that is, both a change in the commodities under the law of supply and demand, as above stated, and a change in the measure itself affecting the price of everything. In fact, it is an admitted doctrine of political economy that there can not be a general rise or a general fall of prices except by a change in the value of money. A general fall or a general rise of prices, when properly understood, means simply that there has been a change in the measure itself.

I might continue references almost indefinitely, but the number given and the eminent sources from which they are derived ought to convince the most sceptical.

When a proposition of this magnitude has received the careful consideration of so many persons, distinguished alike for their honesty and ability, whose conclusions are almost a unit as to its truthfulness, there is no good reason why we should not accept them as final. When this is done our future action regarding the correction or encouragement of the present condition of affairs becomes a sin of commission instead of omission. We act with a full knowledge of the facts before us.

In describing the effects of contraction during Van Buren's administration, Henry Clay said:

"What our present situation is, is as needless to describe as it is painful to contemplate. First felt in our great commercial centers, disasters and embarrassment have penetrated into the interior and at the present time rest like a black cloud over the whole nation."

It has been justly said by one of the soundest and most practical writers that I have ever read, that:

"All convulsions in the circulation of money and in the commerce of any country must originate in the operations of the government, or in the mistaken views and erroneous measures of those possessing the power of influencing credit and circulation, for they are not otherwise susceptible of convulsion, and if left to themselves they will find their own level and flow nearly in one uniform direction."

Our condition is the same to-day as has many times occurred in the history of the past, and has been brought about by the same causes. Our currency has been steadily contracted for many years, and during all that time with but an occasional breathing spell, business has been drooping and values have fallen. We have been tricked, as other nations have been, into placing our national honor into our national credit. We have been induced—or seduced—to believe that our honor as a people consisted in paying our national bonds in gold, one hundred cents on the dollar, which were bought with greenbacks at par, worth only fifty-five cents in gold; and by so doing we have brought business stagnation, and continued financial disaster, from year to year, upon a *confiding* people.

Why should United States bonds, bearing 4 per cent. interest, be worth one hundred and twenty-seven cents on the dollar while good farms cannot be mortgaged for over one-third of their value at 7 per cent. interest? Why is it that bonds go up, and all products of labor, and labor itself, goes down? Is that prosperity?

What labor and products lose in value finds a lodgment in the bonds and mortgages held against this same labor and its products, and all the vantage ground forced from labor and appropriated by capital, is really a loss to society and the nation, and weakens the government instead of giving it strength. The point made by Solon Chase is not only sound in logic but true in fact. He said:

"I bought a yoke of steers a year ago for sixty dollars, fed them all summer and winter, and in the spring was offered but sixty dollars for them in the market. Now, who got the hay?"

What was true in the case of "them steers" is true of every class of property in this country. Now the question is, who gets this lost value? It finds a lodgment somewhere; that place must be with money. For, wherever that may be found it will show an increase in value over products and labor in proportion as products and labor have decreased. Nothing is plainer than this.

The mistake is often made, that prices are not controlled by the volume of money, because they have neither risen nor fallen concurrently with, nor in exact proportion to the increase or decrease of such volume. The precious metals are diffused over so vast a surface, and their current production is so small in comparison with accumulated stocks that it takes considerable time for changes in their yield to so affect their volume relatively to population and business as to produce any sensible effect upon prices. The entire property interests of a country are united in maintaining and, if possible, in advancing the price of property, and in resisting to the uttermost any decline. A temporary maintenance of nominal prices, even in the presence of a shrinking volume of money, is especially practicable with imperishable property, such as real estate. When money begins to become scarce by reason of a shrinkage in its volume, the first effect upon real estate is found to be, not a decline of its nominal price, but a diminution in the number of transactions. Market reports quote real estate "*dull*," "*few sales, but prices firm*." This stagnation is ascribed to temporary causes, and a speedy recovery predicted. In order to maintain price, the terms of purchase are made easier. The amount of cash payments is reduced, and the deferred payments, secured by mortgage on the property, extended over longer periods. After a time this expedient fails, and, even then, nominal prices are unnaturally held up for a short period by the struggles of those who have purchased upon these extended credits, and by the tenacity of owners who refuse to sell at lower figures, and mortgage their own property to protect their power to hold. The stagnation of voluntary transactions is finally followed by the activity of involuntary ones under the direction of sheriffs and by the foreclosure of mortgages.

Upon any material decline in the price of real estate, a large class of investors, believing that the bottom has been reached, and desiring to profit by the reaction which they think is sure to come speedily, enter the market and temporarily check the decline. Another fall in prices sweeps them and their margins away, and a third class of dealers, now absolutely certain that bottom prices have been reached, and sure that a further decline is impossible, come in as purchasers. Each succeeding purchaser fortifies his conclusion, that present prices are bottom prices, by comparing them with and finding that they are no higher than the prices of some period in the past which is arbitrarily assumed to be a standard level, below which subsequent prices could never permanently go.

It is overlooked that price is only the expression of a relation, and that no correct conclusions can be drawn from a comparison of the prices of two periods, unless comparison be also made of the money stock, population, and exchanges of both periods. Contrary to all calculations, as the volume of money shrinks, prices continue to fall, and these dealers encounter the fate of their predecessors. These operations repeat themselves until universal distrust prevails, and until it is found that, when money is decreasing in volume, prices have no bottom except a receding one, and that they are inexorably ruled by the volume of money. The effects of a decrease of the volume of money in a particular country, arising from its abnormal outflow, or from its withdrawal from the channels of circulation through the distrust which prevails when unsound and speculative undertakings are breaking down, or when the country is convulsed by political disturbances, are the same as the effects of a general decrease in the volume of money. The result in both cases is a fall in prices. But in the first case the equilibrium is restored by a quickly returning wave of prosperity, and the evils resulting are confined to individuals and to special localities; and those dealers are fortunate who purchase in the first stages of the decline. But in the second case the cause of the fall in prices is radical, and must continue until prices go out of existence, unless the decrease in the volume of money is arrested. In the whole history of the world every great and general fall of prices has been preceded by a decrease in the volume of money. There has never been a decrease in the volume of money, nor has there ever been a stationary volume of money, unless accompanied by a stationary population and commerce, which has not sooner or later resulted in a general fall of prices; and there has never been a recovery therefrom except through a preceding increase in the volume of money. After the volume of money has begun to decrease, every dollar of credit extended at the old range of prices aggravates the disaster which must come sooner or later. Stagnation and panic are nothing more nor less than the results of a struggle to make prices truly express the relation between money and all other exchangeable things.

The true and only cause of the stagnation in industry and commerce now everywhere felt is the fact everywhere existing of falling prices caused by a shrinkage in the volume of money. This is, in part, the misfortune of mankind, as the mines have failed for several years, under energetic working, to yield the precious metals in quantities sufficient to keep pace with the increasing needs of the world for money. But it is in part due to the folly of mankind in throwing away a benefaction of nature by discarding one of the precious metals. Existing evils date with that folly, which precipitated and now enormously aggravates them.

Many learned and excellent persons and associations of persons in all parts of the world, whose instruments of observation seem to have been adjusted for the examination of remote objects, and consequently, unfitted for, and a hindrance to the inspection and examination of anything near at hand, have furnished many far-fetched, incomprehensible and impossible causes for existing evils, which agree in nothing except their remoteness. They have seen through a glass darkly, or they would have discovered that the cause was all around and about them; that it is the same cause that has invariably preceded and accompanied similar evils. They would have seen that money in shrinking volume was engaged in its legitimate work of ruin. This is the great cause. All others are collat-

eral, cumulative, or really the effects of that primal cause.
Practical men see what the mischief is, and they all see it alike,
and, without formulating their ideas in set words and phrases,
they all state it alike. Capitalists, large and small, give one
and only one reason, for refusing to invest in productive enterprises. Uniformly and universally the reason given is that
prices are falling and may continue to fall, and that money is
the best thing to get and hold while that state of things continues. All can see that prices have fallen and are falling,
although they may disagree, or may not trouble themselves to
form any opinion as to the cause of the fall. And all can see,
and do see, that it is falling prices which cause the stagnation
of business, with all its necessarily attendant circumstances of
an increasing pressure of debts, of decreasing employment and
wages of labor, and of diminishing consumption. "Falling
prices" is only another expression for an increasing value of
money, and those who desire still further to appreciate the
value of money by contracting its volume, desire still further
to reduce prices, and still further to widen and deepen the gulf
between money-capital and labor.

Money-capital is the fund out of which wages are paid.
Capital can only fructify through the employment of labor,
and labor is comparatively helpless without capital. It is by
the employment of labor that money-capital is produced and
increased. It is in vain to advise those who depend upon their
daily wages for their support, and who possess no capital but
their willing hands, to change their places of residence and engage in agricultural pursuits. Even had they the means to
emigrate, which most of them have not, they would still have
to be supplied with seed, implements, and animals, and with
support from seed-time to harvest. It is still more plainly futile to advise them to engage in any species of handicraft or
manufacture on their own account.

In modern times human labor is only available in connec-

tion with machinery and appliances.   A policy which tends to
a constant fall of prices, and therefore compels capital from the
justifiable instinct of self-preservation to withdraw from production, is a policy which reduces laborers to a worse condition than if money were wholly abandoned and the system of
barter were re-established.   The conditions of the laborer are
as bad when money-capital is not employed, as if it did not
exist.   The effect of falling prices is the same upon the smallest capitalist as upon the largest.   The hope of gain is for all
of them the only inducement to take the risks and labor of
enterprises, and they will all prefer to consume their accumulations rather than to invest with the certainty of losing them.
They will, of course, consume them as slowly as possible, and
to that end will reduce their expenditures within the smallest
possible limits.   Laborers thrown out of employment must in
some way have a bare subsistence, but there can be no other
sources for it than the scanty earnings of such as are employed,
and the capital in existence, which cannot refuse food to the
starving.

That shrinking money and falling prices are the cause of
existing evils, was pointed out by the London Economist in its
review (1869) of the previous financial year.   It then said:

"It may be safely affirmed that the present annual supply
of thirty millions sterling of gold is no more than sufficient to
meet the requirements of the expanding commerce of the
world, and prevent that pressure of transactions and commodities on the precious metals which means, in practice, *prices
and wages constantly tending toward decline.*   The real danger is that the present supplies should fall off, and among the
greatest and most salutary events that could now occur would
be the discovery of rich gold deposits in three or four remote
and neglected regions of the earth."

Having shown by the testimony of the ablest writers for
long years in the past, together with the experiences of all
nations, as far back as economic writings extend, also by the
best of our own statesmen and our own national experience that

price depends upon the circulating medium, and that the circulating medium makes the ability to purchase, it now devolves the more difficult task of expressing clearly *how* it is done. We see and know that a blade of grass grows and extends with each successive day's sun, but *how* it grows has never, in a successful manner, been explained. If my readers will follow me closely I will give my reasons in as intelligible a manner as possible for the conclusions above stated. Money is the measure of values. That must be an admitted fact at the outset. This being true, all values must be determined by its measurement. As a nation we have selected the dollar to be our unit of value. Hence all values are either multiples or divisions of that unit, the dollar. It therefore follows that the less value the unit or dollar represents the greater *number* of units or dollars a given amount of value will possess. For example, 3600 pounds of wheat will show sixty bushels of wheat with the unit or bushel representing sixty pounds, but change that unit or bushel to represent but thirty pounds and it will increase the measurement to 120 bushels. Increase the unit or bushel to ninety pounds and it will shrink the measurement to 40 bushels. In fact, the value represented by the dollar is always the divisor, the amount of values under consideration the dividend, and the *number* of values the quotient. From this it is plain that the size of the divisor determines the size of the quotient provided the dividend is always the same, which it is in this illustration. Let us represent all labor productions as the dividend, being the whole sum of produced values. When we come to reduce this amount to the unit or dollar of value, does it not follow that the more value the unit or dollar possesses the less number of units or dollars the quotient will give? But to show more plainly my proposition, let us again suppose the whole production of values for the year is represented by a space of 1,000 feet cubic measure, that is 1,000 feet long by one foot in depth and breath. If we had 1,000 measures one foot deep, one foot wide, and one foot in length, they would exactly fill up the 1,000 cubit feet of space. Now if each space or cubic foot represented productive value to the amount of one dollar, the proposition will be stated complete. When the people brought their products to be measured, those who filled ten measures would have ten dollars in value; those who filled 100 measures would have 100 dollars in value; and so on until the whole product had been measured. If the measures remained the same in capacity, producers could calculate exactly upon the value of their productions. But suppose these measures should be increased in number 100 per cent. (bear in mind the space or volume of products remains the same), then the measure would be increased in number to 2,000, and their capacity for measurement would be decreased one-half. Now the measures would contain but one-half of a cubic foot, and when the producer brings his products for measurement as before, he finds that instead of filling ten measures as at first he can fill twenty. The other can fill 200 measures. The result is, that while they received ten, or one hundred dollars before, they now receive twenty, or two hundred dollars as the case may be. But, suppose the number of measures is diminished to 500, then, in order to fill up the space, which includes the entire volume of products, their capacity must be doubled. They must now be two feet long, one foot deep, and one foot in width. The producers come for measurement as before and find that on account of the increased size of the measure they can only fill five and fifty measures respectively, and as a consequence one receives five and the other but fifty dollars. If we represent the period of our business year by the 1,000 feet of cubic space, the measures which fill that space by our circulating medium, and our whole volume of production from business by the products, we then have this illustration applied to the increase or decrease of the value in the unit or dollar of our measurement of values, and showing its resulting effects—

all of which goes to prove the truth of this statement: the cheaper the dollar the more dollars; the dearer the dollar the less dollars.

We see from this conclusion that the man who owns the dollar is interested in having its value increased to the utmost extent, while the man who accumulates products to purchase these dollars is interested in having their value reduced so that he may obtain a larger number of them for a given amount of his products. This being true the right action in the case would be equal justice to both. The laws of every Republic, especially of ours, are founded upon the principle of "the greatest good to the greatest number." In this principle the fact is recognized that the same law will not, in its application, inure to the benefit of all; that some must suffer through its working; but if it is for the interest of the majority the minority must acquiesce.

Now, in this nation, a very large majority of the population are poor. They are people whose only capital is invisible, and whose means of support is through labor. Again, where one person is found free of debt, thirty-three are discovered to be involved. Where three persons are comfortably fed, housed, and clothed without labor, ninety-seven are in reduced circumstances. The census returns show the startling fact that the average of wealth in this nation is but a trifle over three hundred dollars per capita. Imagine the number of paupers to offset the wealth of Vanderbilt.

Then, is it not true, that our economic laws should be so framed as to aid the poor as against the unjust encroachments of the rich? Do not the poor of this land come directly under the application of the foregoing principles? Some will say the rich will take care of the poor. As well might we expect the wolf to rear the young lambs. Not one man in a thousand who becomes wealthy, after having tasted the bitter fruits of poverty, but forgets that he was ever poor and becomes the worst enemy of the unfortunate, and those who inherit great wealth inherit with it a contempt for the laboring classes. Such is the contaminating influence of money.

The only manner by which the general good of the public can be subserved is through the honest application of wholesome general laws rigidly enforced. This is due to the people and this they have a right to expect.

In concluding this chapter I quote from a late writer as follows:

"The scheme of demonetizing one of the metals throughout the western world originated soon after the discovery of gold in California and Australia, at a time when the yield was at what has since proved to have been its maximum, but which was then expected by many to continue on an ascending scale for an indefinite period. An eminent English writer (De Quincey) published at that time an elaborate collation of current accounts, from which he arrived at the conclusion that the annual out-turn of gold would soon reach seventy millions sterling, or $350,000,000. On the basis of such expectations, the governments of Europe were invoked by Chevalier and others to prevent the anticipated depreciation in the value of money, or, in other words, the anticipated rise in general prices, by the demonetization, not of silver, but of gold.

Chevalier (Fall of Gold, 1856-'57) said:

'The quantity of gold annually thrown on the general market approaches, in round numbers, a milliard of francs ($200,000,000).

These two countries (California and Australia) must, for yet a long series of years, produce gold in such quantities and on such conditions as to render a marked decline in its value inevitable.

It is absolutely certain that so vast a production should be accompanied with a great reduction in value.

In no direction can a new outlet be seen sufficiently large to absorb the extraordinary production of gold which we are now witnessing, so as to prevent a fall in its value.

Unless, then, we possess a very robust faith in the immobility of human affairs, we must regard the fall in the value of gold as an event for which we should prepare without loss of time.'

Under these appeals of Chevalier and others, several nations in Europe, notably Germany and Austria in 1857, demonetized gold. It is probable that the movement in that direction would have become universal in Europe but for the resistance of France. It was changed, at least as early as 1865, into a movement for the demonetization of silver. In the convention of 1865, in which the Latin union was formed, Belgium, Italy, and Switzerland insisted strenuously upon the adoption of the gold standard, but were overruled by France. But this change, from demonetizing gold to demonetizing silver, was more of form than of substance. The object aimed at by both was through a disuse of one of the money metals to protect the creditor classes and those having fixed incomes against a fall in the value of money and a rise in general prices. This is the pith and marrow of the monetary discussions of the last twenty-five years."

CHAPTER III.

PRICE AND ITS RELATION TO BUSINESS.

The laboring classes of all civilized nations have been, and are, as a body, poor. All wealth being the production of labor, therefore, laborers could have possessed it, had not something intervened to prevent this natural result. Even in our own country, where the reward of labor is greater than in most others, some cause is operating with continual and growing effect to separate production from the producer. The wrong is evident, but neither statesmen nor philanthropists have traced it to its true source; and hence they have not been able to formulate any plan sufficient for its removal. Believing both cause and remedy lie with our circulating medium, and that the great mass of our people have been led to distrust their own competency to comprehend the subject, I propose to discuss it in the plainest terms possible. In doing so, conclusions must be arrived at after carefully considering all the factors entering into them. Solid facts and not abstruse theories are necessary in the examination of this question.

In a previous chapter I have shown the dependence of

price upon the amount of domestic currency in circulation. In this chapter I shall endeavor to explain the relation that price has to the business of the country. Not to any particular branch, but to the general business conducted among us as citizens.

I shall begin by showing the various stages through which the volume of our currency has passed; the numerous laws bearing upon it, and the evident conclusions to be drawn from the arguments and proofs presented. I shall neither conceal nor color anything to affect or promote my argument, but give plain facts in plain terms.

The awakening interest manifested among all classes of people upon this question, seems to demand a thorough inquiry into the subject matter. Without further delay, only to ask of my readers a careful perusal in a friendly but critical spirit, I will begin the investigation.

The story of currency contraction has become an "oft-told tale"; yet, being a crime of a free government against a free people, and by their own chosen representatives, it should be repeated as often as possible, that all may come to know where, and through whose instrumentality their present distressing condition originated.

After the war closed in April, 1865, the strength of the government had been tested, and the preservation of the Union clearly demonstrated. The people once more directed their attention to the cultivation of the arts of peace. January 1, 1866, found us as a nation about three billions of dollars in debt, made up of interest and non-interest bearing obligations. It is worthy of remark at this point, and is a fact not generally known, that up to the time of Lee's surrender not a single dollar of gold or silver had been subscribed or paid by any banker or capitalist, either in Europe or America, for a bond of the United States. Also, that it was about seven months after that event before a single bond had been sold in the money

markets of the Old World. Thus we see all this vast amount
of debt was being handled by our own people; and their prosperity at that period has never been equaled before nor since.
The reason for this is plain. About one billion five hundred
millions of this indebtedness was being used by the people as
a circulating medium. In that capacity it was giving the government no trouble. Gold and silver were hiding where they
always do in times of trouble, and dared not venture out; consequently, they did not enter into the aggregate of the circulating medium at that time. Among this currency was a large
amount of interest-bearing notes, variously estimated from
twelve to fifteen hundred millions. This with greenbacks and
national bank bills made up the currency of the nation.

Greenbacks had risen from 46 to 71 per cent measured by
gold value; this, too, with over $50 of circulating medium per
capita of population. Our situation at that time indicated
many years of financial prosperity. Our debt was being cared
for, and held among our own people. The men of both armies
had returned home, and were uniting their efforts to rebuild
the wealth of the nation destroyed by merciless war. The impetus given to business and production by this means was truly
marvelous. Not only did this vast increase of the volume of
business call for more currency, but the entire South had to be
supplied. Human wisdom, to-day, can find no reason for the
subsequent course adopted by the government. The fact of
supplying the people of the South from this stock of currency
was, of itself, a question of great moment to the whole nation,
which seems to have been entirely overlooked. There is not
the least doubt, had Congress issued full legal tenders for this
whole amount, they would have appreciated to gold value long
before specie payment was enforced. "After the battle come
the ghouls, to fatten and thrive on its victims." Just so with
regard to our national finances. At that time the bankers and
capitalists came in swarms to enrich themselves by reason of

the nation's disaster. The lamented Garfield said "that the people would remember the bankers and capitalists of Wall street as the Germans remembered the robbers of the river Rhine, who never came out from their strong-holds but to plunder and rob them."

They performed their task so well that at one blow twelve hundred millions of what had been circulating as currency, was converted into 5-20 bonds, bearing six per cent interest, and sold abroad. The interest on these bonds was payable in coin, and since that time we have been raising and shipping corn, wheat, cotton, etc., to pay it. The annals of economic history affords no parallel to this great crime against the industries of a confiding people. The shock that immediately followed beggars description. The people had learned, during the war, to indulge somewhat in luxuries. The desire to live in more ease and comfort had naturally grown upon them during this season of prosperity. They enlarged their business, built new homes, bought new farms and began new enterprises, for which, to a considerable extent, they had gone in debt, anticipating as easy payments in the future as had been made in the past. They dreamed of no change in values, and all was progressing happily and smoothly, when, like a flash of lightning from a clear sky, came this act of Congress which took from them more than one-half of their means of payment. Every debt, national and individual, was by means of that act doubled. This brought financial trouble all over the land. Not satisfied with funding this large amount of circulating medium, early in that year (April, 1866), Congress permitted the Secretary of the Treasury to further contract the currency by burning up on an average five million dollars of greenbacks each month. In order to obtain these greenbacks, he was authorized to sell bonds drawing interest and buy them. This continued until February 4, 1868. By that time a wail had gone up from the people that even Congress could not ignore, and an act was passed forbidding the Secretary of the Treasury reducing the circulating medium further. President Grant refused to sign the bill, and it became a law without his signature. In the mean time failures had increased from 495 in 1863 to 2,864 in 1868. Our currency had been reduced in volume from $1,863,409,216 in 1866 to less than $794,756,112 in 1868. We learn from these figures both the cause and the effect.

One other feature of the question that escapes notice is, at this time bonds were selling at a premium. If that fact was significant in any sense, did it not show the rapid appreciation, in gold value, of our currency as it then was constituted?

About this time there was also considerable discussion through the press as to what these bonds should be paid in. It was plainly apparent that the government would take advantage of its option and soon begin to call them in.

From 1863 to 1867 there had been bonds sold amounting to $1,429,392,400. These were all paid for in greenbacks at par. Reckoning the discount between greenbacks and gold we find that the price paid in gold value was only $945,251,-220, leaving a difference of $484,141,180. It requires no great thought to understand that when these bonds were declared payable in coin their value was increased by this difference.

March 18, 1869, the following act was passed by Congress:

"That in order to remove any doubt as to the purpose of the government to discharge all just obligations to the public creditors and to settle conflicting questions and interpretations of the law by virtue of which such obligations have been contracted, it is hereby provided and declared that the faith of the United States is solemnly pledged to the payment in *coin* or its equivalent of *all the obligations of the United States* not bearing interest, known as United States notes, and of *all the interest-bearing obligations* of the United States, except in cases where the law authorizing the issue of any such obligations has expressly provided that the same may be paid in lawful money or other currency than gold and silver."

When this became a law the bondholders had thereby made, through its operation and effects, the sum of $484,141,-180, in the exchange of greenbacks for bonds that were to be paid in coin.

That the original contract between the people and the bondholder implied their payment in lawful money, either paper or coin, I quote the following as proof.

In a speech delivered in the Senate February 27, 1867, John Sherman said:

"Equity and justice are amply satisfied if we redeem these bonds at the end of five years in the same kind of money, of the same intrinsic value it bore at the time they were issued. Gentlemen may reason about this matter over and over again, and they cannot come to any other conclusion; at least that has been my conclusion after the most careful consideration. Senators are sometimes in the habit, in order to defeat the argument of an antagonist, of saying that this is repudiation. Why, sir, every citizen of the United States has conformed his business to the legal tender clause. He has collected and paid his debts accordingly."

In 1868 he wrote to a friend as follows:

"*Dear Sir;* I was pleased to receive your letter. My personal interests are the same as yours, but like you, I do not intend to be influenced by them. My construction of the law is the result of careful examination, and I feel quite sure an impartial court would confirm it, if the case could be tried before a court. I send you my views as fully stated in a speech. Your idea is that we propose to repudiate or violate a promise when we offer to redeem the 'principal' in legal tenders. I think the bondholder violates his promise when he refuses to take the same kind of money he paid for the bonds. If the case is to be tested by the law, I am right; if it is to be tested by Jay Cook's advertisements, I am wrong. I hate repudiation or anything like it, but we ought not to be deterred from doing what is right by fear of undeserved epithets. If under the law as it stands, the holders of the 5-20's can only be paid in gold then we are repudiators if we propose to pay otherwise. If the bondholder can legally demand only the kind of money he paid, then *he* is a repudiator and extortioner to demand money more valuable than he gave.

Truly yours,

JOHN SHERMAN."

Again in 1869, in another speech in the Senate, Mr. Sherman said :

"The contraction of the currency is a far more distressing operation than Senators suppose. Our own and other nations have gone through that process before. It is not possible to take *that* voyage without the sorest distress. To every person, except a capitalist out of debt, or a salaried officer, or annuitant, it is a period of loss, danger, lassitude of trade, fall of wages, suspension of enterprise, bankruptcy and disaster. It means the *ruin* of all dealers whose debts are twice their business capital, though one-third less than their actual property. It means the fall of all agricultural productions without any great reduction of taxes. What prudent man would dare to build a house, a railroad, a factory, or a barn, with the *certain* fact before him that the greenback that he puts into his improvements will, in a few years, be worth 35 per cent. more than his improvements are then worth? When the day comes, every man, as the sailor says, will be close-reefed ; all enterprise will be suspended ; every bank will have contracted its currency to the lowest limit, and the debtor compelled to meet in coin a debt contracted in currency will find the coin hoarded in the treasury, and no representative of coin in circulation ; his property shrunk, not only to the extent of the contraction of the currency, but still more by the *artificial* scarcity made by the holders of gold. *To attempt this is to impose upon our people;* by arresting them in the midst of their lawful business, and applying a new standard of value to their property without any deduction of their debts, or giving them any opportunity to compound with their creditors, or to distribute their losses ; and would be an act of folly without example in evil in modern times."

Hon. B. F. Wade, known from Maine to California for his sterling honesty and incorruptibility, in a letter to a friend, said :

"VICE-PRESIDENT'S CHAMBER, }
WASHINGTON, Dec., 13, 1867. }

Yours of the 8th inst. is received, and I must cordially

agree with every word and sentence of it. I am for the laboring portion of our people. The rich can take care of themselves. While I must scrupulously live up to all the contracts of the Government, and fight repudiation to the death, I will fight the bondholder as resolutely when he undertakes to get more than the pound of flesh. We never agreed to pay the 5-20's in gold; no man can find it in the bond, and I never will consent to have one payment for the people. It would sink any party, and it ought to. To talk of specie payments or a return to specie under present circumstances, is to talk like a fool. It would destroy the country as effectually as a fire. And any contraction of the currency at this time is about as bad. But I have not time to give my ideas in full.

Yours truly,

BENJAMIN F. WADE.

Capt. A. Denny, Eaton, O."

Garrett Davis offered the following amendment:

"That the just and equitable measure of the obligations of the United States upon their outstanding bonds, is the value in gold and silver coin of the paper currency advanced and paid to the Government on these bonds."

He declared the resolution "robbery and would make the people pay nearly $900,000,000 more than by law and equity they should pay."

Senator Bayard seconded the arguments of Senator Davis:

"Suppose instead of issuing paper money, it had pleased Congress to order an abasement of our national coinage. Suppose twenty-five per cent. more of alloy or worthless metal had been interjected into our currency, and with that base coinage, men had come forward to buy your bonds. What would be thought of the man who, when the day of payment of those bonds arrived, should say, 'I gave you lead, or lead in certain proportions; but for all the worthless metal I handed you, you must give me back pure gold.' Whether he was more maddened or more dishonest would be the only question arising in men's minds."

The facts are, the Government received nothing but greenbacks for the bonds, dollar for dollar, during the entire war; that we never agreed to liquidate the principal of the debt in gold, the original contract being far from so stipulating; and that the contract in question was ignored and another substituted in the interest of the bondholders, it being this latter that provided for the redemption of the bonds in coin. The ablest men in all parties and in Congress have made that acknowledgment. To quote the language of the late Senator O. P. Morton, of Indiana:

"We should do foul injustice to the Government, and to the people of the United States, after we sold those bonds on an average for not more than sixty cents on the dollar, now to propose to make a new contract for the benefit of the bondholders."

And that noble old Commoner, Thaddeus Stevens, expressed the sense of every true patriot in the House of Representatives when he uttered the following emphatic declarations in 1868, his voice trembling with emotion at the outrage which it was sought by powerful combinations to put into effect in the interest of the bondholders in changing the 5-20's into gold bonds:

"If I knew that any party in this country would go for paying in coin that which is payable in money, thus enhancing it one-half; if I knew there was such a platform and such a determination this day on the part of any party, I would vote for the other side, Frank Blair and all. I would vote for no such swindle upon the tax-payers of this country. I would vote for no such speculation in favor of the large bondholders, the millionaires who took advantage of our folly in granting them coin payment of interest."

The object of the framers of the law could not have been to strengthen the public credit. The amount of credit which either a nation or an individual can possess, depends upon the strength and extent of the belief among lenders and capitalists that the borrower is both able and willing to meet the exact terms of his obligations. An offer to do more would subject the debtor to well-merited suspicion and distrust. He can not improve his credit by promising to pay a larger amount of money, or money of greater value, than the terms of the obligations held against him require.

The sufficient, best, and only means of improving credit, public or private, is exact performance of contracts. The debtor that insists upon all his rights and at the same time performs all his duties, is the one most confided in. Credit can be strengthened by *fulfilling* contracts, but not by *changing* them ; by performing all promises and not by making new ones. Nor could the honest object of the framers of the law have been to advance the value of bonds already sold and in the hands of purchasers. It would be of great public importance to enhance the value of bonds which the Government was proposing to sell, but to overload the country with additional burdens for the purpose of enhancing the value of outstanding bonds, would be to subserve gratuitously and unjustly, private interest at the public expense. It would be very gratifying to national pride to have the bonds of the United States, now in private hands, command the highest prices in the markets of the world, but it could scarcely be deemed a wise financial policy in the present condition of the country to obtain that gratification by paying a premium for it. If, however, it were deemed advisable to enhance the value of bonds already sold, it should have been done by some plain and direct method, and in such a way that the country might know exactly what it was going to cost—as for instance, by increasing the principal or rate of interest of outstanding bonds. It should not have been done by the indirect method of changing the medium of payment from gold or silver, at the option of the Government, to gold alone. The additional burden which that might impose, from a rise in the value of gold, is incalculable.

The passage of this act, while it declared the bonds payable in coin, was done when coin was at a premium of nearly 25 per cent, which, of course, added at once 25 per cent of value to the bonds, and at the same time lessened the means of payment to the same extent by its effects in producing a general decline of prices. Why it was necessary at that time to strengthen the public credit, and why it was an act of justice (?) to the people of the United States to have the whole basis of their indebtedness changed and increased by fully one-fourth its amount, will always remain a mystery to every student of political economy.

This was the first time the contract between the people and the bondholder had been changed. I quote from an eminent English author on this point, Professor McCulloch. He says:

"To make any direct change in the terms of the contract entered into between individuals would be too barefaced and tyrannical an interference with the rights of property to be tolerated.

Those, therefore, who endeavor to enrich one part of society at the expense of another, find it necessary to act with great caution and reserve, and to substitute artifice for open and avowed injustice. Instead of directly altering the stipulations in the contract, they ingenuously bethought themselves of altering the *standard* by which the stipulations were to be adjusted.

They have not said, in so many words, that 10 or 20 per cent should be added or deducted from the mutual debts of society, but they have, nevertheless, effected this by making a difference in the value of the currency." (Increased or diminished its quantity.)

But, as the sequel shows, this was only a portion of the scheme. The next year, July 14, 1870, Congress passed a funding bill which authorized the sale or exchange at par for other bonds, fifteen hundred millions of interest-bearing bonds to run 10, 20 and 30 years, with interest and principal payable in coin. After the funding of these bonds had been accomplished the last act was to be perpetrated. Feb. 12th, 1873, Congress passed an act dropping the standard silver dollar from our coinage, and in 1875 demonetized it. This act made our whole national indebtedness payable in gold and necessarily creating a new basis for the payment of all debts, public and private.

This again added to the burden of debt and also increased the difficulties of payment. The contract had been changed again. It seems as though the moneyed men on either side of the Atlantic owned our Congress; and the people, to whom we must look for means of payment, were ignored entirely.

The fact that over eleven thousand failures were reported during these two years is sufficient proof of the manner it was "benefiting" the nation. But this was not enough. Jan. 14, 1875, the specie resumption act was passed. It authorized the Secretary of the Treasury to first sell bonds to buy silver for the purpose of exchanging and withdrawing the postal currency and scrip from circulation. About eighteen millions of 5 per cent bonds were sold for that purpose. There were also sixty-five millions of 4 1-2 per cent, and twenty-five millions of 4 per cent bonds sold for the purpose of retiring legal tender notes, which are still drawing interest. Here we see bonds of the United States sold on a long time that are now worth, and command a premium of 27 per cent, to take from the people the best small currency they ever had, and to retire from circulation the best medium of exchange known to any civilized nation.

The failures following this, 1875-6-7, for each year respectively were 7,740, 9,092 and 10,480. This indicates the "*success*" of the experiment. The silver commission, in their report, say:

"Its true character, as now interpreted, was neither avowed in Congress nor understood by the country at the time of its passage. The phraseology of the act created the impression that there was to be no reduction of the aggregate of paper money, but that legal-tender notes were to be diminished only as bank-notes were increased. As the act is administered in practice, both classes of notes are being reduced at the same time, while the population of the country is expanding. The words of the act may justify this method of administration, but it was not with that understanding that it was sanctioned by Congress.

A more fatal misconception grew out of the ignorance that prevailed almost universally until after the passage of the resumption act, that silver had been demonetized, and hence, that a law providing for specie payments was really a law for gold payments. The people were not aware that coin then meant gold, and that coin payments involved the shriveling of all values to the measure of a single metal. They were in favor of resumption but not confiscation, and they were not aware that resumption as proposed was but another name for spoliation. Although the period fixed for this spoliation was nominally in the future, it actually commenced at once, and is now proceeding day by day. It having been made certain, so far as the law could make it certain, that each dollar of the actual money of the country would, on a given day in the near future, be raised to the value of a gold dollar, the universal tendency was, and has continued to be, to change all forms of property into money, and to refuse investment in either property or productive enterprises. Moneyed capitalists, knowing the disastrous effects which the impending fall of prices would have on the financial condition of borrowers, prudentially withdrew or diminished all credits and hastened to realize on securities. They have never been deceived, for one moment, by the idle fallacy that resumption in gold involved an appreciation in the value of the legal-tender notes and a fall in prices only to the extent of the present difference between the value of those notes and gold. They knew that the appreciation of legal-tender notes must reach that vastly higher level which the value of gold must reach when hundreds of millions of it were and are demanded for resumption, and that prices would sink to a corresponding point of depression."

In the campaign of 1876 there appeared a new feature in the economic views entertained by the people. Previous to that time they had considered "finance" too deep a study, and in consequence it had been left almost entirely with their congressional representatives for a solution. But, then, the question of American finances began to be discussed by them—the acts of Congress and votes of members were freely criticised. Ugly questions were being asked, which soon developed the fact that the average Congressman was about as ignorant of the effect of his vote as were his constituents. All that was necessary to pass an act touching the finances was to "convert" the few leaders.

The most striking evidence, perhaps, of the public inattention to the effect of the coinage act of 1873, is the fact that President Grant, who signed it, and who was critically observant of the legislation of Congress, had no knowledge of what it really accomplished in relation to the demonetization of silver, and was still uninformed about it as late as the following October. If the President of the United States, in daily intercourse with the public men of the country, had failed to hear during certainly eight months that the laws no longer permitted money to be coined from silver, it must be true that the ignorance on the subject was general and profound.

In a letter written October 3, 1873, to Mr. Cowdrey, General Grant said:

"I wonder that silver is not already coming into the market to supply the deficiency in the circulating medium. * * * Experience has proved that it takes about $40,000,000 of fractional currency to make the small change necessary for the transaction of the business of the country. Silver will gradually take the place of this currency, and further, will become the standard of values, which will be hoarded in a small way. I estimate that this will consume from two to three hundred millions in time, of this species of our circulating medium. * * * I confess to a desire to see a limited hoarding of money. But I want to see a hoarding of something that is a standard of value the world over. Silver is this.

Our mines are now producing almost unlimited amounts of silver, and it is becoming a question, 'What shall we do with it?' I suggest here a solution which will answer for some years, to put it in circulation, keeping it there until it is fixed, and then we will find other markets."

This may, to some extent, perhaps, explain how John Sherman and Hugh McCulloch became millionaires, and why Robert Schenck was sent to the Court of St. James to teach the English people how to play "draw poker." However this may be, a cry went up from the people for relief. Agitation and discussion disclosed many of the frauds embodied in the acts of Congress, and through fear of political destruction, on the 28th day of February, 1878, the standard silver dollar was rehabilitated with its legal-tender power, and the coinage of at least two millions per month was made compulsory.

The act of May 31st, of the same year, forbade the further retiring of greenbacks. During this year business failures in the United States amounted to more than $234,000,000—the most disastrous since the almost total extinction of values in 1857, which was at that time produced from the same causes. We notice also that the aggregate of failures from 1866 to 1878 amounted to the enormous sum of $1,784,394,132. During the years 1863-4-5, when we had an abundance of money in circulation, there were only 1545 failures, amounting to $34,-103,000, while during the succeeding eleven years of contraction there were 67,422 failures, amounting to the vast sum given above.

Who can examine these figures and not come to the conclusion at once that contraction was the prime cause of these bankruptcies, and the governing factor in this wide-spread destruction?

On January 1st, 1879, specie payment was resumed, and with it came the inevitable lessening of the means of payment. Although Congress had remonetized silver and ordered its continued coinage, each Secretary of the Treasury, in collusion with banks and bankers, has succeeded in keeping it out of circulation up to the present time. Every document coming from the Treasury department has contained a carefully prepared paper upon the evils of silver coinage; and the silver dollar that ought to be controlled by and belong to the people, has never had a friend in any administration since. Everything is being done to add to the coinage of gold, while every obstacle possible is thrown in the way of the coinage of silver.

Congress passed an act permitting the issue of silver certificates upon deposits of silver with the Treasurer, and after repeated insults from the banks, in a lucid interval, passed another act that no National Bank should belong to a clearing house that would not receive these silver certificates in settlement of balances. This law the New York and other banks in large cities have persistently ignored. In order to assist in the evasion of the law the Secretary of the Treasury resorts to the following scheme as shown by one of the leading journals. The local editor of the New York Tribune, a paper which has been distinguished for its zeal in supporting the refusal of the banks to receive silver certificates, gives in that paper of February 11th, the following account of the motives of the banks in seeming, on the 9th, to have relaxed in their exclusion of silver :

"It is understood that the Monday payment by the Sub-Treasury was intended to accomplish two objects—to soothe any jealousy on the part of country banks and to enable the Secretary of the Treasury to answer satisfactorily the congressional inquiry whether any National Banks or clearing-house associations refused to accept silver or silver certificates. As the New York clearing house has now accepted silver in payment of balances both it and the Sub-Treasury have complied with the Federal law. It is generally understood by bank officers that payment in silver will not be repeated except in cases of emergency."

In issuing bonds under the act of July 14, 1870, the United States took the risk of a rise in the value of both the metals. The parties accepting the bonds took the opposite risk of a fall in the value of either of them. The chances against the United States were wars and political disturbances in the mining countries, such as caused a decrease in the production of gold and silver between 1809 and 1848, or that the mines would be, from any other cause, less productive, or that countries not using gold or silver might decree their use as money, and thus make a new demand for them, or that a change of fashion might increase the consumption of the metals in the arts. Either of these circumstances, or all combined, might raise the value of the metals very materially. On their part, those who accepted the bonds took the risks of an increased production of either or both of the metals by the discovery of new gold and silver mines, or by the more vigorous working of old mines, or that commercial countries *might demonetize one or both of the metals,* or that great amounts of gold or silver might be liberated by the suspension of specie payments in important countries, or that the habits of the world might be so changed that less amounts of gold or silver would be used for other purposes than as money. Either of these circumstances, or all combined, might depreciate the value of one or both of the metals very materially.

One fact, not a matter of chance but of reasonable certainty, operates steadily against the United States. This is the advance of the world in population, wealth, and exchanges, and the consequent requirement of more money, with no certainty that the mines will produce more.

The risks were and are mutual. Is it supposable that, upon the occurrence of any or all of the circumstances which would tend to raise the value of both metals, and thereby increase the burdens of the obligations payable in them, the United States would ask or that the bondholder would agree to a corresponding scaling of the contract? Has a bargain been made where the creditors, under all vicissitudes, stand to win and not to lose ? Is the United States bound to the obligations and penalties of the contract, and debarred from all the advantages conferred by its terms? These interrogatories admit of but one reply.

There is no dispute about the facts of the case, or the law. A contract has been entered into between the government and its creditors involving contingencies which may favor either party, and both parties must abide the issue, whatever it may be. It would be beneath the dignity of the Government to demand any advantages of the Government which the law and the contract made under it do not confer. It would be a violation of justice and a betrayal of the great interests confided to its charge to accept anything less. The Government is an agent and not a principal. It is the trustee of the nation, and must find the charter and guide for the administration of the affairs intrusted to it in the law and not in sentimental emotions.

The creditor would have no reason to complain of the law or the fact if he were now paid in silver. The contingencies which have happened have not been favorable to the United States, but otherwise. Not only has the value of both the metals risen, but a comparison of gold prices in 1870 with silver prices in 1885 will show that the value of silver in buying the products of labor is now greater than the value of gold was then. Payment to-day in silver would not only give the creditor all he is entitled to under the law and the contract, but would mete out to him more than equity would demand.

It is sometimes said that the more recently issued bonds should be paid in gold, because the United States received gold for them. The obligations of a bond are not governed by the price or the species of money, or the nature of the consideration received by those who issued it. They are governed by the terms of the bond, and not by what it is sold for. A bond sold at 105 can have no other construction than a similar bond sold at 50, and a bond sold for gold can have no other construction than a similar bond sold for silver or greenbacks, or given in payment for supplies and services. The promise, and not the consideration, governs. If it were really true that what is received for bonds determines what they promise, the holders of a majority of the outstanding bonds of the United States would be in a much less favorable position than they now occupy.

In consequence of this war on silver, a large sum lies idle in the vaults of the national Treasury, with a fixed determination on the part of the Secretary and the Government that not one dollar shall be paid for the redemption of bonds. The plea of unfairness is made, that silver has depreciated in value, and is now at a discount compared to gold. With a hundred millions or more of bonds subject to call, which should be paid, thereby putting into circulation the same amount of currency, and relieving the Nation of the interest on that amount of bonds, all this vast sum is held idle in the Treasury because the bondholders control the administration.

Let us go to the facts and ascertain whether these bonds can be honorably paid in silver. The law passed February 25, 1862, provides that coin, and coin alone, shall be received for customs dues. That law has never been changed. It also provides for the disposal of the coin so received as follows :

"Section 3694.—The coin paid for duties on imported goods shall be set apart as a special fund, and shall be applied as follows :

First—To the payment in coin of the interest on the bonds and notes of the United States.

Second—To the purchase or payment of one per cent. of the entire debt of the United States, to be made within each fiscal year, which is to be set apart as a sinking fund, and the interest of which shall in like manner be applied to the purchase or payment of the public debt, as the Secretary of the Treasury shall from time to time direct.

Third—The residue to be paid into the Treasury.

Since the passage of the above-mentioned act, millions of silver has been received into the Treasury from customs, and not one dollar of it applied, as the law directs, in the purchase or payment of bonds, while the act expressly provides for the payment of one per cent, each year, of the entire debt with this coin.

In 1870, when our present bonds were issued, they were sold in accordance with the following act of Congress :

"Chap. 256.—An Act to Authorize the Refunding of the National Debt.

Be it enacted by the Senate and House of Representatives

of the United States of America in Congress assembled, That
the Secretary of the Treasury is hereby authorized to issue, in
a sum or sums not exceeding in the aggregate two hundred
million dollars, coupon or registered bonds of the United
States, in such form as he may prescribe, and of denominations of fifty dollars, or some multiple of that sum, *redeemable
in coin of the present standard value,* at the pleasure of the
United States, after ten years from the date of their issue, and
bearing interest, payable semi-annually in such coin, at the rate
of five per cent per annum; also a sum or sums not exceeding in the aggregate three hundred million dollars of like
bonds, the same in all respects, but payable at the pleasure of
the United States, after fifteen years from the date of their
issue, and bearing interest at the rate of four and ahalf per
cent per annum; also a sum or sums not exceeding in the aggregate one thousand million dollars of like bonds, the same in
all respects, but payable at the pleasure of the United States,
after thirty years from the date of their issue, and bearing
interest at the rate of four per cent per annum; all of which
said several classes of bonds and the interest thereon shall be
exempt from the payment of all taxes or duties of the United
States, as well as from taxation in any form by or under state,
municipal or local authority; and the said bonds shall have set
forth and expressed upon their face the above specified conditions, and shall, with their coupons, be made payable at the
Treasury of the United States.   But nothing in this act, or in
any other law now in force, shall be construed to authorize any
increase whatever of the bonded debt of the United States."

This is section first of the act approved July 14, 1870.
Can language be plainer than this? Notice the express provision, "redeemable in coin of the present standard value."
What was the standard value of silver then? 412 1-2 grains,
the same as now. But for further proof I give below the exact
wording of *the bond itself.* This wording is on the original
and all subsequent renewals:

"This bond is issued in accordance with the provisions of
an act of Congress entitled ' An act to authorize the refunding
of the national debt,' approved July 14, 1870, as amended by
an act approved January 29, 1871, and is redeemable at the
pleasure of the United States after the first day of July, 1907,
in coin of the standard value of the United States on said

July 14, 1870, *with interest in such coin* from the day of the date hereof at the rate of four per cent per annum, payable quarterly, on the first day of October, January, April and July in each year. The principal and interest are exempt from the payment of all taxes or duties of the United States, as well as from taxation in any form by or under state, municipal, or local authority.

Washington, July 1, 1877."

The act creating the bond, as well as the bond itself, specifically declares that coin of the standard value of 1870 shall be the standard of payment. The contract was changed in 1875, but restored to its original conditions in 1878. Since that time we have had a double standard of payment in fact, but only one in practice. From a recent report of the Secretary of the Treasury I clip the following :

"Although the act of July 14, 1870, provides for the issue of United States bonds, '*redeemable in coin of the present standard value*,' whereby were included both gold and silver coin of that value, yet as by the act of Feb. 12, 1873, the further coinage of silver dollars was prohibited, and the revised statutes declared gold coin only to be for sums exceeding five dollars, equity, if not strict construction of law, requires that the holders of such bonds should receive payment therefor in gold or its equivalent."

The above statement of the Secretary of the Treasury falls flat when we consider the fact that the law of 1873 did not *demonetize* the silver dollar, but simply stopped its coinage. The act of June 22, 1875, sections 3585 and 3586 took from it its legal tender properties.

Beginning with the date, June 22, 1875, and tracing the laws to February 28, 1878, when silver was remonetized, the amount of bonds sold under the act referred to, was: 5 per cent bonds, due 1881, $156,216,950 ; 4 1-2 per cent bonds, due 1891, $140,000,000.

Of this amount the bonds due in 1881 have all been paid or reissued in some other form. Of the bonds due in 1891 there is only about $128,000,000 outstanding. From these figures we can discern the last flimsy foundation upon which the advocates of a single gold standard of payments base their arguments.

Hon. Edwards Pierrepont, Attorney General of the United States, and Minister to England, in a letter to the New York Times of April 18, 1884, says:

"There is not an outstanding bond, coupon or greenback issued by the United States which may not be lawfully paid in silver. Not one of them on its face or back, or in the statute authorizing the issue, or in declaration, or in resolution of Congress, has any proviso that they shall be paid in gold. And the act of Feb. 28, 1878, directing the coinage of silver dollars, declared that such dollars shall be a legal tender at their nominal value for all debts and dues, public and private, except where otherwise expressly stipulated in the contract."

The most conclusive evidence of all is in the following resolution. This completely explodes the idea of a single standard of gold in payment for bonds.

The following resolution passed the United States Senate January 25, 1878, and the House of Representatives January 28, 1878, by a vote of 42 to 20 in the Senate and 189 to 79 in the House:

"That all the bonds of the United States issued or authorized to be issued under the said acts of Congress hereinbefore recited are payable, principal and interest, at the option of the government of the United States, in silver dollars of the coinage of the United States, containing 412 1-2 grains each of standard silver; and that to restore to its coinage such silver coins as a legal tender in payment of said bonds, principal and interest, is not in violation of the public faith nor in derogation of the rights of the public creditor."

It is both interesting and instructive to examine the list of those voting for and against the resolution then and note their positions at this time.

Neither do I believe there is a bond or debt of any description against this Government bearing interest, but can be called in at any time and paid. I hold it to be the duty of this

Government to call in any of these bonds and rid the treasury
of its surplus in their payment.   What is the meaning of the
following quotations, if it does not convey that power?

In the Credit-Strengthening act, passed March 18, 1869, it
is provided as follows:

" But none of said interest-bearing obligations shall be redeemed or paid before maturity, *unless* at such time United
States bonds shall be convertible into coin at the option of the
holder, *or unless* at such time bonds of the United States bearing a lower rate of interest than the bonds to be redeemed can
be sold at par in coin."

It may be urged that this language refers solely to the
currency sixes.   Granting this for the sake of argument, we
find in Sec. 3,693 of the Revised Statutes the following provision:

" But none of the interest-bearing obligations not already
due shall be redeemed or paid before maturity, unless at such
time United States notes are convertible into coin at the option
of the holder, or unless at such time bonds of the United States
bearing a lower rate of interest than the bonds to be redeemed
can be sold at par in coin."

A recent writer says:

"If this language means anything, it means that Congress
then recognized the fact, which no one will seriously dispute,
that the Government had the undoubted right to pay its bonded
indebtedness at any time.   But, owing to the peculiar condition of the currency at that time, Congress provided by a solemn pledge that it would not exercise this right until the conditions named existed.   Both conditions now exist.   United
States notes are exchangeable for coin at par, and bonds bearing a lower rate of interest than the bonds to be redeemed can
be sold at par in coin.   It follows that a strict construction of
the law under which these bonds were issued fully warrants
their payment at any time.   If it is urged that it would cause
loss to the holders of the bonds; the answer is that such holders
had full knowledge of the law, and also that the Government
owes to the debtor class, and to the people generally, just as
much care and fidelity as it owes to the bondholders."

It is asserted in the Secretary's report that one of the consequences of the payment by the Government of all its debts in silver would be the impairment of the national credit, although no explanation is given how a refusal to pay gold can injure the character of a country which has never promised to pay gold, and which has a law on its statute-books admonishing everybody who deals with it that the standard silver dollar is, and shall be, a tender for everything which it owes, unless it is "otherwise expressly stipulated in the contract."

The Economist says "nearly every nation on the face of the globe is indebted to us, and the result of an appreciation of gold is that we obtain a larger quantity of their commodities" in settlement of our claims.

H. H. Gibbs, an ex-governor of the Bank of England, says in an article in the British National Review for July, 1883, that the following ideas being precisely those of the Economist, are constantly pressed upon the English public:

"England is a creditor nation. The scarcity of gold has made that metal more valuable, and she must needs be the gainer by this, and must continue to be still more the gainer if gold becomes scarcer still. Is it to be expected that she should throw away this advantage?"

The same reasons which make gold monometalism a favorite policy in England make it a favorite policy in every country, and in every section of all countries in which the creditor classes are dominant. Quite as naturally it is not a favorite policy in countries and sections of countries which are heavily loaded with public, corporate and private debts.

The honor of the Government was no more sacredly pledged to the bondholder, that the principal and interest of bonds issued under the act of July 14, 1870, should be paid in coin of the standard value of that date, than it was to the people that they should have the option and privilege of paying the bonds issued under that act in either of the classes of coin of the standard value of that date. There are two parties to these contracts, the bondholder on the one side and the masses of the people on the other. The rights of the one are as sacred as the rights of the other.

Even Great Britain, for many years during the present century, paid the interest of its public debt, a large proportion of which had been contracted in coin, in inconvertible bank notes, whose depreciation sometimes reached as high as thirty per cent. While nearly all nations have, on various occasions, met their obligations in a money less valuable than they agreed to pay, the Government of the United States stands alone and pre-eminent in the generosity and in the folly of paying in a money more valuable than it agreed to pay. The only compensation which it has received for the added burdens thrown upon its citizens by an over-performance of its contracts is the interested praise of those benefited, which is as insincere as it is interested. Those who obtain an unjust advantage have a real contempt, however concealed, for the weakness that concedes and allows it. That sensitiveness so morbidly manifested by some in respect to the estimation in which this Government may be held by its creditors, here and abroad, and their indifference as to the estimation in which it shall be held by the great mass of its own citizens, instead of being the evidence of proper national pride, is an exhibition of weak and puerile vanity. That sentimental idea of honor which requires the abrogation of the plain terms of a written contract by one of the parties to it, against its own interest and at the demand of the other party, while suited to youthful fancy, and refreshing in the pages of cheap literature, should find no place in official interpretations defining the rights and duties of a nation under contracts whose written terms are so precise as to exclude implication, and were framed by eminent patriots who had the welfare of the nation always at heart.

Senator Beck in a recent speech placed this idea in a convincing light:

"There is no more effectual or pernicious method of contracting the currency than by collecting by taxation a large sum in excess of the needs of an economically administered Government, and locking it up in the Treasury. Every dollar needlessly taken from the tax-payer, wrongfully deprives him of that much capital which he needs and labored to obtain, and when it is locked up, the circulating medium, which all the people want, is wrongfully withheld from them. The thief who steals and squanders an unneeded surplus locked up in the Treasury vaults would inflict less injury on the country and its business if the money he stole was put in circulation, than a Secretary who holds and hides in vaults currency which the people want and refuses to use it to pay the debts, especially interest-bearing debts, which the men who own this money owe. It is easy to raise a clamor about a surplus, but it will be more difficult to explain to the people why such vast amounts of the money they have been so heavily taxed to furnish is lying idle in the overloaded Treasury vaults, and they deprived of its use, while interest is running against them on bonds which can be and ought to be paid. The idle money when paid out for interest on bonds would at once be released and restored to circulation."

The Senator continues his remarks on this question further. He says:

"If the gold mines of California and Australia had continued to produce abundantly, and the Comstock lode and the Leadville mines had not produced silver, so that the market value of the two metals as bullion in London had been reversed, the argument could be made quite as plausibly that the silver dollar was the constitutional unit of value in 1870, which the bondholders have a right to demand.

There is not an outstanding obligation of the United States, nor of any state, municipality, corporation, or individual, which can not be legally and honorably discharged by the payment of the present standard silver dollar. What right has Congress to deprive the debtor of that right by adding more silver to the coin than he agreed to pay, or by stopping its coinage so that he can not obtain it? It is as palpable a violation of a contract to increase the obligation of the debtor as it is to impair or reduce the standard value of the coin which the creditor stipulated in his contract should be paid to him. I repeat: Why should it be stricken down, or its purchasing power further increased 20 per cent. by adding 40, 50, or any other number of grains to its weight? · In other words,

why should every producer and debtor have to give 20 per
cent. more of the products of his labor to obtain either a new
silver dollar or gold coin with which to pay his debts than he
does now, when he is already paying his obligations according
to the terms of his contract in a coin which will procure for its
owner much more of all he needs than it would in 1870? It
is only another phase of the constant struggle of the rich to
grind the faces of the poor, and of the favored few to enrich
themselves by class legislation.

While no one can deny that every obligation of the United States and every contract within our own borders can be
discharged honorably with the present silver dollar, we are told
that our foreign obligations and relations are such that gold
will be at a premium very soon, and we will be on a basis of
degraded silver at once if we do not increase the weight or stop
the coinage of silver; that all Europe is horrified at our stupid-
ity or dishonesty, or both.

Fortunately the official reports overthrow all the reckless
assertions of the gold worshipers. The Register of the Treasury (see report for this year, page 4), shows that out of $1,-
071,460,262 registered bonds of the United States outstanding
only $11,927,900, or a little over one-tenth of 1 per cent. is
held abroad, and of those which can be paid before 1892, foreigners hold only $34,150, which is less than the interest on
the money now lying idle in the Treasury for one day at 3 per
cent. per annum.

These facts, coupled with the fact that our exports of
goods exceeded our imports $130,000,000 this year, and our
imports of gold exceeded our gold exports $18,213,804, an
amount greatly exceeding all our bonds held abroad, settle the
question. The falsity of the clamor about foreign complica-
tions or gold premiums is made too apparent for any sensible
man to be deceived by it.

The press is filled with articles day by day which seek to
make people believe that all other nations have ceased to coin
silver, and that we alone are stubbornly persisting in forcing it
upon this country after it has been abandoned everywhere else.

I propose to disprove these allegations by officially stated
facts. The Director of the Mint in his last report shows
(pages 131, 132) that for the year 1884 the world's production
of gold was $95,292,569; of silver, $115,147,878; and that
$99,459,240 of gold was coined, while the coinage of silver last
year amounted to $90,039,443, of which the United States
coined $23,991,756 of gold, and $28,534,866 of silver. Other

nations, therefore, coined in 1884 $61,504,577 of silver, show-
ing that we are far from being alone in the coinage of that
metal. England coined $3,204,824 of silver last year and $6,-
201,517 the year before, to add to her stock which has been accumulating for generations; while she has coined silver for
India in the last three years to the value of $68,234,000.

The workers for wages in England to-day get their pay in
silver coin, and the question is never mooted by them as to the
comparative bullion value of the silver and gold coin of that
country. Even Germany, notwithstanding she pretended to
have demonetized silver twelve years ago, coined in 1882 $6,-
407,157 of it to add to her vast stock on hand; her laborers are
paid in it now. No complaint is made anywhere, here or in
Europe, about silver coin except by the holders of our bonds,
who seek to increase largely the purchasing power of gold, or,
which is the same thing, reduce the value of all our property
from 25 to 50 per cent. below its present value when tested by
the single standard of gold, which they claim shall be paid by
us to them and to them alone. They do not seek to establish
the single gold standard, they say; they are bimetallists.
They agree that silver is a legal tender for all debts and obligations of the Government, except those held by them. It is
good enough to pay the laborer, the soldier, the sailor, in short,
all who work for the United States, but they insist that it is
dishonest in us to pay it to them, although their bonds and obligations all show on their face that it is a legal tender in payment of them all so long as it is coined of the standard value
fixed by law, July 14, 1870, as it is now and always has been.

Our dollar is more valuable than that coined by most of
the other leading nations, France included, theirs bearing the
relation of 15 1-2 to 1 with gold, while ours is 16 to 1. I need
not repeat in detail what the official reports show in regard to
the gold, silver, and paper currency of the several countries.
It is sufficient to prove by them that while the difference in
the market value of gold and silver in London operates to degrade their silver coin more than it does ours, France and other
countries maintain their silver and paper in all transactions,
public and private, at par with gold under far greater difficulties
than we have to contend with, no matter from what stand-
point the comparison is made."

All that is now, or ever has been necessary to keep silver
where it belongs and in its proper ratio with gold is for the
officers of the Government to obey the law. Let them say to

the bondholders, here is coined silver of the required fineness and weight; take it in payment for your bonds. It is all you can legally or morally ask, as it is strictly in accordance with the bond you compelled us to give. When this is done, and these patriotic gentlemen known as the nation's creditors, are made to understand that in the near future they will be the owners of this tabooed silver dollar, the cry against silver coinage will cease, and this howl about a buzzard dollar will be heard only as an echo from foreign lands. This war is not made against silver, but against the *quantity* of money in the hands of the people, and for the purpose of restricting the means of payment now within the reach of the debtor class of our citizens. When we understand this truth, all· the acts of Congress which have been directed by our moneyed men will be made plain. They want the volume of currency reduced, well knowing that the value of what remains will be enhanced.

There is another factor which has aided in the contraction of our currency, to-wit: The continued attacks upon it by the banks and capitalists, and their constant harping against the constitutionality of the legal-tender greenback. These persistent assaults upon the greenback led to a trial in the Supreme Court of the United States of the legality of their issue, with the following result as reported by the Associated Press:

DECISION OF THE SUPREME COURT.

"WASHINGTON, March 3, 1884.—A decision was rendered by the Supreme Court of the United States to-day in the long pending legal tender case of Augustus D. Jilliard *vs.* Thomas S. Greenman, brought here by writ of error from the Circuit Court of the United States for the southern district of New York. The question presented by this case as stated by the Court is, ' whether notes of the United States issued in time of war under acts of Congress declaring them to be legal tender in payment of private debts, and afterward, in time of peace, redeemed and paid in gold coin at the treasury, and then reissued under the act of 1878, can under the constitution of the United States be legal tender in payment of such debts.'

The Court is unanimously of opinion that the present case cannot be distinguished in principle from cases heretofore decided and reported under the names of 'legal tender cases' (12 Wall 457) 'Dooly vs. Smith' (13 Wall 604), 'railroad company vs. Johnson' (15 Wall 195), and 'Maryland vs. railroad company' (22 Wall 105), and all the justices except Justice Field, who adheres to the views expressed in his dissenting opinion in those cases, are of opinion that they were rightly decided. The Court holds, therefore, that Congress has power to issue obligations of the United States in such form and to impress upon them such qualities as currency for the purchase of merchandise and payment of debts as accord with the usage of a sovereign government. The power as incident to power of borrowing money, and issuing bills and notes of the government for money borrowed, of imposing upon those bills or notes the quality of being legal tender for the payment of private debts, was a power universally understood to belong to sovereignty in Europe and America at the time of the framing and adoption of the constitution of the United States. This power of making notes of the United States legal tender in payment of private debts being included in the power to borrow money and to provide a national currency, is not defeated or restricted by the fact that its exercise may affect the value of private contracts. If upon a just and fair interpretation of the whole constitution a particular power or authority appears to be vested in Congress, it is no constitutional objection to its existence or to its exercise that property or contracts of individuals may be incidentally affected.

The Court says in conclusion:

Congress, as the legislature of a sovereign nation, being expressly empowered by the constitution to levy and collect taxes, to pay debts and provide for the common defense and general welfare of the United States, and to borrow money on the credit of the United States, and to coin money and regulate the value thereof and of foreign coin, and being clearly authorized to coin as incidental to the exercise of those great powers, to emit bills of credit, to charter national banks, and to provide a national currency for the whole people in the form of coin, treasury notes and national bank bills, and the power to make notes of the government a legal tender in payment of private debts, being one of the powers belonging to sovereignty in other civilized nations, and not expressly withheld from Congress by the constitution, we are irresistibly impelled to the conclusion that impressing upon treasury notes of the United States the quality of being legal tender in payment of private debts is an appropriate means conducive and plainly adapted to execution of the undoubted power of Congress consistent with the letter and spirit of the constitution; therefore, within the meaning of that instrument necessary and proper for carrying into execution the powers vested by this constitution of the Government of the United States.

Such being our conclusion in the matter of law, the question whether at any time in war or peace the exigency is such by reason of unusual and pressing demands on the resources of the government or of inadequacy of the supply of gold and silver coin to furnish the currency needed for uses of the government and of the people, that it is as a matter of fact wise and expedient to resort to this means is a political question to be determined by Congress when a question of exigency arises, and not a judicial question to be afterward passed upon by the courts. It follows that the act of May 31, 1878, is constitutional and valid, and that the Circuit Court rightly held that a tender in treasury notes reissued and kept in circulation under that act was a tender of lawful money in payment of the defendant's debt to plaintiff.

The judgment of the Circuit Court is affirmed.   Opinion by Justice Gray, JusticeField dissenting.

JUSTICE FIELD DISSENTS.

Justice Field, in a long and carefully prepared opinion, dissents from the opinion of the Court and from all arguments advanced in its support. He says:

'If there be anything in the history of the constitution which can be established with moral certainty, it is that the framers of that instrument intended to prohibit the issue of legal tender notes both by the general Government and by states. The argument presented by the Court, and by advocates of legal tender, amounts to this: The object of borrowing is to raise funds; the annexing of the quality of legal tender to notes of the Government will induce parties to take them, and funds will thereby be more readily loaned. But the same thing may be said of the annexation of any other provision which would give to the holders of notes some advantage, as for instance a provision that notes of the Government should serve as a free ticket on public conveyances of the country, or give free ingress to places of amusement, or entitle him to a percentage from the revenue of private corporations. The same consequence—a ready acceptance of notes—would follow, and yet no one would pretend that annexation of provisions of this kind with respect to property of others, over which the borrower has no control, would be in any sense an appropriate measure to the execution of power to borrow. There is no invasion by the Government of the rights of third parties which may not be thus sanctioned under the pretense that its allowance will lead to the ready acceptance of the Government's notes and produce the desired loan.'

In conclusion Justice Field says:

'From the decision of the Court I see only evil likely to follow. If Congress has power to make notes of the United States legal tender, and to make them pass as money, it may be asked what necessity was there to invest it by the constitution with power to borrow money? If it can make money, why borrow it? and if notes of the United States with the legal tender quality are money, or equivalent to money, why should Congress not at once issue a sufficient amount to pay all bonds of the United States? Why pay interest on $1,000,000,000 bonds when in one day it can make money to pay them? It would not indeed surprise me if there be a call from many quarters upon the Government to issue such notes for bonds. Who can object to it if the doctrine declared by the Court is sound? and why should there be any restraint upon unlimited appropriations by the Government for all imaginary schemes of public improvement if the printing press can furnish all the money needed for them?' "

That Court, the highest authority in the land, declares in substance, first, that the Government has the power to issue legal-tender paper money, and second, that Congress is the sole judge as to when, and in what quantity it may be issued. This decision is the end of the whole matter. It is final. We have now compassed the whole story of contraction, and from the facts given are prepared to judge of the conflict that began with the civil war and is raging at the present time. When it will cease and what will be the final result no man can predict. One thing, however, is certain. This concentration of values— this building up of giant monopolies—this increasing power of wealth over labor and its products, cannot continue many years and our nation remain a free Republic.

I will now proceed to compare the volume of domestic

currency in the hands of the people for the years 1866 and
1885. There seems to be a difference of opinion among writers
in regard to these ratios. I have made a thorough investigation of the public records and have made my table from them
alone. The task is a difficult one, but in a book of this character
it becomes absolutely necessary. I have given the amount of currency among the people each year. In doing so I have
deducted from the gross amount of currency, all reserves held in the United States Treasury and the banks.
From 1875 to 1885 I have made a very conservative deduction
for lost or destroyed currency. There has been issued and reissued $1,640,559,947 of U. S. notes, and nearly double this
amount of national bank bills. Of course there must have
been a per cent. of this paper money as well as coin lost
and destroyed.

The public debt statement of June 30, 1866, was as follows:

Ten-forty 5 per cent bonds.............................$	171,219,100.00
Pacific Bonds...	6,042,000.00
Five-tweny bonds due 1882-4-5........................	722,205,500.00
Six per cent. bonds due 1881.........................	265,317,700.00
Six per cent. bonds due 1880.........................	18,415,000.00
Five per cent. bonds due 1874........................	20,000,000.00
Five per cent. bonds due 1871........................	7,022,000.00
Temporary ten-day loan...............................	120,176,195.65
Certificates of Indebtedness..........................	26,391,000.00
Six per cent. bonds due 1868.........................	8,908,341.80
Six per cent. bonds due 1867.........................	9,415,250.00
Compound notes......................................	159,012,140.00
Seven-thirty notes...................................	806,251,550.00
United States notes	400,891,368.00
Fractional currency..................................	27,070,876.96
Gold certificates....................................	10,713,180.00
Texas indemnity.....................................	559,000.00
Bonds due and not in................................	3,815,675.80
Total.....................................$	2,783,425,878.21
Cash in Treasury......................................$	132,887,549.11

Amount and kind of currency June 30, 1866, was as follows:

One year notes of 1867...............................$	8,908,341.00
Two year notes of 1868..............................	9,415,250.00
Compound interest notes.............................	159,012,140.00

Seven-thirty notes	806,251,550.00
Temporary loan, ten days	120,176,196.00
Certificates of indebtedness	26,391,000.00
United States notes (greenbacks)	400,891,368.00
Fractional currency	27,070,876.00
Gold certificates	10,713,180.00
National bank notes	294,579,315.00
Total	$1,863,409,216.00

Amount and kind of currency June 30, 1886, was as follows:

United States notes (greenbacks)	$ 346,681,016.00
National Bank notes	277,847,168.00
Gold and silver	820,998,837.00
Total	$1,445,527,021.00
Less reserves in banks and treasury	$ 727,122,021.00
Less reserves in State Banks	125,000,000.00
Less National Bank currency destroyed	15,000,000.00
Less greenbacks destroyed	30,000,000.00
Less gold and silver coins	15,000,000.00
Total	$ 912,122,021.00
Leaving in circulation	$ 533,405,000.00

CIRCULATION PER CAPITA.

Year.	Circulation.	Population.	Per Capita.
1866	1,863,409,216	35,819,281	$52.01
1867	1,350,949,218	36,269,502	37.51
1868	794,756,112	37,016,949	21.47
1869	730,705,638	37,779,800	19.34
1870	691,028,377	38,558,371	18.70
1871	670,344,147	39,750,073	16:89
1872	661,641,363	40,978,607	16.14
1873	652,896,762	42,245,110	15.45
1874	632,032,773	43,550,756	14.51
1875	630,477,609	44,896,705	14.04
1876	620,316,970	46,284,344	13.40
1877	586,328,074	47,714,829	12.28
1878	549,540,187	48,935,306	11.23
1879	534,424,248	50,155,783	10.65
1880	528,524,267	51,660,456	10.23
1881	610,632,433	53,210,269	11.48
1882	657,404,084	54,806,577	11.97
1883	648,205,895	56,450,714	11.48
1884	591,476,978	58,144,235	10.17
1885	533,405,001	59,888,562	8.90

These amounts are taken from reports to Congress, and the returns are from those of the director of the mint and the Comptroller of the currency. They must, therefore, be considered as authentic. A careful study of the above should convince any person of the justice of the cause I am pleading—more domestic currency for the people.

Some, even now deny that the 7-30 bonds enterd into our circulating medium. Everyone in business at that time knows they did. And Treasurer Spinner in his report to Congress for the years 1869 and '70 (page 244) heads the estimate of outstanding currency with a certain amount of 7-30 bonds. This authority ought to settle the question. Others deny that there has been any contraction in our domestic currency, claiming there is as much money now as there ever was. To such I refer to the above table. That it has been the settled purpose of the Government for the past 20 years to contract the circulating medium to the lowest possible amount, I refer to the following extract taken from the report of Hugh McCulloch, Secretary of the Treasury, to Congress in 1866, page 17:

"Anxious as he (the Secretary) is to lighten the public burdens and reduce the public debt, he does not hesitate to say that these notes (legal tenders) should be withdrawn from circulation and that the furnishing of what paper currency may be required be left to corporations. The reduction could be increased from four millions to six millions per month for the present fiscal year and to ten millions per month thereafter."

At the time of this recommendation, the only manner that these notes could be withdrawn was by purchasing them with interest-bearing bonds. Yet this profound financier was willing to burden the people with more debt in order to hire the national banks to issue our currency. This idea has governed our financial system for the past 20 years, and is with us to-day.

These tables show $8.90 per capita in circulation among the people at the present time; and when we reflect that hard times compel wage-workers and producers to hoard their earnings, no matter how small the amount, we can readily see that there is not over $5 per capita in actual circulation; as a dollar

laid away in a man's pocket is as surely out of circulation as if
it were in the bank.   Hoarded money is as much out of circulation as though it remained in the mines.

In connection with the above figures I give the list of
failures for each year named.   From them will be seen the
dreadful effects caused by a shrinkage in the circulating medium.   With contraction come failures in business as surely as
night follows day.   These figures speak with greater power
and eloquence than I can find language to express.

From 1866 to 1886, the failures in the United States number 109,682, with liabilities amounting to $2,744,525,880.
Comment is unnecessary :

In 1867 there were	2,780	failures ; liabilities, $	96,666,000.
In 1868 "	2,608	" "	63,694,000.
In 1869 "	2,799	" "	75,054,000.
In 1870 "	3,551	" "	88,242,000.
In 1871 "	2,915	" "	85,252,000.
In 1872 "	4,069	" "	121,036,000.
In 1873 "	5,183	" "	228,499,000.
In 1874 "	5,830	" "	155,239,000.
In 1875 "	7,740	" "	201,000,000.
In 1876 "	9,092	" "	191,117,000.
In 1877 "	8,872	" "	190,669,000.
In 1878 "	10,478	" "	234,383,132.
In 1879 "	6,658	" "	98,149,053.
In 1880 "	4,735	" "	65,752,000.
In 1881 "	5,582	" "	81,155,932.
In 1882 "	6,738	" "	102,000,000.
In 1883 "	9,184	" "	172,874,172.
In 1884 "	10,968	" "	226,343,427.
In 1885 "	11,211	" "	267,340,264.

From $52.01 per capita with 520 business failures aggre-
gating $8,579,000 in 1864, we have reduced the amount in cir-
culation to $8.90 per capita with a result of 11,211 failures
amounting in the aggregate to $267,340,264 in 1885.   What a
record is this for the greatest, freest and most enlightened nation
on earth!   What a record for a nation, possessing such bound-
less resources of soil, mines, inventive genius and labor, with

every facility to promote the happiness and prosperity of the people, is here chronicled! What reasons can be assigned for the alarming fact, that from 1866 to 1886, 109,682 of our honest, industrious business men were given over by law to a remorseless financial destruction?

There are no reasons, founded in justice, or based on the correct principles of political economy, for the bankruptcies, ruin and almost constant business depression of the last twenty years in this country; for, of all nations, ours should by right, be the most prosperous, and its people the most happy of any on earth.

The effect of these different acts of Congress, alluded to, was to lessen the amount of the circulating medium, and by this contraction the value of labor and all its products was reduced.

The proposition that the *amount* of an obligation does not consist in the number of dollars it contains, but in the ability to pay, is sound in all respects, and will hold good in public as well as private transactions.

Yet, in all this legislation the people, who were the actual debtors, and owed the money, and from the products of whose labor it all must in the end be paid, were ignored, in the law, and their wants and rights overlooked.

It is a well known trick of capital to appeal to the honor of the nation to place the credit of the nation above the credit of its people. What does it matter to me if our national bonds are selling at a premium when my own debts on that account are unpaid and perhaps increased?

Capital—gold and silver—as an evidence of wealth, is always the first to hide when there is any trouble, and the last to reappear and enter the field of traffic when the trouble is over.

These acts of Congress were passed purely in the interest of parties who held our Government bonds, and those who possessed wealth in currency; for by these very acts the difference between a paper and a gold dollar was added to the debt. By the first act, no one can dispute that 484 million dollars was thereby added to the debt and to the taxation of the people. By the two last, God only knows to what extent the amount was increased, and how far-reaching were their effects.

Such, in brief, is the history of contraction. And in that shameless history we find the reason for all the widespread destruction and want, bankruptcy and distress we now see on every hand. What is the situation of our people to-day in regard to national and other indebtedness? Let us ascertain, if possible,—for the great mass of the people are anxious to know the cause of these hard times—why they can't pay their own debts; why wheat, pork, beans, beef and all products are so low as not to pay even a small profit; why our national debt is virtually as large as ever. They know that a few years ago, with much less population than now, pork was worth ten dollars per hundred; now it is selling for five. It takes as much labor to raise the corn and fatten the pork now as then. The grains of gold and silver in the dollar remain the same now as then. Why is it that it takes twenty pounds of pork to buy a dollar now, when it took only ten pounds at that time? Our mortgages and notes are the only things that seem to escape the general shrinkage. Can these questions be answered? They must be. In 1866 we had $52 per capita in currency. We then had plenty of business, plenty of work; tramps were unknown, and labor riots were yet to be seen. Now, after twenty years of contraction, we have less than $8.90 per capita in circulation, with all business demoralized. Our land is filled with tramps, and strikes are the order of the day.

In 1866 our national debt amounted to nearly three billions of dollars. Now it is about 1500 millions, or a little less than one-half the original amount. Nearly 1900 millions have been paid in interest, but nevertheless, the debt is at present really as large as ever, judged by the ability of payment. It will take more pounds of the five great staples of this country—wheat, iron, cotton, meat and wool—to pay what remains of the debt, at present prices, than it would to have paid the whole at the prices when the debt was contracted. A comparison of prices will prove this true. From it we gather the following startling facts:

Original debt, $3,000,000,000. Paid on debt, $1,300,000,-000. Paid in interest, $1,900,000,000. Total paid, 3,200,000,-000. What remains will require more of labor and its products to pay than has been already paid, as before stated; because prices have shrunk at least 65 per cent. Is not this statement plainly true? If true, is it not, in the light of our present civilization, *disgracefully* true?

This process is technically known as making the dollar good, and it is all done in the interest of the workingman, "so that when he earns a dollar, he can buy a dollar's worth with it." Here is a table showing the debt of the United States on the first day of July, 1866 and 1884, including non-interest bearing greenbacks, expressed in dollars, and also in the things working folks have to produce in order to get the dollars with which to pay debts and interest:

Debt in	1866.	1885.
Dollars	2,773,000,000	1,830,000,000
Beef, barrels	129,000,000	135,000,000
Corn, bushels	2,000,000,000	3,000,000,000
Wheat "	800,000,000	1,740,000,000
Oats, "	3,262,000,000	4,357,000,000
Pork, barrels	82,000,000	96,000,000
Coal, tons	213,000,000	400,000,000
Cotton, bales	12,000,000	34,000,000
Bar iron, tons	24,000,000	40,000,000

Almost every product of labor shows the same result. We paid, from 1866 to 1884, on the public debt: interest, $1,870,-000,000, and principal about 12 hundred millions, yet we find that what there is left of it, when measured by labor or the products of labor, is 50 per cent greater than the original debt. This is equally true with regard to State, city, corporation and

private debts, which reach a sum estimated at twenty billions
of dollars.

Every honest man ought to know and feel that a national
contract of this character, running as it does for a long term of
years, should not be changed. The bonds in 1866 were payable in lawful money, of which there was about 1500 millions
used as domestic currency. The act of March 18, 1869,
changed the contract between the people and the bondholders,
and made the bonds payable in coin. At that time there was
not a dollar of gold or silver in circulation. Both were at a
premium of nearly 30 per cent. The acts of 1873-5 which demonetized silver changed the contract again, and made the
bonds payable in gold instead of gold or silver, and at this time
neither gold nor silver was in circulation except at a premium of
about 13 per cent. During the period from 1865 to 1873 paper money had appreciated from 46 to 88 cents on the dollar
in gold. The act of 1875 fixed the date of January 1, 1879,
as the time for resumption of specie payments. These four
acts of Congress have no parallel in the history of the world.
Other nations have been plundered by their rulers; but never
has a people been so wantonly robbed, so infamously cheated
of their hard earnings under the disguise of statesmanship before. Nor have they allowed such brigandage of their rights
to go unpunished. But here, in this country—a Republic—
some of the very men who participated in this unrighteous
proceeding have been kept continually in office by the people
who have meekly borne the sufferings caused by their misgov-
ernment. As Madame Roland said: "O! Liberty; what crimes
have been committed in thy name!"

During all this time there has been a constant contraction
of our currency. Its volume has grown less with each succeeding year, and the price of labor and its products has in
the same ratio declined, until there is scarcely a living profit in
any legitimate business. The people are as anxious to gather

riches as ever, but the laws of the Government regulating the distribution of wealth are framed by the hand of moneyed men. This gives them power over labor, and they have used that power in a merciless manner. Hence the conflict between capital and labor. No matter how much may be said about there being no antagonism or conflict between capital and labor; that their interests are identical, etc. I say there *is* a war, there always has been a war, and always will be a war, bitter and ugly between them. Their interests are *not* identical, but are diametrically opposed to each other. Money wants cheap labor and a dear dollar; the toiler wants dear labor and a cheap money. How, then, can there be anything at best but an armed neutrality between them? Each stands ready to take advantage of the other. Law seems to be the only regulator or arbiter of their differences. If labor can force a law that will reduce the abnormal and unjust profits of capital it will hasten to do so. If capital can enslave labor it does not hesitate or fail to make the point. For more than a century the laws of this nation have favored the rich. But since 1861 the whole machinery of government has been actually in their possession. Our Senators and Representatives in Congress, with very few exceptions, become wealthy, perhaps millionaires, in a few years of service. All seem to fatten upon something—a *plant* growing out of their official positions—intangible to the masses, but not difficult to name. The scrutiny of the people will soon disclose it.

Every law that has passed Congress since 1861, regulating the financial condition of the Government and people, has been in favor of the rich and against the poor. Because of this, great monopolies have grown up. Immense corporations have sprung into existence and flourish. All business is done upon a scale that makes it impossible for the small dealer or tradesman to endure the competition and continue his business. Not only this, but farming is fast approaching the same condition. Soon, unless these conditions change, our small farms will be a thing of the past, and a system of tenant farming will take its place.

In view of the fact that the contract between the people and their creditors has been changed three times, and each time against the interests of the tax-payers; that, owing to the righteous indignation of the sufferer, an act was passed giving back the silver dollar to the people, in part, with full legal tender qualities, would it not be fair and just to further benefit them by passing one more law restoring the original contract in letter and spirit to the nation?

Burke said (recognizing that there is a faith due to the people as well as to the holders of public securities):

"It is to the property of the citizen, and not to the demands of the creditor of the state, that the original faith of society is pledged. The claim of the citizen is prior in time, paramount in title, superior in equity."

This astute English Statesman condenses the truth of the whole question in the paragraph quoted. These measures were denounced by the best and truest men of our country, and their prophecies as to the consequences resulting from the enactment of the laws referred to have proved true.

That a want of sufficient currency is the cause of distress and bankruptcy among nations cannot be denied; and that a sufficient supply completely reverses this condition of affairs must be admitted, I will point to our own condition of financial prosperity or adversity as the case may be, and quote from the history of other nations and from other dates to prove these statements true.

On page 439 in the appendix, Bancroft cites the following intelligence from New York, under date of June 4, 1785:

"There is no trade with any but the British, who alone give the credit they want, and draw off all the bullion they can collect. They see no prospect of clothing themselves, unless they had the circuitous commerce they formerly enjoyed with Great Britain, which many think a vain expectation, now they are no part of the empire. The scarcity of money makes the produce of a country cheap, to the disappointment of farmers and the discouragement of husbandry. Thus the two classes of merchants and farmers, that divide nearly all America, are discontented and distressed. Some great change is approaching."

Beginning on page 355, Belknap particularizes some of the extreme measures which popular clamor and the severity of the emergency compelled several of the Legislatures to adopt, in an attempt to alleviate the intolerable situation of the community. He says:

"Similar difficulties at the same time existed in the neighboring State of Massachusetts, to remedy which, among other palliatives, a law was passed called a *tender act*, by which it was provided that '*executions issued for private demands might be satisfied by cattle and other enumerated articles, at an appraisement of impartial men under oath.*' For such a law the discontented party in New Hampshire petitioned; and to gratify them, the Legislature enacted, 'that when any debtor shall tender to his creditor, in satisfaction of an execution for debt, either real or personal estate sufficient, the body of the debtor shall be exempt from imprisonment; and the debt shall carry an interest of six per cent., the creditor being at liberty either to receive the estate, so tendered, at a value estimated by three appraisers, or to keep alive the demand by taking out an *alias*, within one year after the return of any former execution, and levying on any estate of the debtor which he can find'. At the same time an act was made enlarging the power of the Justices of the Peace to try and determine actions of debt and trespass to the value of ten pounds. These laws were complained of as unconstitutional; the former as being retrospective, and changing the nature of contracts; the latter as depriving the creditor, in certain cases, of a right to trial by jury. But so strong was the clamor for redress of grievances, and so influential was the example of the neighboring State, that some of the best men in the Legislature found it necessary to comply, whilst another part were secretly in favor of worse measures."

Belknap, on page 357, further said:

"The scarcity of money was still a grievance which the laws had not remedied, but rather had a tendency to increase

To encourage its importation into the country, the Legislature exempted from all port duties, except light-money, every vessel which should bring gold and silver only; and from one-half of the duties, if a sum of money equal to one-half of the cargo should be imported. But it was to no purpose to import money, unless encouragement were given for its circulation, which could not be expected whilst the 'tender act' was in force; for every man who had money thought it more secure in his own hands than in the hands of others."

Under date of September 20, 1786, Otto, the French Minister in New York, wrote home to his Government, as follows:

"In the small state of Connecticut alone more than five hundred farms have been offered for sale to pay the arrears of taxes. As these sales take place only for cash, they are made at very low price, and the proprietors often receive not more than one-tenth of the value. The people feel the deadly consequence of this oppression, but not being able to discover its true cause, it turns upon the judges and the lawyers. In the States which have paper money, the rigor of the laws is less desolating for the former, since he can always get paper enough to satisfy his engagements; and, besides, the creditors are less urgent."

Beginning on page 35 of "The New Olive Branch," Mathew Carey says:

"I have in 1786 seen sixteen houses to let in two squares of about eight hundred feet in one of the best sites for business in Philadelphia. Real property could hardly find a market. The number of persons reduced to distress, and forced to sell their merchandise, was so great, and those who had money to invest were so very few, that the sacrifices were immense. Debtors were ruined without paying a fourth of the demands of their creditors. There were most unprecedented transfers of property. Men worth large estates, who had unfortunately entered into business, were in a year or two totally ruined; and those who had a command of ready money quadrupled or quintupled their estates in an equally short space. Confidence was so wholly destroyed that interest rose to two, two and a half, and three per cent. per month. And bonds and judgments and mortgages were sold at a discount of twenty, thirty, forty, and fifty per cent. In a word, few countries have experienced a more awful state of distress and wretchedness."

Chief-Justice Marshall, taking a general survey of the

situation throughout the Confederation, says, in the fifth volume of his "Life of Washington," beginning on page 88:

"In many of those states which had repelled every attempt to introduce into circulation a depreciated medium of commerce, or to defeat the annual provision of funds for the payment of the interest, the debt sunk in value to such a degree that those creditors who were induced by their necessities, or want of confidence in their rulers, to transfer their public securities, were compelled to submit to a loss of from ten to sixteen or seventeen shillings in the pound. However unexceptionable might be the conduct of the existing Legislature, the hazard from those which were to follow was too great to be encountered without an immense premium. In private transactions, an astonishing degree of distrust also prevailed. *The bonds of men whose competency to pay their debts was unquestionable, could not be negotiated but at a discount of thirty, forty, and fifty per centum: real property was scarcely vendible; and sales of any article for ready money could be made only at a ruinous loss. The prospect of extricating the country from these embarrassments was by no means flattering.* Whilst everything else fluctuated, some of the causes which produced this calamitous state of things were permanent. The hope and fear still remained that the debtor party would obtain the victory at the elections; and, instead of making the painful effort to obtain relief by industry and economy, many rested all their hopes on legislative interference. *The mass of national labor, and of national wealth, was consequently diminished.* In every quarter were found those who asserted it to be impossible for the people to pay their public or private debts; and, in some instances, threats were uttered of suspending the administration of justice by private violence. About three hundred mutineers met near Exeter to break up the courts of justice; but Governor Sullivan, a distinguished officer during the war, instantly put himself at the head of the militia, dispersed the insurgents, and dispersed the chiefs of the revolt. The people of Connecticut have equally made some efforts for the abolishment of debts and breaking up of the courts of justice, but the vigilance of the Governor has thus far prevented any overt act. *It must be agreed that these insurrections are in great part due to the scarcity of specie.*"

Minot, in his "History of the Insurrection in Massachusetts," page 27, summing up the causes of public disorder, proceeds as follows:

"From the short view we have taken of the affairs of the Commonwealth sufficient causes appear, to account for the commotions which ensued. A heavy debt lying on the State, added to burdens of the same nature upon almost every incorporation within it ; a decline, or rather an extinction, of public credit ; a relaxation of manners and a free use of foreign luxuries ; a decay of trade and manufactures, with a prevailing scarcity of money ; and, above all, individuals involved in debt to each other, are evils which leave us no necessity of searching further for the reasons of the insurrection which took place."

Henry Clay said :

"The revulsions of 1837 produced a far greater havoc than was experienced in the period above mentioned. The ruin came quick and fearful. There were few that could save themselves. Property of every description was parted with at sacrifices that were astounding, and as for the currency, there was scarcely any at all. In some parts of the interior of Pennsylvania, the people were obliged to divide bank notes into halves, quarters, eighths, and so on, and agree from necessity to use them as money. In Ohio, with all her abundance, it was hard to get money to pay taxes. The Sheriff of Muskingum County, as stated in the Guernsey Times, in the summer of 1842, sold at auction one four-horse wagon at $5.50 ; ten hogs at 6 1-4 cents each ; two horses (said to be worth from $50. to $75. each) at $2. each ; two cows at $1. each ; a barrel of sugar for $1.50, and a 'store of goods' at that rate. In Pike County, Missouri, as stated by the Hannibal Journal, the Sheriff sold three horses at $1.50 each ; one large ox at 12 1-2 cents ; five cows, two steers, and one calf, the lot at $3.25 ; twenty sheep at 13 1-2 cents each ; twenty-four hogs at 25 cents for the lot ; one eight-day clock at $2.50 ; lot of tobacco, seven or eight hogsheads, at $5 ; three stacks of hay at 25 cents each."

Also :

"By the contraction of money in England, from 1816 to 1825, more than *four-fifths* of the land owners were robbed of their estates, the whole number in the Kingdom shrinking from 160 thousand to 30 thousand."

When Louis Phillippe, in 1848, escaped from his outraged people, the financial condition of the nation was about as bad as it could be compatibly with existence.

The British Embassador wrote in March that year, as follows:

"The scarcity of money became so great that a sovereign passed for four and forty francs. Many persons sent their plate to be coined into five franc pieces. It was melancholy to see the most civilized capital in the world suddenly reduced to the primitive conditions of barter."

In December, 1848, the London Times, with its ordinary Delphic dogmatism, announced the inevitable failure of the French Republic and disintegration of French society in the near future, but so wise was the administration of the statesmen of that nation that two months later the calumniator was forced to eat his own words, saying in his columns (The Times), February 16, 1849:

"As a mere commercial speculation with the assets which the bank held in hand it might then have stopped payment and liquidated its affairs with every probability that a very few weeks would enable it to clear off all its liabilities. But this idea was not for a moment entertained by M. D'Argout, and he resolved to make every effort to keep alive what may be termed the *circulation of the life-blood* of the community. The task was overwhelming. Money was to be found to meet not only the demands on the bank, but the necessities, both public and private, of every rank in society. It was essential to enable the manufacturers to work, lest their workmen, driven to desperation, should fling themselves amongst the most violent enemies of public order. It was essential to provide money for the food of Paris, for the pay of the troops, and for the daily support of the *ateliers nationaux*. A failure on any one point would have led to a fresh convulsion. But the panic had been followed by so great a scarcity of the metallic currency, that a few days later, out of a payment of 26 millions fallen due, only 47 thousand francs could be recorded in silver.

In this extremity, when the bank alone retained any available sums of money, the Government came to the rescue, and on the night of the 15th of March, the *notes of the bank* were by a decree, made a *legal tender*, the issue of these notes being limited in all to 350 millions, but the amount of the lowest of them reduced for the public convenience to 100 francs. One of the great difficulties mentioned in the report was to print these 100 franc notes fast enough for the public consumption. In ten days the amount issued in this form had reached 80 millions.

To enable the manufacturing interests to weather the storm, at a moment when all the sales were interrupted, a decree of the National Assembly had directed warehouses to be opened for the reception of all kinds of goods, and provided that the registered invoice of these goods, so deposited, should be made negotiable by endorsement. The bank of France discounted these receipts. In Havre alone eighteen millions were thus advanced on *Colonial produce*, and, in Paris, fourteen millions on *merchandise;* in all, sixty millions were thus made available for the purposes of trade. Thus, the great institution had placed itself, as it were, in direct contact with every interest of the community, from the Minister of the Treasury down to the trader in a distant out-port. Like a huge hydraulic machine, it employed its colossal powers to pump a fresh stream into the exhausted arteries of trade, to sustain credit, and *preserve the circulation from complete collapse.*"—*The Bank Charter Act, and the Rate of Interest,* London, 1873, pp. 123-5.

Sir Archibald Allison saw as clearly as the noon day sun the possibilities of such a calamity when he wrote, in 1852:

"Gold is a very good thing, and necessary for foreign exchanges, but it is not worth purchasing by the ruin of the country.

In every one of the great monetary crises which have occurred every five or six years during the last thirty, from $500,000,000 to $750,000,000 have been destroyed. Is the retention of gold worth purchasing at such a price?

It may be safely affirmed that if the requisite change is not made, the nation will continue to be visited every four or five years by periods of panics which will destroy all the fruits of former prosperity, and the people, like the unfortunate culprits who under the former inhuman system of military law— when sentenced to 1,000 or 1,500 lashes—were brought out at successive times to receive their punishment by installments as soon as their wounds had been healed in the hospital."

The speech of General Gordon in the United States Senate, devoted largely to the point that the disasters which had overtaken the business of the country were the direct results of the contraction of the currency, was promptly met with ridicule and indifference. His argument was irresistible, notwithstanding: " In the discussion of this question no tongue is so eloquent as facts. As overtopping the eloquence of any man upon this subject—which reaches into all our homes—we offer the record of these melancholy years that cover the story of contraction.

In tracing the story of bankruptcy and hard times during the decade from 1866 to 1877, the table we submit will be profitable for instruction and reproof. The facts it sets forth, the business failures and business depression, bear the relation of cause and effect. Disaster grew with contraction, step by step. The woes that have fallen upon business have trod upon the heels of contraction of the machinery created for the conduct of business with painful and unmistakable precision. The enormous remorseless contraction has done its work. The number of annual failures has increased from less than 500 to about 14,000, and the liabilities involved in these failures have grown from nine millions a year to more than 300 millions. The table shows why:

STATEMENT OF THE PUBLIC DEBT OF THE UNITED STATES.

Bonded debt, including Loans of various dates, Five-twenties, Ten-forties, etc.:

June 30, 1866	$1,090,198,126
June 30, 1867	1,439,838,676
June 30, 1868	1,959,995,357
June 30, 1869	2,031,684,235
June 30, 1870	2,015,637,640
June 30, 1871	1,967,076,167
June 30, 1872	1,870,497,982
June 30, 1873	1,825,235,077
June 30, 1874	1,745,996,115
June 30, 1875	1,783,245,331
June 30, 1876	1,764,469,481
June 30, 1877	1,714,479,082

Circulating medium, including Treasury notes, gold certificates, fractional currency, demand notes, United States notes, etc.:

June 30, 1866	$1,693,379,753
June 30, 1867	1,091,360,338

June 30, 1868... 676,126,507
June 30, 1869... 614,879,520
June 30, 1870... 479,420,378
June 30, 1871... 450,721,775
June 30, 1872... 433,386,848
June 30, 1873... 473,870,528
June 30, 1874... 510,511,248
June 30, 1875... 498,984,711
June 30, 1876... 466,549,097
June 30, 1877... 477,445,221

Annual contraction:

June 30, 1867... $602,019,415
June 30, 1868... 415,233,831
June 30, 1889... 61,346,987
June 30, 1870... 135,459,147
June 30, 1871... 28,698,603
June 30, 1872... 17,334,927
June 30, 1875... 11,526,537
June 30, 1876... 32,435,614

During three years of this time there were temporary or accidental pauses in this policy of contraction, closing with the years as follows:

June 30, 1873... $40,583,680
June 30, 1874... 36,640,720
June 30, 1877... 10,896,124

The panic of 1873 compelled the chief variation from the otherwise uniform and pitiless policy.

This is the record of contraction. What is the corresponding record of prosperity? The argument of facts must now be heard. That country is prosperous in which every frugal and industrious man can pay his debts. Even the money-lender must admit this. But without discussion, let us place side by side the record of "prosperity" and the record of contraction.

The era of abundant money began in 1862. The era of contraction began in 1865-6. This is the accompanying business history. In 1863 there were but 485 failures in the United States, with liabilities of but $6,864,700. In 1864 there were but 520 failures, with liabilities of but $8,579,000. In 1865 there were but 530 failures in the country, and the liabilities involved were but $17,625,000. At this time, or a little before, contraction commenced the destruction of the business

of the country, as shown above. The result has more than
once been exhibited in detail. The annual number of failures
has grown from 500 to 14,000, and the liabilities from $9,000,-
000 to $330,000,000." This is the argument.

In 1879 Thomas Ewing said:

"Resumption does not mean the equalization of paper
money with gold; it means an addition of from 50 to 66 per
cent to the burden of all debts and taxes to be paid by the
people. Will the people permit adding to the burden of their
taxes, their national, state, municipal, railroad and individual
debts, not less than $5,000,000,000 by forcing prices down to a
gold level? Unless the demands of the people are complied
with by the passage of some such bill as this, the whole resumption scheme will be smashed, even though some political
parties may have to be smashed."

In 1815 the war closed by the capture of Napoleon at
Waterloo. The scourge of war now being removed, it seems
to have been thought that the country could endure without
entire destruction a scourge far worse than the war; and the
Shylocks, with Sir Robert Peel at their head, or as an associate,
began to insist strenuously upon a law for resumption of specie
payments. And then what took place? Let Thomas Doubleday, in his financial, monetary and statistical History of England, tell. He says:

"Prices fell on a sudden to a ruinous extent—banks
broke—wages fell with prices of manufactures; and before the
year 1816 had come to a close, panic, bankruptcy, *riot and dis-
affection* had spread through the land. Vast bodies of starving
and discontented artisans now congregated together and demanded reform of the Parliament. The discontents, as usual,
the Government put down by an armed force. As the memorable first of May, 1823, drew near, the country bankers, as
well as the Bank of England, naturally prepared themselves by
a gradual narrowing of their circulation for the dreaded hour
of gold and silver payments on demand. * * * The distress, ruin and bankruptcy which now took place were universal, affecting both the great interests of *land* and *trade.*"

The great Scotch economist and scientist, Professor Mc-
Culloch, says:

"Thus it appears that, whatever may be the *material* of the money of a country, whether it consists of gold, silver, copper, iron, cowries or paper, and however destitute it may be of any intrinsic value, it is yet possible, by sufficiently limiting its quantity, to raise its value in exchange to any conceivable extent."

The following tables of facts and results, compiled from official statistics, tell a tale worth a dozen theories that panics and periods of good and bad times naturally follow each other like the troughs and waves of the ocean. We give below the volume of money and results at certain dates:

1811—$	28,000,000		Hard times
1816—	110,000,000		Good times
1818—	40,000,000		Panic.
1832—	60,000,000		Fair.
1837—	150,000,000		Booming times.
1843—	58,000,000		Panic.
1847—	105,000,000		Good times.
1857—	215,000,000		Booming times.
1858—	150,000,000		Panic.
1865—	1,651,282,373,	failures 530....	Booming times.
1873—	738,219,749,	" 5,183	Panic.
1877—	696,443,394,	" 8,872	Prostration

These figures demonstrate that those who control the money volume control the times, as much as he who controls the helm controls the course of the ship.

I might quote similar statements from a hundred different works on money, but the ground is more completely covered by simply stating that *no* economist or scientist who has written on money for the past three-quarters of a century denies this truth regarding money—in fact, *it is incontrovertible.*

I will quote from an article in the New York Tribune of late date in further proof of the propositions heretofore made in relation to the effect that the volume of money has on price. The dates given in the tables comprise the periods of contraction from 1865 to 1885. The results are obtained from the only fair method of computation and comparison that has yet been devised. A careful study of the figures given in these tables will be of service to the reader, and enable him to discover the causes operating to produce either financial dis-

tress, or universal prosperity among the people.   The quotation
is as follows:

"It must suffice here to state that quotations of about 200
articles are compared since 1850, and the amount of money is
ascertained which would purchase at different dates of these
various articles, quantities corresponding as closely as possible
to their ascertained consumption in 1880, the date of the last
census.   Among the articles compared are wheat, corn, oats,
rye, barley, beans and peas, mess pork, bacon, ham, live hogs,
lard, fresh beef, tallow, live sheep, poultry, butter, cheese,
eggs, milk, hay, potatoes, turnips, cabbage, onions, apples,
raisins, sugar, brown and crushed; molasses, coffee, tea, tobacco, whisky, malt and hops, mackerel, codfish, salt, rice, nut-
megs, cloves, pepper, cotton, print cloths and standard sheet-
ings, wool of different qualities, blankets, carpets, flannels,
leather, boots, shoes, hides, silk, India rubber, iron (pig and
bar), nails, steel rails, coal, oil (crude and refined), tin and tin
plates, copper, lead, hemp, lumber, spruce and pine, oak, ash,
walnut, and white wood, lath, brick, lime, turpentine, linseed
oil, soap, glass, paper, white lead, and twelve other kinds of
paints, fertilizers, and over fifty kinds of drugs and chemicals.
Constant quantities of all the articles, proportioned as accurately as I am able to the quantities actually entering into consumption in 1880, could have been bought at the quotations
on or nearest to the 22d for $74.56, and the same quantities
would have cost twenty years ago, November 1, 1865, no less
than $174.77.

A part of this change has obviously been due to the depreciation in the value of the legal tenders, now equal to gold,
but of which it took November 1, 1865, about $1.45 7-8 to
purchase $1 in gold.   But we have no right to assume that the
prices of this year measure the purchasing power of gold,
rather than the prices of May 16, 1882, when $106.59 was re-
quired to purchase the same quantities of the same articles that
cost in August last $74.56.   Here has been a decline of more
than $32 in the gold price of the entire list of commodities,
legal tenders having been equivalent to gold for several years
prior to 1882.   The sums in currency which, from data thus far
obtained, appear to be equivalent in purchasing power at different periods, selected to illustrate the extremes of upward or
downward movements, are given in the first column of the following table.   It is proper to add that the completion of the
inquiry may warrant small changes in these figures, but proba-

bly not changes of importance.   In the second column is given
the price of gold in currency the dates named, and in the third
column the gold value of the sums in currency which appear
to have had equivalent purchasing power at the different dates
prior to resumption: •

COST OF CONSTANT QUANTITIES OF PRODUCTS AT DIFFERENT DATES.

PRIOR TO THE WAR.

	Cost in Currency.	Price of Gold.	Cost in Gold.
1860, May 1.................$100,00		$100.00	$100.00

AFTER THE WAR.

1865, Nov. 1.................$174.77		$145.87	$119.81
1866, May 1 .... 157.60		125.12	126.04
1866, Nov. 1................. 170.31		146.25	117.82
1871, Nov. 1................. 122.03		112.00	108.95

THE PANIC RECORD.

1872, May 1.................$137.13		$112.50	$121.81
1873, Nov. 1................. 115.14		108.50	106.01
1874, May 1................. 122.77		112.87	108.77

PREPARATION FOR RESUMPTION.

1875, Jan. 1........ ....$118.01		$112.37	$100.37
1876, Oct. 1................. 97.30		110.00	88.45
1877, May 1................. 99 29		106.75	93.01
1878, May 1................. 82.09		100.37	81.81
1878, Oct. 18................. 77.94		100.37	77.65

RESUMPTION.

1879, Nov. 1.................$ 93.48		$....	$....
1880, Jan. 1................. 103.42		....	....
1881, Jan. 1................. 95.98		....	....
1882, May 16 .... 106.59		....	....

THE RECENT DECLINE.

1883, March 13.................$ 97.82		$....	$....
1883, Nov. 1.,................. 88.71		....	....
1884, Jan. 1 .... 88.37		....	....
1884, Nov. 21................. 78.47		....	....
1885, Jan. 1................. 79.66		....	....
1885, May 9................. 80.22		....	....
1885, Aug. 22 .... 74.56		....	....
1885, Nov. 1................. 75.35		....	....
1885, Close................. 78.53		....	....

It is not only clear from this comparison that the prices of
1885 have been the lowest in our history for twenty-five years,
but that there has been a general tendency toward lower prices.
From 1866 to 1871, and again from 1872 until 1878, and again
from 1882 until 1885, prices fell quite steadily.   Indeed, had
not the short crop of 1881 caused a temporary advance in the

spring of 1882, the range of January, 1880, would have been the highest of the later period, and it might have been said that the present era of declining prices had continued with little intermission for six years. None will fail to observe how swift and sharp the advances have been—about 12 per cent. from November, 1871, to May, 1872, and 25 1-2 per cent. from October, 1878, to January, 1880. But these spasmodic advances, by which the general tendency downward is interrupted, only serve to make it more clear that prices have been tending irresistibly toward a lower level than that of 1860, not only during the period of paper depreciation, but since gold has been the measure of value."

One remarkable feature in this connection is that such an article should have appeared in a journal making a bitter war on silver. If the above tables prove anything, they prove that gold has advanced in value 23.86 per cent. since 1860. There must have been a general decline in the price of all the products of labor as well as in labor itself, or else an advance in the value of gold. Which is most reasonable? Gold being a commodity like all the other products named, it is not reasonable to presume that gold alone has remained unchanged. Besides this, a constant and lively competition has been going on for the purchase of this gold among the most powerful nations of the earth. England, France, Germany, the Netherlands, as well as America, have all struggled to obtain their share, and even more than the conditions of their commercial relations would admit.

Statistics show that the supply of coined gold is being gradually encroached upon by reason of its increased uses in the arts—they show there is not gold enough in the world among civilized nations to pay 5 per cent. of their indebtedness. Then, why should we ask, in the face of these facts, whether all other products had fallen in price, or gold appreciated? Further, this comparative decrease in prices incident to an increase in the value of gold follows in direct ratio with the increase and decrease of the circulating medium. No

stronger argument can be made, showing the truth of the last
proposition, than the figures above quoted. Since 1866 prices
have fallen. This has been the general rule. During all this
time the volume of money has been shrinking, and, as a natural result, gold has appreciated in value—it having, by law
and executive coercion, been made the basis of all paper circulation.

The real cause of the present universal derangement of
commerce and industry must be ascertained before the proper
remedy can be devised. The causes assigned are various and
contradictory. Many of them never had any existence in fact.
Others are inadequate or absurd in themselves, or by reason of
being confined to narrow localities or special interests, cannot
have produced a mischief which reaches all places and all productive interests.

Overproduction is one of those alleged causes, although
food, clothing, houses, and everything useful to mankind, are
and probably always will be in deficiency as compared with
the needs of them if the means were at hand to purchase.
The constant effort of the human race is, and ought to be, to
multiply production. The aggregate effective demand for
products, that is to say, the aggregate demand accompanied by
an ability to purchase, always increases with production. Supply and demand mean substantially the same thing, and are
nothing but two faces of the same fact. Every new supply of
any product is the basis of a new demand for some other product. The capacity to buy is measured exactly by the extent of
production, when the medium of exchange is sufficient, and
there is practically no other limit to consumption than the
limit of the means of payment. Overproduction of particular
things may occur, but that is soon corrected by the loss of
profits in their production. Overproduction in general and in
the aggregate is impossible as far as the natural and positive wants
of mankind are concerned. The contrary opinion will be held

only by those who regret the discovery of the steam-engine, the spinning-jenny, and the sewing and threshing machines, and who believe that while mankind has the skill to devise methods of increased production they have no capacity to provide for the distribution of industrial products. Production is the sole and only source of wealth, and in fact is but another name for wealth. Overproduction must therefore mean superabundant wealth, and the idea that superabundant wealth or superabundant facilities for producing it can be the inciting cause of wide-spread poverty is repugnant to the common sense of mankind. All reputable authorities concur in treating the idea of overproduction as the idlest of fancies and wholly unworthy of serious notice.

Too many railroads are said to have been built, when it is clear there is an urgent need for more. Undoubtedly a too rapid construction may create an abnormal demand for and a rise in the price of the special materials required in railroad building, and may possibly cause an abnormal advance of the interest on money by absorbing too much floating capital in a fixed form, but such evils are self-corrective. Railroad building will always halt under such circumstances until the cost of materials and of capital ceases to be excessive. The tendency of industry to take profitable directions, and to withdraw from those found to be unprofitable, needs no other regulation than to be let alone.

Money sunk in railroads prematurely built and at present unproductive, is another cause assigned for the existing condition of things. But the loss resulting from labor misdirected is no greater than the loss resulting from the non-employment of labor. One single year of the loss now sustained through the stagnation of industry, caused by falling prices, is a calamity of greater proportions than the total loss from all the badly planned or unfortunate railroad enterprises of a decade. If it were really true that the labor lost in unproductive works is the cause, or one of the principal causes, of the present distress, the future must be dark indeed for this country, which has had an army of unemployed laborers since 1873 that is still being recruited as industries break down, one after another, under a shrinking volume of money and falling prices. If a few years of misdirected labor of 100,000 or even 500,000 men, has brought on conditions under which 3,000,000 are forced to be idle, the evils to come hereafter from the present idleness of that vast number must be incalculable and self-perpetuating. They must prove an endless chain freighted with a constantly accumulating volume of disaster, a Pandora's box with hope left out.

That species of speculation in property and securities which is described as reckless and unsound, is said to be one of the causes of the present distress. But even in gambling, there can be no more lost than there is won, and the material damage to the community cannot exceed the worth of the time of those engaged in it. The rating of property at higher or lower prices could not result in a destruction of the property, or even in the impairment of its productiveness. It would be deplorable if it were true, but happily it is wholly untrue, that the prosperity of the prudent and industrious is at the mercy of gamblers, of whatever species or degree.

It is sometimes said that what is being witnessed is a coming down to solid bottom in prices. But the question of prices is a question of the standard in which they are measured. Wages at $2 per day, with a currency of gold and silver, are as much on solid bottom as they would be at a lower range with a currency of gold alone, and what are called bottom or bed-rock prices when the standard is gold, would in their turn be described as inflated if a new policy should decree that money should consist only of diamonds. Prices are nothing but the expression of the relation between money and other things, and in the end cannot express it otherwise than correctly, and when so expressed, prices are at the bottom wherever that may be, and the range of prices, whether higher or lower, depending on the relation between the volume of money and other things. Money is bought with products. Products are bought with money. An increase or decrease in the volume of either will raise or lower the price.

It is maintained by many that existing evils are the results of a loss and lack of confidence, and that the sufficient remedy would be found in its restoration. On all occasions they portray in glowing phrase the abounding prosperity which would follow if moneyed and other capitalists would freely exhibit confidence by inaugurating industrial and commercial enterprises. But it is to be observed that they content themselves with recommending confidence to others, while they are careful not to make a practical exhibition of any on their own part. They seem, in short, to be unconsciously influenced by the view that while they might profit by the confidence of others, confidence on their own part might involve them in losses. The real mischief is not the lack of confidence, but the lack of any legitimate grounds for confidence, and there neither will be, nor ought to be, any revival or extension of confidence, so long as the volume of money continues to shrink, and prices continue to fall. The word "*courage*" and not "*confidence*" should be used in this connection, for it implies the hardihood to face imminent and certain danger. Under existing conditions, if by any possibility confidence could be inspired, the consequences would be baneful rather than beneficial.

Similar conditions to those which preceded the panic of 1873, in the main, exist to-day. The volume of money is shrinking absolutely and relatively to other things, although perhaps not as rapidly as between 1865 and 1873, and the prices of property are gradually shriveling. The principal difference is, that since 1873, the credits extended by moneyed institutions have been largely curtailed or cut off altogether,.

and consequently the material of which panics are made is not in as great abundance as then. The collapses which are constantly occurring do not make as much noise, nor attract as much attention as the explosion of 1873, because they do not occur simultaneously and conspicuously with public institutions, such as banks, in 1873, but nevertheless they are constantly taking place in all parts of the country, and in increasing numbers. All that is necessary to change this monotonous clatter of isolated collapses into a general crash is to restore a courageous confidence and credit without any change in existing conditions. As the collapse of 1873 is generally attributed to an overextension of confidence and credit, a restoration of such confidence now, when the conditions are the same, must pave the way to a new collapse and would be placing dynamite for future explosions under the foundations of business.

It is very necessary to understand in what particulars confidence has been lost before deciding that its healthy restoration is either possible or under existing conditions, desirable. It has not been lost in the intrinsic value of real estate or of any *useful* thing. It has not been lost in the fruitfulness of the soil, or in the ingenuity, industry, or integrity of the people, the stability of the Government, or in the productive powers of labor and machinery. Confidence has not been lost in anything except the possibility of maintaining prices while the volume of money is being shrunk by existing legislation. Confidence has been lost in the idea that capital invested in productive enterprises can be returned with a profit, or even intact, to the investors. Its restoration while present conditions remain is impossible, and would work mischief if it were possible.

It is stoutly affirmed by many that the present stagnation is the result of uncertainty as to the future value of the paper money of the country. If there were any such uncertainty, and consequently, if there were possibilities of a rise as well as of a fall in prices, the adventurous temper of the business men and the people generally would cause active investments and purchases, as was illustrated during and immediately after the civil war, when such an uncertainty really existed. The true cause of the stagnation is to be found in the opposite fact. Instead of it being an uncertainty as to the future value of paper money, it is the absolute certainty that, under present legislation, paper money must still increase in value, and that prices must continue to fall.

From the facts, figures and statistics given in this chapter we cannot shut our eyes to the truth that price is the controlling factor in business. There can be no business without it, and the greater the price the greater will be the aggregate of business done. We also learn that the relation existing between price and business is of such a character that both rise or fall together. The factor which commands and controls both *is the volume of currency.* In a previous chapter I have shown very plainly that price depends upon the amount of currency in circulation in the nation where the price is established. I have shown in this chapter how business depends upon price, and that both are entirely dependent upon the amount of currency in use.

"As before stated, *money is a standard of payment, fixed and immutable.* You can, by changing the quantity of the money, or the quantity of the *uses* for the money, make it necessary for you to part with more of your labor or your property—to any conceivable extent—in order to obtain a dollar, but when obtained it will not pay one whit more of your debts. *By changing the quantity of the money, or by omitting to increase it as the uses for it increase, you change the price that can be had for your property or your labor, but you do not change the debt; that stands as fixed and unchanging as the north star.*"

CHAPTER IV.

KIND AND AMOUNT OF CURRENCY.

We want a currency thoroughly American. One that will represent our peculiar American ideas and traits of character. A currency that carries with its use independence of thought, coupled with that advanced and enlarged conception of social and business life now constituting the one great feature of Americanism. There are but few things—in fact a full-fledged native American has but little in his composition—found in common with citizens of other countries. Our great lakes and rivers, our vast forests and broad prairies, our diversity of soil and climate, our high mountains and rich valleys, our enormous treasures in minerals, the constant push and hurry of trade—all conspire to broaden and deepen the minds of an American citizen upon all economic subjects far beyond that of any other nationality. We, as a nation, have but little in common with the balance of the world that can affect our financial system or the measure of our productive industries that brains and energy cannot improve. We ignore their customs, despise their laws and, as a rule, are indifferent to their teachings. In our national affairs our actions are governed—and almost everything is done—from our own conceptions of justice and equity among the citizens of this Republic; and we ask no concurrence in our measures by the balance of mankind. We are a distinctive people, isolated commercially, independent socially; and by habit, thought and teaching are continually diverging from the beaten paths of other nations. Our ideas of trade and commercial intercourse with nations, colonies and dependencies are inimical to those of any other country. Being thus independent in almost every other respect, why should we not have a distinctive American system of currency? Why should not this great and progressive Republic take care of its own financial system, and have a currency that will completely represent and promote the economic ideas of our own people. If other nations are not satisfied with it, and will not accept it, as reaching their conceptions of what a national currency should be, we are surely in a condition to assume the responsibility of the issue. We are commercially, financially and intellectually qualified to stand the pressure of such national isolation. We forget that other nations have far more need of us than we have of them. We do not always remember that our products are only taken when they can be purchased the cheapest; that prejudice, friendship and national lines are entirely lost sight of in the great struggle for commercial ascendency.

All that the nations of Europe have done for us, by example and otherwise, has proven a positive injury and impediment to our progress. Our very existence as a Government would be wiped out by them if it were possible. Why, then, should we be compelled to accept their system of currency? A system fashioned and molded by the royal and aristocratic hands of kings, emperors and money-lords, to the end that equity and justice in commercial exchanges might be wrested from the producers of wealth. Such a system, if fully adopted here and put into constant effect by the Government, would in time produce the same results as in Europe. Even now we are beginning to realize the existence of a similar condition.

We want a circulating medium exclusively our own; one that will not force itself beyond the boundaries of our own country. We do not want our money made of so valuable a material as to be sought for abroad.   We want it kept in use at home, so that we may enjoy the benefits and reap the rewards of its influence on the great business interests of our people.   We want much less talk about that impossible thing, "the money of the world," and much more action in regard to what shall be the money of America.

It is not generally known that at the present time our Government has commissioned a gentleman to take in the sights of the Old World, and, as he journeys along, ask such non-partisans as Gladstone, Bismarck and others, as to the wisdom or unwisdom of continuing the coinage of silver.   Such childlike simplicity in these times of intrigue and deception is, to say the least, refreshing.   Of course, their advice, under the circumstances, would bear the stamp of disinterestedness. What a spectacle for 60 millions of intelligent people to witness!   Where are our statesmen, our scholars and other men of brains?   Are we bankrupt in that respect, or are they following their plows and forging at their anvils?   The latter is probably true.

We hear and read much concerning the stability of foreign ideas regarding money; that we must copy and endorse their customs and laws, or so much of them as affect our financial condition.   Were that the case, we would make a sorry mess of it.

Professor Levi says:

"Frightened, and not without reason, at the *possible* consequences, some countries heretofore anxious to attract and retain gold in circulation, even at great sacrifices, showed a feverish anxiety to banish it altogether.   In July, 1850, Holland demonetized the gold ten-florin piece and the Guillaume.   Portugal prohibited any gold from having current value except the English sovereign.   Belgium demonetized her gold circulation (that is, repealed the laws making it legal money).   Russia prohibited the export of silver; and France, alarmed but less hasty, issued a commission to look into the matter."

In 1855 Germany demonetized gold, and made silver the

only legal money. But in 1870, after the silver mines had begun to issue vast sums of silver money, and the annual issue of gold money had declined from 146 millions to 98 millions, she demonetized silver and made gold the only legal money.

I might give similar instances of fluctuations and changes in the views of European nations in regard to the use of the precious metals as money. From those given we learn that even those nations which have existed longest are not fully determined upon any fixed line of action. We infer from this that there is a probable chance for improvement with them. Hence I claim as we are or ought to be a distinctive nation in nearly all that the term implies, an effort on our part to improve the methods of issuing a circulating medium would not, if disastrous, stand alone.

In a literal sense every nation has a distinctive circulating medium and no other, for there is no such thing as " a money of the world" any more than there is a market of the world. Where the market or the money is found, it is evident that both or either exist under the laws and regulations governing traffic in each individual nation. What I intend to convey is, a currency not differing in its organic construction from that of other nations. Nothing could be more disastrous to trade and commerce than for all nations to adopt the same monetary system. What affected one, in such a case, would affect all.

In Holland silver was the sole standard until 1816. In that year the double standard was adopted with the legal relation between the metals of 15.873 to 1, which undervalued silver and practically banished it from the circulation. In 1847 silver was again adopted as the sole standard, not, as claimed by some, in consequence of the discovery of gold in California, but just before that event. The principal reason assigned by the statesmen of Holland for this change in 1847 was, that it had proved disastrous to the commercial and industrial interests of Holland to have a money system identical with that of England, whose financial revulsions, after its adoption of the gold standard, had been more frequent and more severe than in any other country, and whose injurious effects were felt in Holland scarcely less than in England. They maintained that the adoption of the silver standard would prevent England from disturbing the internal trade of Holland by draining off its money during such revulsions, and would secure immunity from evils which did not originate in and for which Holland was not responsible.

This proposition is undoubtedly sound, and is being so recognized by the best economic writers on both sides of the water.

As the most important function of money is to measure values and to establish equities in time transactions, the great bulk of which are internal and between citizens of the same country, and all of which are expressed in the money of some particular country, it follows that any system of money that is common to several countries is a vicious one, in that it subjects the entire internal business of each of them to all the disasters originating in the political or financial mismanagement of the Government, or in the political disturbances, follies, misfortunes, or reckless speculations of the inhabitants, of any one or all of the others. That money is simply the instrument of commerce and industry and not their object; that a sufficiency of it is better than more, and infinitely better than less; that the outflow of money from one country to another having money systems in common, is a double injury. It is an injury to the country that receives it and a greater injury to the country that parts with it. It tends in the one instance to produce crises by inflation, and in the other panics through contraction. And that in addition to this is an injury to each on account of the derangement of the trade of the other; that their invention of money is but half completed when the necessary limitations and regulations of its quantity, and consequently of its value, are remitted not only to the vicissitudes and chances of mining, but to the vicissitudes in the business and legislation of foreign countries; that these facts and considerations, and many others which might be urged, show that metallic money is an inaccurate money, and fills only in a moderate degree any of the requirements of a perfect system, while, in essential particulars, it so far fails to fill them as to render it unfit for an advanced civilization.

On the other hand, every requirement of a perfect system can be met more nearly and more certainly by paper money than by any other ever devised. Not paper money based upon gold, silver, or any other fluctuating commodity, whose measure it should be, nor upon a promise of commodities, near or remote, definite or indefinite, of governments or banks; nor like the French assignats, based upon lands; nor fastened to gold or silver by a chain sure to snap when the metals are wanted; nor convertible into bonds and thereby offering the bribe of interest for its withdrawal from circulation; nor of any use to its owner except when parted with; nor capable of yielding profit except when employed in the production and distribution of wealth; but an absolute money, whose value, conferred by the sovereign authority, and regulated by a pre-arranged and perfected system, and not by the passions and caprices of the hour, would rest impregnably on functions essential to civilization and progress.

Bryant, in his discussion of the question, says:

"The *power* of money to fix the *condition* of man in all human affairs, is supreme, absolute—*sovereign*.

The condition, then, of those who *gain* the money *must* rise, while the *condition* of those who *lose* it *must* sink—*no alternative is possible.* Hence, to *possess* the money becomes, as it were, the life-and-death struggle of civilization—of man's existence. Now, it is obvious that, if the money of *several* nations *be of the same* kind—in fact or in principle—then this *merciless* struggle for the money—*for existence*—will be of one nation against all the others, and of all against all.

To make a money that is *common* to several nations is to

set up a huge auction-block, upon which Prices will officiate as a heartless and soulless auctioneer. The money will be knocked down to those who bid the most for it—of their labor or its productions.

The *highest* bidders for the money will *ever* be those whose *necessities* are the greatest.

What the *necessities* of a people are, is largely fixed by the institutions—the government—under which they live. That great statesman, Lord Chatham, has most truly and wisely said: 'The *ruin* or *prosperity* of a state depends so much upon the *administration* of its government, that, to be *acquainted* with the *merit* of a ministry, *we need only observe the condition of the people.*'

If among these several nations having the *same kind of money*—in fact or in principle—there is *even one* nation whose institutions are such as enslave the masses to an aristocracy who own the capital and the land, then that curse spreads itself—*inevitably*—over all the other nations. The *necessities* and *miserable* condition of *that* people *forces* them to offer the most of their labor or its productions for the money. As the money flows to them their condition rises—they prosper. But those from whom it ebbs, sink. Nor can any human power arrest their sinking condition, until they have reached a point where their *necessities* make them the highest bidders for the money. A system of money common to several nations guarantees *two* things: First, that the condition of the producing and industrial classes will be about the same in each and all. And the *condition* of these classes *fixes* the condition of fully 85 per cent of the total population. The condition of the manufacturer for *home* consumption, the merchant, the professional man, etc., etc., sinks with the foundation. Second: It guarantees that no one of the nations will ever enjoy more than three or four *successive* years of prosperity. Their prosperity is *ever* born of the *dire* necessity which forces them to bid the most for the money; but in gaining it they *reduce* some other nation to adversity, which, in turn, bids it *away* from them again. It is a tide that ebbs and flows like that of the seas. In connection with this, it is of the highest importance to consider the following fact, namely: For each year of *prosperity* there will be four or five of adversity; for a period of *three or four years* of prosperity there will be one of *twelve to fifteen* of adversity. The prosperity of the *few* years is due to the fact that the purchasing power or value of money is sinking, while that of labor and its productions are rising—

less and less of labor and its productions going to the money-loaner, and more and more to *general* society. The *many* years of adversity are due to the opposite fact—more and more of labor and its productions are required to cancel the demands of the money-loaner, and less and less are left to the patronage of general society. So that, while it is a system of money that sometimes bears upon the money-loaner, we see that for each year of *his* adversity he is enriched by four or five of prosperity; while general society has *five* of adversity to *one* of prosperity. Society *always* gets into debt to the money-loaner *when the value of the money is depreciated, and is forced to go out of debt when its value is appreciated; when it borrows two dollars it obtains one day's work, and when it pays the two dollars it gives two days' work;* and merchants and others—supposed to be intelligent—say that it is 'hard times.' The periods 1812 to 1816, 1834 to 1837, 1853 to 1857, in all a period of eleven years, were 'good times'—in each there was a great increase in the quantity of the money. From 1817 to 1833, 1838 to 1852, and 1858 to 1872—but for the war—in all, a period of 44 years, were 'bad times,'—in each there was an enormous contraction of the money. It is four or five to one in favor of the money-loaner. And, as an inevitable consequence, that portion of society which produces *all* the wealth are largely bankrupts or paupers, while those who do not produce a single farthing of it are largely millionaires. And all that portion of society subsisting between the money-loaner and the producer are ever seized with the 'chills and fever,'—a short season of *fever* and a long one of *chills.*"

No matter how large or small the exchanges are between nations, the difference must be leveled up with commodities. The balancing commodity used may be either wheat, corn, meat, gold or silver; yet, it must be paid out and received as an article of commerce having its value fixed by the nation receiving it. Nothing American is money when taken from under the jurisdiction of the stars and stripes. All articles of commerce are then simply exported commodities, and are put upon the market at a price to be fixed by foreign purchasers. We are told that gold and silver are the recognized money of the world. That is an error. The gold and silver coins of one nation are received by another only as so much bullion, and its value is estimated by its weight and fineness. Wheat, cotton, meat and manufactured articles are used as the basis of more foreign exchange in one week than gold and silver is in a whole year. Gold, silver, copper and iron are the products of labor the same as all the other articles enumerated, and all nations, in their exchanges, treat them as such; consequently, the domestic currency of a nation does not, in the least, conflict with its foreign commerce. This being true, of what benefit is an expensive currency to any nation? The more precious the material the more expensive the currency. If gold was the only metal used for money, it would cost much more than silver, and if silver was the only metal used it would cost much more than gold, while paper costs comparatively nothing. The entire expense of a dear currency is made simply to gratify an exploded idea. Outside of the legal quality that goes with the stamp of the government is the guarantee that the metal upon which it is impressed is of a certain weight and fineness. Of what use to the people, then, is all this expense of coining gold and silver into money when it can be used as such only among ourselves? When used abroad it is weighed and bought as produce, notwithstanding its costly and handsome coinage. Why not keep it in bullion, and when an adverse balance is to be settled, send it in that form in payment of the difference, if required.

As I said before, both gold and silver are too expensive for the uses they are put to as legal money. For instance, take a paper dollar and a gold dollar. Suppose both are lost at sea, what is the difference in the effect of their loss? With the paper dollar the individual loses a dollar in value, and the nation gains it. With the gold dollar both the individual and the nation are losers—two dollars are lost, for the nation paid an equivalent for the metal before it was coined. This, of itself, amounts to a large sum in the course of years. Of the 45 millions of fractional currency issued, 15 millions have been lost or destroyed. This would happen with silver or gold certificates in like manner—the nation would gain what the individual lost, instead of both being losers in the same calamity.

I do not believe in deceiving the people in any manner, much less in regard to the great question of domestic currency. Squarely and honestly told, the only money in this nation to-day is gold and silver coin; all else is a fraud, a delusion inspired by undue confidence in a coin basis. National bank bills are redeemable in greenbacks, and greenbacks are redeemable in coin. Now, if the people should bring all their promises to pay to the banks and treasuries of the United States, and demand their redemption at one time, the nation would suspend payment, become bankrupt, and the banks would prove insolvent. We are led to believe that there is a coin dollar back of each paper dollar that is in circulation. This is not true. National bank bills are redeemable in greenbacks. These banks had in circulation Oct. 1, 1885, $268,869,597. The amount of greenbacks outstanding at that date was $346,-681,016, making a total of $615,550,613. To redeem this amount the Government held $100,000,000. Here is an example of 100 millions of money secured by a coin reserve and 515 millions of absolute frauds.

Ask one hundred men you may meet in your walk, if our currency national bank bills and greenbacks have a coin reserve to protect their redemption, and ninety-nine will say they have. When, in fact, the only issue that has an absolute coin basis is the certificates which are not legal tender. Domestic currency is one thing, but legal money is another. This paper money the Government and banks compel the people to receive in payment of all their dues, but the Government, under the present law, can only receive it from the people for certain specified payments, and for this reason I claim again it is a fraud. If an individual will not take his own debt in payment for a credit he holds, plain people will call him a scoun-

drel, and justly, too. All this masquerading and financial jug-
glery is concocted simply to deceive a trusting people, with the
object of robbing them of their earnings. Why not present
the bare facts, cut the matter open, and let the light of wisdom
and common sense in to dispel the darkness?

I would have gold and silver, if they are to be used as
money, coined free and unlimited, or gold and silver certificates issued on bullion deposited at any of the mints or sub-
treasuries, equal to the amount of coin, and in convenient denominations for circulation. That much currency would be
bottomed on the precious metals. Then I would issue Government notes or greenbacks in sufficient quantities to give the
people currency enough to keep capital, labor and its products
independent of each other, and bottom this issue on taxation.
Let the Government pay it to the people for what it wants of
their labor, and products, and receive it of the people for all
dues. With such a currency there could be no deception nor
depreciation.

I quote from Thomas Jefferson on this question:

"And so the nation may continue to issue its bills as far
as its wants require and the limits of its circulation will permit.
Those limits are understood to extend with us at present to
$200,000,000, a greater sum than would be necessary for any
war. But this, the only resource which the Government could
command with certainty, the States have unfortunately fooled
away, nay, corruptly alienated to swindlers and shavers, under
the cover of private banks. Say, too, as an additional evil,
that the disposal funds of individuals to this great amount
have thus been withdrawn from improvement and useful enterprise, and employed in the useless, usurious and demoralizing
practices of bank directors and their accomplices. In the war
of 1755 our State availed itself of this fund by issuing a paper
money bottomed on a specific tax for its redemption, and to insure its credit, bearing an interest of 5 per cent. Within a
very short time not a bill of this emission was to be found in
circulation. It was locked up in the chests of executors, guardians, widows, farmers, etc. We then issued bills bottomed on
a redeeming tax, but bearing no interest. These were readily

received, and never depreciated a single farthing.—*Opinions of Thomas Jefferson in* 1813; *his letters to John W. Epps, June* 24, 1813; *Jefferson's Works,* volume 4, pages 40, 41.

The question will be asked, and ought to be looked at, what is to be the recourse if loans cannot be obtained? There is but one—"*Carthago delenda est.*" Bank paper must be suppressed, and the circulating medium must be restored to the nation to whom it belongs. It is the only fund on which they can rely for loans; it is the only recourse which can never fail them, and it is an abundant one for every necessary purpose. Treasury bills, bottomed on taxes, bearing or not bearing interest, as may be found necessary, thrown into circulation will take the place of so much gold and silver, which last, when crowded, will find an efflux into other countries, and thus keep the quantum of medium at its salutary level. Let banks continue, if they please, but let them discount for cash alone or for Treasury notes."—*Letter September* 11, 1813, volume 6, pages 199, 200, 201.

Bear in mind the first issue of our greenbacks was upon this identical plan. They were received and taken for all dues, and in consequence remained equal with gold and silver, while those subsequently issued under a law discriminating as to their uses, to a large extent depreciated in value. Or, if this will not do, I would demonetize both gold and silver, and issue all the currency direct from the Government in legal tender notes. For my part, I am inclined to the latter idea. It would avoid confusion and deception regarding the true status of our currency, and make it unnecessary to further discuss the question of a single or double standard of payments. It would entirely eliminate the little understood question of a ratio between the two metals, and give us a currency that could not be increased or decreased in value only by limitation in quantity, which legislation could regulate. Every nation of the world is, at the present time, trying to solve this greatest factor in human progress—the best currency. And I expect to live to see the time when silver and gold will be considered, by all students of political economy, as unfit for money—as simply a commodity of considerable intrinsic value; and the cheapest of all materials—paper—solely used to bear the stamp of power or governmental authority, which alone *makes money*. Then each Government will have its one distinctive currency, that cannot be impaired or depreciated by the financial or commercial success of any other country.

I here quote from the report of the Silver Commission:

"Describing our situation summarily, it may be said that our commercial intercourse with Western Europe consists of two parts:

First, the export of articles indispensable to Europe, such as cotton, the cereals, tobacco, and the products of animals, a trade which needs no stimulation or favor of any kind.

Second, the import from Europe of manufactures. This is a trade which all parties and the representatives of all shades of economical opinion in this country wish to see steadily diminished and eventually terminated. The reasons which conduce to this uniformity of desire are very diverse, as also are the modes proposed to accomplish the object sought. Some propose protective tariffs and high duties as the best means. Others maintain that the better if not the only way to keep out European manufactures is by the production in this country of superior articles at lower prices, and that this is only possible with free trade or simply a revenue tariff and cheap raw material. But, by whatever way it may be reached, a diminution, tending always to an extinction of imports from Europe, is universally desired in this country.

It is in trade with other parts of the world, in less advanced stages of civilization, or with essentially different systems of civilization, or with essentially different raw products resulting from marked diversity of climates, that we find the natural outlets for our manufactures, and in many cases the opportunity for a mutually advantageous exchange of native productions. It is not perceived that that trade can become too large. All interests and opinions favor its expansion, and, unlike the trade with Western Europe, its existence and extent depend upon the wisdom and vigor of our efforts to secure and increase it. Our trade with England would be but little affected if we should be entirely passive in relation to it. With China, on the other hand, we have no trade which we do not actively seek. Commercial nations will seek after our trade. We must ourselves seek after trade with the non-commercial nations.

It is by no means clear that trade between nations is either increased or facilitated by a concurrence in their standards of money. But even if it were so, the double standard would meet all requirements better than the single standard. It would tend to keep constantly available a sufficient stock of both metals for the trade of either gold or silver standard countries.

However it may be in respect to trade with non-commercial countries, it has never been shown that diversities of money, however arising, whether from single standards of a different metal, or from systems of irredeemable paper currency, are any hindrance to trade between commercial countries. Whatever the moneys of such countries may be, they are always interconvertible at known and not widely-variant rates. There is no property on sale in London for which the holder would refuse payment in silver or in greenbacks at the current rates of exchange; and there is no property on sale in New York for which the holder would refuse payment in Bank of England notes at the current rates of exchange. Greenbacks are not a legal tender in London. Silver is not a tender there. Neither are American gold eagles, and both greenbacks and silver are as readily convertible into sterling money as gold eagles are. The irredeemable paper currency existing in this country since 1862 has not obstructed its European trade in any degree whatever. The trade of England with commercial countries was not obstructed when it had an inconvertible paper currency from 1797 to 1821. The paper moneys of Russia, Austria, Italy, France and Brazil, although differing greatly in their value relatively to gold and silver, are no hindrances to their trade with each other, with the United States, or with European countries having metallic standards. Various nations in Europe, in close proximity to each other, or having large intercourse with each other, have had different single metallic standards, without experiencing any inconvenience from that circumstance. The single silver standard existed in Holland from 1847 to 1875, and in Germany from 1857 to 1871, but the large trade of both with England, having a single gold standard, was carried on during those periods with undiminished facility.

The long and still continuing difference of currency between England and its greatest dependency, India, is a striking illustration of the fact that trade between distinct peoples is not obstructed by the difference in their money standards. Both are parts of one empire, and the coinages of both are impressed with the head of the same ruler, but the British sovereign is not a good tender for a debt in Calcutta, nor is the Indian rupee a good tender for a debt in London. Cases are said to have occurred of such extreme financial pressure in both those cities that loans of money, that is to say, silver, have been refused at Calcutta on a pledge of sovereigns, and that loans of money, that is to say, gold, have been refused in London on a pledge of rupees. No difficulty has ever arisen in the immense trade between Great Britain and India from this difference of currencies, although this is doubtless due in part to the exceptional circumstances which have given to England a large and constant supply of silver, notwithstanding that its standard money is gold.

A fact, less striking in some aspects, but more so in others, is the difference in the actual currencies of the Atlantic and Pacific States of this Union. The difference is not made by law, but is a matter of choice on the part of the people of the Pacific slope. They judge that it has advantages for them, and both they and the people on the Atlantic perceive that it is not in the least degree obstructive to their mutual intercourse. There is no more difficulty in translating the greenback prices of New York into the gold prices of San Francisco, than there is in translating pounds avordupois into French kilograms.

A distinguished writer, J. E. Cairnes, professor in the University College of London, in a recent work (1874) on Political Economy, says:

'It appears to me that the influence attributed by many able writers in the United States to the depreciation of the paper currency, as regards its effects on the foreign trade of the country, is, in a great degree, purely imaginary. An advance in the scale of prices, *measured in gold*, in a country, if not shared by other countries, will at once affect its foreign trade, giving an impulse to importations, and checking the exportation of all commodities other than gold. A similar effect is very generally attributed by American writers to the action on prices of the greenback inconvertible currency. But it may easily be shown that this is a complete illusion. Foreigners do not send their products to the United States to take back greenbacks in exchange. The return which they look for is either gold or the commodities of the country; and if these have risen in price in proportion as the paper money has been depreciated, how should the advance in paper prices constitute an inducement for them to send their goods thither? The nominal gain in greenbacks on the importation is exactly balanced

by the nominal loss when those greenbacks come to be converted into gold or commodities. The gain may, in particular
cases, exceed the loss, but, if it does, the loss will also, in other
cases, exceed the gain. On the whole, and on an average, they
cannot but be the equivalents of each other.' "

The nations of Europe are not prepared to decide whether
gold or silver is preferable for money. Centuries of study
and experience does not appear to solve the question. The
general money system of Europe had been that of the double
standard until 1873. The conspicuous exceptions were Holland, which had been during much the larger part of its history a single silver standard country, and England, which had
adopted the single gold standard, in 1816 by law, and in 1821
in fact. In consequence of the apprehensions of a fall in the
value of money, or, what amounts to the same thing, a rise in
wages and the value of property, excited by the Californian
and Australian yield of gold, Belgium adopted a single silver
standard in 1850, and the German States in 1857. Belgium,
however, returned to the double standard in 1861.

Germany and the United States demonetized silver in
1873. At that time it was neither depreciated nor unsteady in
value, nor had any change occurred in the relative production,
consumption or distribution of the precious metals to indicate
its depreciation in the future, nor was any actual or probable
depreciation assigned as a reason for its demonetization. The
average flow of silver to India was undisturbed, and the big
Bonanza in the Comstock lode was undiscovered. Manifestly,
the real reason for the demonetization of silver was the apprehension of the creditor classes that the combined production of
the two metals would raise prices and cheapen money, unless
one of them was shorn of the money function. In Europe,
this reason was distinctly avowed. This is no doubt the true
reason for all this outcry against silver. The war against it is
not made to destroy its commercial value, but to destroy its use
as money, and thereby to lessen the volume of circulating me-

dium. Evidence like this ought to be sufficient to condemn both metals as a basis for currency.

A transition in this country from paper to coin involves a struggle for the needed coin with other countries, no one of which has any that is not urgently needed for its own payments and necessities. The United States will be at the disadvantage of struggling for the coin, of which other countries are in possession. It can be successful only by a reduction of prices in this country, not merely to the present level of coin-prices throughout the world, but to that lower level to which they must descend under such a new and great demand for coin as the resumption of specie payment in this country has occasioned. This crash in prices cannot be avoided by confining our demand for the metals to the products of our own mines. That product is a part of the current supply of the world, and to subtract from that supply is the same thing in its practical effect as subtracting from the stocks of the world, because the entire current supply is not more than sufficient to keep the existing stocks unimpaired. It cannot be avoided by borrowing coin abroad upon our bonds. No such borrowing will be permitted to reach the gold of the great European banks, and must be confined to the small quantities floating in commercial hands. But the decisive consideration is, that even if gold should be obtained in that way, it could be kept here upon no other condition than a reduction of our prices to or below the coin prices of the world.

My objections to a metallic basis for a circulating medium are:

1st. All currencies based on metallic values must vary more or less as the supply of these metals increase or diminish.

2nd. No two metals can bear the same ratio of value to each other for any considerable length of time, owing to the above reasons.

3d. When one metal is made the standard or unit of

value, all other metals are forced to become subsidiary.

4th.   When one metal is named as the sole measure of value, it immediately contracts the circulating medium of the country to the amount of that one metal, because all other currency is measured by the existing standard.   This increases the value of the one metal at the expense of all other kinds of currency.   It makes this one metal the arbiter of all values, thereby giving it a power never intended in the economy of the exchanges of the world.

5th.   It makes the volume of circulating medium entirely dependent upon the success or failure attending the discovery and operation of gold mines.   With an increase of gold mining our circulation would expand; with a decrease in that enterprise, our circulation would contract.   This would place all commercial values, both of products and labor, in a vacillating condition, rising or falling in proportion to the success or failure of this one branch of business.

6th.   The effect is bad enough when the condition of prices rests upon the success or failure of the two enterprises—the mining of gold and silver—together, but when reduced to the single venture resulting from a gold standard, the effect is reduced to a degree of uncertainty that is generally disastrous to business.

7th.   Our business prosperity should be placed beyond any such contingency, because a failure in the business of mining the precious metals would react on all other branches of industry, and make their success depend entirely upon the good or bad luck of mining ventures.   All our industries outside of mining are based upon close calculation, while the success of mining is simply and only the result of chance.

8th.   The value of both gold and silver frequently change, and for this reason it is difficult to determine whether other commodities have depreciated, or gold and silver appreciated in value.

9th.   Gold and silver being simply commodities, it is neither logical nor philosophic to say that one commodity shall measure the value of another.

10th.   The only currency that will perform the functions of an equitable exchange and   measure   of values is the inconvertible paper dollar or unit, in *itself* incapable of increasing or diminishing intrinsically, and based on the wealth and ability of the whole people, and the power of the general government to levy taxes, thereby making it for the interest of every citizen of the Republic to support and maintain our national integrity.

11th.   There is no such thing as a recognized money of the world.   Outside of each nation all money is sold for its commodity value in pounds, ounces, etc.   The oft-quoted idea has no foundation in fact, and only obtains through the ignorance of the people on financial questions.

12th.   A nation with the diversified interests that ours possesses should have a currency of its own, a currency that if used and passed outside of our borders, beyond our national lines, would be without our consent; and that for every dollar so used by foreign nations we should be that much the richer instead of becoming poorer, as now, by a constant drainage from our circulation of the precious metals.

"Government paper money has always enriched a nation when properly issued, restricted, and secured.   It has ever been a success.   Specie, for a domestic currency, or as a basis for paper, has been a failure without a solitary exception.

Napoleon, at St. Helena, claimed that England beat him with her spindles, but it was her paper money that kept the spindles in motion.   Specie in its stead would have given him the victory.

England's entire disregard of specie and copious issue of paper money after the suspension of specie payments in 1797 till 1819 were the most prosperous days that England ever saw.

This wise policy, to which she was driven by necessity, together with the bills of credit issued by the United allied powers, and which were not only as good, but superior   to gold, from 'Kamschatka to the Rhine,' turned the tide of war against Napoleon, and won the decisive battle of Waterloo, saving England from becoming a province of France."

In order to discuss the question of a supply of currency understandingly, we should first examine the sources from which this supply is obtained, which are as follows:

1st. The coinage of gold, which is free and unlimited.

2nd. The coinage of silver, which is not free, and is limited to two millions per month.

3rd. The issuing of legal tenders by the Government, which is limited to about 347 millions in amount.

4th. The issuing of bank notes, which is unlimited in amount, but is not made compulsory.

Through these four channels must come all the circulating medium of the nation. A glance at the above statements will show how completely the supply of currency is in the hands of moneyed men, and how strongly they are entrenched behind the law.

The coinage of gold is absolutely without expense; that is, any one who has gold can have it coined into money free of charge. This gives to that metal a premium over silver, and creates at the outset a discrimination against it.

The coinage of silver is limited to a certain amount each month, and the Government reserves the right to purchase it, wherever it can be bought the cheapest. This makes competition among the silver producers, which also tends to discredit that metal, for no matter how much may be mined, ready for coinage, this arbitrary act of Congress limits the amount to two millions each month—all of which creates a feeling of distrust that is not favorable to silver, and is beneficial to gold.

The issuing of more greenbacks is forbidden by law; hence, a further supply from that source is impossible.

The only recourse seems to be with the national bank issue. This, at first glance, seems to be sufficient and reasona-

ble, but to examine it closely dissipates all such hopes. There
is nothing, absolutely nothing, that compels a bank to take out
any currency. Many banks do not. The only inducement for
them in that direction is the question of profit. If it will pay
to issue their bills, the banks issue them; if it will not pay,
they not only refuse to issue any, but retire what they have
issued. So the amount of national bank currency does not depend on the wants or demands of the people, but the profit
accruing to the banker; the people in the mean time pay
to the banks this profit. In proof of this, we have 2,714
banks, with a combined capital of $527,524,410; these banks
are entitled to 90 per cent. of this amount in currency, which
would be $474,771,969. Instead of that amount, there is but
$268,869,597 of national bank bills in circulation, a difference
of $205,902,372. If it should appear to their advantage, the
whole might be retired, and the circulating medium reduced to
the extent of their whole issue. Such an act on their part
would certainly bankrupt the nation. This is a power for evil
that is delegated to no other corporations on the face of the
earth. It absolutely dictates the values of everything in our
country, fixes the price not only of labor, but all the productions and accumulations of labor. The fact that gold is not
mined in sufficient quantities to satisfy the demand even for
the manufacture of ornaments, and that the stock of coin and
bullion has been encroached upon, is not very encouraging for
a greater supply from that source. Men well posted in the
supply of that metal declare that within the next decade the
present stock of gold coin will be lessened by a large per cent.
for purposes outside of money use. The world has been ex-
plored to its uttermost parts for this metal, and the time seems
near at hand when that industry will prove to be unremunera-
tive at its present value. Even now its value is enhancing with
every year. The supply for the purpose of money will grow
less as the demand for it for other purposes increases, because

money is gold in its cheapest form. People will pay more for it to use as ornaments than can be paid for it to use as money. It is its value as a commodity, and not as money, that is considered. Gold is now rapidly appreciating in value, and the time will soon come when for that reason alone it can not be utilized in that capacity. When that time comes, silver will go through with the same course, being the next most precious metal, and without doubt the appreciation in value will force it from the metals out of which money is made. Enough good reasons have presented themselves to me to justify the idea that sooner or later the supply of currency must come from the Government direct. That we must have free, unlimited coinage of gold and silver, and a certain amount of Government issues per capita of the people, with an increase as the nation becomes more populous.

The late decision of the Supreme Court has shown us that the Government can issue legal tender paper money at such times and in such quantities as Congress may determine. Why should the Government not put that prerogative in force? Why should the people be compelled to pay for its being done by heartless corporations? In a debate in Congress upon this question a member said:

"On the other hand, take away the profits on issuing currency, and the banks will take away the currency itself. This is the condition of things now. It comes to this then: If you make it their interest to do so, the banks will put out an abundance of currency, even to the wildest inflation; but if it is not made their interest to do it, they will not put out any."

Under the present banking laws, the banks of this country could inflate the currency to the extent of one or more billions of dollars in less than six months' time, and in the same time contract it by that amount. This is a power granted to a monopoly by our laws. This power is not only dangerous to the nation, but disastrous to the common welfare of the people. What we need is a steady volume of currency, increasing with our population, and the growing demands of business. This cannot be brought about through delegated power. Such power is almost always used in the furtherance of selfish purposes. Class legislation will prove ruinous to any nation. There should be, and might be, a happy medium between the debtor and creditor classes, the buyer and seller, the producer and consumer, in which the rights of each should be impartially considered.

After careful examination, I am led to believe that we should have at least fifty dollars per capita of currency in the United States. Our industries are so diversified and the extent and area of our land so great that we require more circulating medium to do the same amount of business than other nations whose populations are more condensed. This amount should be increased in volume in proportion as the country increases in population and business. With a currency of this volume, issued as before stated, universal prosperity would prevail throughout our land.

We might with profit ascertain as nearly as possible what amount of work a dollar is required to do during one year of business. But few, I venture to say, can even approximate the truth in this respect.

First, we will take up the actual debts of the country from our best authorities—known and estimated as follows:

Our National Debt proper is.............................	$2,149,725,277.02
Bonds to Railway Companies...........................	64,623,512.00
Interest on Bonds.......................................	18,627,743.43
Unsettled liabilities (estimated).......................	250,000,000.00
State and Municipal....................................	1,000,000,000.00
Loans, etc., by National Banks........................	944,233,304.22
Loans, etc., by State Banks, etc.......................	514,081,496.90
Loans, etc., by same in twenty-eight States, etc. (estimated)	1,500,000,000.00
Individuals to each other, etc., (estimated)	2,000,000,000.00
Funded, etc., of Railroads.............................	1,511,578,944.00

Making the fearful total of.................$9,952,870,266.67

This aggregate is almost incomprehensible.

Add to this the returns from the clearing-houses for one

year. A comparison of the business of all the clearing-houses of the United States is afforded by the following table, compiled from the figures furnished for the year ending December 31, 1884, and representing the clearings of each institution:

New York	$30,985,871,170
Boston	3,243,327,658
Philadelphia	2,514,028,803
Chicago	2,259,680,392
St. Louis	785,202,177
Baltimore	631,687,135
San Francisco	556,857,691
Pittsburg	469,316,010
Cincinnati	460,600,000
New Orleans	454,500,000
Providence	217,448,300
Louisville	211,700,000
Milwaukee	178,995,637
Kansas City	177,175,467
Detroit	133,611,910
Minneapolis	110,556,620
Cleveland	106,044,770
Hartford	81,834,837
Indianapolis	73,213,168
Memphis	60,040,361
New Haven	57,799,870
Portland	45,421,102
Peoria	44,058,884
Worcester	39,610,041
Springfield	37,585,774
Columbus	34,858,428
St. Joseph	34,657,818
Norfolk	34,158,781
Syracuse	27,266,247
Lowell	24,460,396
Total	**$44,091,569,447**

To this enormous amount we will also add:

Agricultural Products	$ 3,600,000,000
Manufactured "	6,000,000,000
Mining	1,500,000,000
Imports	650,000,000
Taxation	300,000,000
Freights	1,000,000,000
Labor	3,000,000,000
Total.	**$16,050,000,000**

But this is only a commencement. If the clearing-house returns alone show 44 billions, how much would all the business of the nation outside of what I have mentioned, aggregate? I have placed it at one hundred times as much. Let us recapitulate:

1st, Debts	$	9,952,000,000
2nd, Clearing-house Returns	.	44,091,000,000
3rd, Products, etc.		16,050,000,000
4th, All other transactions		6,900,000,000,000
Total		$6,970,093,000,000

The above sum is beyond human conception. With the present amount of currency among the people, say 500 million dollars, each dollar would have to change hands at least 46 times per day, or nearly five times during each business hour.

Bankers will say, and truly, too, that 94 per cent. of all business is done with checks, drafts, etc. In view of this fact, which is more important than all others, we, as a people, should have an increase of currency sufficient to reduce this per cent. of business, which has really been transacted on inflated credits, to a point as near to a cash basis as human wisdom can determine. For the reason that the great volume of all the business of the country has long been done through a system of inflated credits, we notice with alarm that the wealth of the many is rapidly concentrating in the hands of the few. This kind of currency was invented for the rich—those who are able to have bank accounts; and, bear in mind that 99 per cent of our people never had a bank account. None but the wealthy can use these substitutes for a circulating medium. Of all the inventions that man has devised to add riches to the rich at the expense of the poor; of concentrating business in large monopolies and soulless corporations, thereby driving out all the smaller industries; of making one portion of our people masters and the others slaves—I believe this system of check, draft and exchange paper inflation is the most ingenuous and destructive substitute for money ever known.

It is not maintained that a compensation can be made for a shrinkage in the volume of money by an increase of such banking expedients as checks, bills of exchange, and clearing-houses. These expedients are now resorted to, and because profit is found in their use, always will be availed of to the utmost possible extent. It is manifest, therefore, that, whatever the proportion or per centage they bear to the volume of money, it cannot be increased except through an increase in that volume. And it is as manifest that, when the volume of money is diminished, these expedients must diminish, and prices must fall in a corresponding ratio. Money is the prime and governing force, whose functions cannot be superseded by any device whatever, and whose volume or existence does not depend on banking expedients, while these expedients grow out of money and could not exist without it. The farthest extent to which they can be used is already practically reached, and they can only increase, and must decrease, as the volume of money increases or diminishes. This reasoning partially applies as to the effect of credit on prices.

It would seem to be reversing the natural order of things to maintain that prices are controlled by the volume of credit, instead of by the volume of money. Without entering into an elaborate discussion of this intricate question, it may be said that prices were affixed to property at the time when the invention of money superseded barter. Fluctuations of prices frequently arise from special causes, but they are local and temporary in their character.

Even were it possible to devise a money system so perfect that steadiness in the general level of prices would be absolutely assured, there would still occur occasional fluctuations in the prices of particular commodities, arising from a temporary glut or scarcity of such commodities in the general markets, caused by exceptionally favorable or unfavorable conditions, which might suddenly enlarge or diminish their production, or vary the demand for them. Such fluctuations cannot be avoided. They mark the ebb and flow of business, and no more affect the general level of prices or prosperity than the ebb and flow of the tides affect the general level of the ocean. The producers of and dealers in each article should be better able than anybody else to foresee and guard against them, and have no reason to complain of them. But they may well complain when the general level of prices is disturbed by monetary legislation which they could not foresee, are not responsible for, and whose injurious effects they could not, by any degree of prudence, avoid.

As I have stated before, all the nations of the world, at the present time, seem to be striving for the possession of gold, and are determined, if possible, to make it the sole standard of payment. The only means by which it can be obtained is by the sale and exchange of the products of labor. The nation that will part with its products the cheapest will obtain the gold and hold it until some other nation forces the price of products down to a still lower point. This is the cause of such a general depression in business all over the world. This strife has been so bitter and earnest that the price of all productions has shrunk below the range of any profit, and even below the cost of production. Consequently, we find bankruptcies and business failures throughout the civilized globe. No matter if all adverse balances are leveled up with exchangeable commodities, they must first be measured by the prevailing standard of payments of the country to whom the balance is paid. We now find England, France, Germany, Holland, the Scandinavian States, and the United States all struggling for gold, because that metal, by secret governmental interference, has virtually become the standard of payments. We might, in certain cases, with some degree of safety, attempt to establish a gold standard by law, but with all these nations attempting to do the same thing, and competing with us for the gold necessary to keep the standard good, it would be the height of folly for this nation to adopt it. It would wreck the entire industries of the country.

I quote from a London paper:

" Probably, if there were gold enough for all the world, it would be best that there should be only a single standard of value throughout the world, and that one—gold. But this is impossible. Some have doubted whether there is gold enough even for the nations which now intend to use it; and there certainly is not enough for all the world."—*London Economist*.

One writer claims there is not gold and silver enough in the world to pay the interest on the world's indebtedness.

If our currency could be expanded sufficiently to enable at least a majority of business transactions to be conducted with money, the wealth of the nation would seek its level, and each individual would, in a much larger degree, reap the reward of his own energies.

All of the truly great economists and scientists of the world freely admit that both gold and silver have ever been, and from the nature of things, must ever be imperfect money, and an unjust standard or thermometer of prices. And they also admit, that a paper money issued solely by the Government, under a system that would duly and properly limit its amount—would be the most perfect economic and just money of which the present knowledge of man is able to conceive. Those who deny that such is the position held by the great economists of the world, and also the truth that has been established by some thirty centuries of mankind's experience, have failed in their study of the world's history, and any one who is inclined to doubt these statements can verify them by recourse to the proper course of reading.

Those economic laws which may be perfectly sound and correct under certain customs and conditions, would, if carried into effect with us, be suicidal. The laws of many nations are made for dense populations, where there is and always has been, the rigorous rules of caste ; where men are born as lawmakers, instead of being selected by the people. There is hardly a condition in our social and economic life where the same rule of action would apply to both.

Then why should we not be nationally independent in that greatest of all factors entering into our individual prosperity and happiness—*the currency of our country?*

Instead of being led by the older nations of Europe, why do we not turn our attention to the vast field for operations at home, and lead the South American States and Mexico up to the plane of civilization, financially and socially, that we occupy? It would be satisfactory, remunerative and beneficent to the entire people.

CHAPTER V.

VALUE AND ITS RELATION TO MONEY.

"Money is, as it were, the substitute for legal demands (for payment) and hence it has the name *vouioua* (that which is established by law), because it is not so by nature, but by law; and because it is in our power to change it and render it useless."—*Aristotle.*

In the minds of most people there is a sort of superstitious awe about money. Why it is money and how did it come to be such, are queries that have generally been vaguely answered. The word is invested with a kind of glamour that keeps its real properties and functions from being investigated and made plain. No person ever handled a dollar, any more than he ever held in his hand a days' work. A dollar is an abstract idea, not the name of a thing, but the name of a quality of a thing. Take for example a gold dollar. Its superscription denominates it a dollar. Place it beneath the blows of a hammer, and deface the inscription. Now, what is it; a dollar? No. It is a quantity of gold. The dollar is gone, without any loss of metal. No one saw it go from the metal. Neither can it be found. This dollar is an idea—a mental conception—and has no relation to value in itself whatever. Neither can it be value of itself in any sense.

One class of writers state their case as follows: The dollar measures values the same as the yard-stick measures yards. The dollar is made of a certain number of grains of gold or silver. The yard-stick is composed of thirty-six inches linear measurement. From this they argue: Is it right that the yard-stick should measure thirty-three inches to-day, and thirty-eight to-morrow? Where would the just standard of measurement be found? If it is not right to change the yard-stick it cannot be right for a dollar to be of one value at one time, and increase or diminish in value at another. This argument appears plausible and quite unanswerable. Let us examine it.

In the first place, it is not true that the dollar measures value as the yard-stick measures the yard. In the one case both are considered actual substances, while in the other both are mental conceptions or ideas. But suppose they were alike. In order to measure yards it is necessary to have yard-sticks; also to measure value we must have the dollar or unit of measurement. It would follow, therefore, that the more yards to measure the more yard-sticks would be necessary. Likewise, the more value to measure, the more dollars would be needed. We will not stop here. If the yard-stick should be made more than 36 inches in length, the seller would lose and the buyer gain, because the measure is increased and the number of measurements lessened. If the value of the dollar is increased, its capacity for measurement will be increased, and the number of measures lessened. Suppose a government should set its people to manufacturing cloth by offering special inducements, and at the same time make up a quantity of yard-sticks for their use. At first there might be yard-sticks enough and to spare, but as business increased, they would become more and more in demand, until the time came when there would not be enough to measure the cloth as fast as it came from the looms. Now, suppose these yard-sticks were made from some rare material, difficult to find, whose very possession was the result of chance, and the making and furnishing was monopolized by the government. Suppose under these conditions the people clamored for more measures, saying their goods were unmeasured, and, consequently, for a lack of sufficient measures remains unsold. What would be the wise course for that government to pursue? Would it break up a large per cent. of the measures on hand and in constant use? Would it say to its people—go out among the swamps and through the timber, and perhaps you may find some of the material out of which these measures are made. You can make no absolute calculation as to its location, but must depend entirely upon chance to obtain it, and if luck should be in your favor, bring the material to me, and I will make you a certain number of measures each month. Would this be the wise course to pursue? Certainly not. The government should ask how many measures were needed, and then take the most convenient commodity, and make as many as its people needed, and also provide for future wants. How does this illustration apply to the dollar? Congress said, when the people were using three measures of value, "You have too many; we will destroy a portion of them," and it did. It claimed the measures were made of too many kinds of material—paper, silver and gold; therefore, we will limit their composition to two of these—silver and gold. Again, it said, "We will limit the measures to one material, and that shall be gold alone." It was done. No matter how great the need of the people for these measures, no matter how much they clamored for them, the Government said, "Go to the hills and dig, and if you are successful, bring the results to me, and I will make the measures for you as I think you need." Would it not be better for the Government to say to the people, "You shall have all the measures that your business demands, and for fear some evil disposed persons might in some manner get possession of too large a portion of them, and levy a contribution for their use, I will furnish an abundant supply."

Notwithstanding the fact that time and human progress has changed nearly everything else in our economic existence, we find ourselves paying out to-day, silver, the current money of the merchants, the same as Abraham did more than 4,000 years ago, when he bought the cave of Machpelah. We are digging for the same material, gold, for which Solomon so anxiously struggled.

The most ancient idea connected with the temporal relations of man is that of gold and silver as money. No other idea, among the millions that have been advanced, relating to the social and business conditions of the human family, has withstood the changes of progressive civilization and maintained its original character as has this idea of money.

In those days of nomadic governments, this idea became general for obvious reasons. It continued down through the history of weak and unstable nations preceding the fifteenth century, and began to be relaxed with the invention of bills of exchange, or paper money, in the sixteenth century. As bills of exchange, checks, and paper money have increased in use, mankind have, without understanding its import, in direct ratio to that increase, yielded to the solid fact that there can be no intrinsic value in money.

During the reign of Augustus Cæsar, the gold and silver money of the whole world amounted to less than the present amount of gold and silver in the United States. During the Dark Ages, from the fourth to the fifteenth centuries, the mines having failed, this amount was diminished to about 200 millions. The gold and silver mined and used, following the discovery of America, combined with the use of bank paper, rekindled the glimmering fires of civilization, and made possible the grandeur of the nineteenth century. We are met here with representatives or substitutes for money.

If money must have value intrinsically—a certain amount of either gold or silver—then there is no method known by which it can be increased in amount, only by an increase in the quantity of the metals. If they are represented or substituted, they must remain at their maximum to redeem their representatives or substitutes. They cannot perform both functions at once. When there are more substitutes than principals, the overplus ceases to be substitutes, and necessarily becomes a fraud. It is impossible to represent value, when there is no value to represent. A thousand paper dollars cannot be represented by five hundred coin dollars, both being possessed of equal debt-paying power. Yet, if this doctrine of intrinsic value in money should be strictly applied, there is not enough of this kind of value to redeem one per cent. of the money obligations of the world. There is not enough to pay one-half the yearly interest on national and corporate indebtedness.

This idea has been so far exploded that ninety per cent. of all the business of the world is done with money having no intrinsic value. Some will say these representatives of money are good. That may be true, but their worth comes only through a strained confidence in business men. The persons issuing them may be rich in *property*, but property is not money. The fact is, this kind of money is good as currency until the principal is called for, then the fact of its being a representative of an obsolete idea becomes painfully apparent.

The material upon which the imprint that makes money is stamped may have a commercial value, but the money—the insignia of a nation's sovereign authority—never.

The precious metals change less in value than other commodities, silver much less than gold; but both being products of labor, and controlled by the same factors that control all other labor-products, must fluctuate in value as the circumstances under which they exist change. These two metals, aside from their money functions, are governed by the same rules which govern all other metals, and are exempt from none. They are more valuable because of their scarcity, and more precious because of the difficulty connected with their acquisition. If gold was as plenty as iron, it would not be as valuable, because it could not be as useful to man as iron. The ex-

periment has been tried for a long series of years to maintain
a certain ratio between silver and gold for the purpose of
securing a uniform standard of payment. While these two metals are less apt to fluctuate than others, it is certain that they
do vary, and have maintained their ratios but for short periods
at a time. In this relation they act as a check upon each other
and should never be separated in their legal functions.

That gold and silver fluctuate in value, I quote:

" By limiting the quantity of money, it can be raised to
any conceivable value. It is on this principle that paper money circulates."—David Ricardo.

"Thus it appears that, whatever may be the material of
the money of a country, whether it consists of gold, silver,
copper, iron, salt, cowries, or paper, and however destitute it
may be of any intrinsic value, it is yet possible, by sufficiently
limiting its quantity, to raise its value in exchange to any conceivable extent."—Prof. McCulloch.

"It is well known that the discovery of America (with its
rich deposits of gold and silver) was followed by a great and
permanent fall in the price—purchasing power—of the precious
metals, which reduced it to one-fourth of their previous relative value to all other commodities."—Albert Gallatin.

"From 1789 to 1809 gold fell 45 per cent. From 1809 to
1849 it rose in value 145 per cent."—William Stanley Jevons.

Humboldt says that the gold and silver money in circulation in the eighteenth century is—at the time he wrote—thirty
times greater than in the fifteenth century, and that its value
or purchasing power was only one-twelfth of what it then was—
that is, 8 1-2 cents would then buy as much as 100 would at
the time he wrote.

Prof. Bonamy Price says that the purchasing power of
the so-called precious metals has fallen fourteen times since the
reign of the Henrys—that is, 7 1-7 cents would then buy as
much as 100 will now.

Laveleye illustrates this very handsomely in this paragraph:

"This immense stock of the precious metals lessens the
variations in the value which might result from the variations
in the annual supply, just as the level of a great lake is little

affected by any changes in the discharge of the rivers which flow into it."

Adam Smith, Wealth of Nations, p. 38, says:

"Gold and silver, however, like every other commodity, are sometimes cheaper and sometimes dearer; sometimes of easier and sometimes of more difficult purchase. The discovery of the abundant mines of America in the 16th century, reduced the value of gold and silver in Europe to about one-third of what it had been before, and this revolution in their value, though perhaps the greatest, is by no means the only one of which history gives some account. But, as a measure of quantity, such as a foot, fathom, or handful, which is continually varying in its own quantity, can never be an accurate measure of the quantity of other things, so a commodity which is itself continually varying in its own value can never be an accurate measure of the value of other commodities."

* "Silver, in bullion or money, changes its value from any change in its quantity, or in the demand for it. In either of these cases goods are said to be dearer or cheaper; but 'tis silver or money is dearer or cheaper, being more or less valuable, and equal to a greater or lesser quantity of goods."

† "The value of money is inversely as general prices: falling as they rise, and rising as they fall.   *   *   *
Let it, therefore, be remembered—and occasions will often arise calling it to mind—that a general rise or a general fall of *values* is a contradiction, and that a general rise or general fall of prices is tantamount to a rise or fall in the value of money."

‡ "But there is abundance of evidence to prove that the value of gold has undergone extensive changes. Between 1789 and 1809, it fell in the ratio of 100 to 54, or by 46 per cent., as I have shown in a paper on the variation of prices since 1782, read to the London Statistical Society in June, 1865. From 1809 to 1849 it rose again in the extraordinary ratio of 100 to 245, and by 145 per cent., rendering government annuities and all fixed payments, extending over this period, almost two-and-a-half times as valuable as they were in 1809. Since 1849, the value of gold has again fallen to the extent of at least 20 per cent., and a careful study of the fluctuations of prices, as shown either in the American Reviews of Trade of the Economist newspaper, or in the paper referred to above,

---

*John Law: Money and Trade Considered, chap. v.
†J. S. Mill: Principles of Political Economy, page 267-297
‡W. Stanley Jevons' Mechanism of Exchange, p. 325.

shows that fluctuations of from 10 to 25 per cent. occur in every credit cycle."

* "The precious metals are often spoken of as 'the standard of value,' which is true only in a restricted sense. A standard must remain the same, however other things change; and this is certainly not true of gold and silver. Their purchasing power has been continually varying, generally declining, as the natural deposits of their ores have been laid bare, and the resistance of nature to those who searched for them has diminished."

REPORT FROM THE SELECT COMMITTEE ON THE HIGH PRICE OF GOLD BULLION.

(Ordered by the House of Commons, to be printed, June 8, 1810.)

"The Select Committee appointed to enquire into the cause of the High Price of Gold Bullion, and to take into consideration the state of the Circulating Medium, and of the Exchanges between Great Britain and Foreign Parts;—and to report the same, with their Observations thereupon, from time to time, to the House;—Have, pursuant to the Orders of the House, examined the matters to them referred; and have agreed to the following report:

Your Committee proceeded, in the first instance, to ascertain what the price of gold bullion had been, as well as the rates of the foreign exchanges, for some time past; particularly during the past year.

Your Committee have found that the price of gold bullion, which, by the regulations of His Majesty's Mint, is 3l. 17s. 10 1-2d. per ounce of standard fineness, was, during the years 1806, 1807 and 1808, as high as 4l. in the market. Towards the end of 1808 it began to advance very rapidly, and continued very high during the whole year 1809; the market price of standard gold in bars fluctuating from 4l. 9s. to 4l. 12s. per oz. The market price at 4l. 10s. is about 15 1-2 per cent. above the Mint price.

Your Committee have found, that during the first three months of the present year, the price of standard gold in bars remained nearly at the same price as during last year; viz., from 4l. 10s. to 4l. 12s. per oz. In the course of the months of March and April, the price of standard gold is quoted but 4l. once in Wettenhall's tables, viz., on the 6th of April last, at 6s. which is rather more than 10 per cent. above the Mint price.

It will be found by the evidence, that the high price of gold is ascribed, by most of the witnesses, entirely to an alleged

*R. E. Thompson: Social Science and Nat. Economy, p. 160.

scarcity of that article, arising out of an unusual demand for
it upon the continent of Europe. This unusual demand for
gold upon the continent is described by some of them as being
chiefly for the use of the French armies, though increased also
by that state of alarm, and failure of confidence, which leads
to the practice of hoarding."

Mr. Patterson :

"The effect of the Eastern Trade upon the value of the
precious metals has hitherto attracted but little attention; yet,
without a perception and appreciation of the facts which we
have now set forth, the events connected with the value of
money during the last quarter of a century would be wholly
inexplicable. It has been the drain of the precious metals to
the East, to meet the requirements of Indian trade and investments, which alone has falsified the confident predictions of all
the highest authorities as to a stupendous fall in the value
of money, and especially of gold. But one remarkable circumstance still remains to be explained—namely, the recent
fall in the value of silver; which event, likewise, is the very
opposite of what was expected. The currency of the East is
silver, and consequently it is in silver that the greater part of
the enormous payments of specie to India have been made.
How, then, does it happen that it is silver, and not gold, that
has fallen in value?—fallen, or apparently fallen, in the West,
while its value is still maintained in the East?

.When the new gold-mines were discovered it was universally predicted that, while gold would lose a great part of its
old value, the value of silver would be fully maintained. And
had the extraordinary expansion of the Eastern trade been
foreseen, it must have been predicted that silver would not
only maintain its old value, but rise almost to a famine-price.
As is well known, silver did for several years rise in value
compared to gold; although we think there is ground for believing that the rise was not absolute—i. e., as measured in
general commodities, but was only equal to, and produced by,
the contemporaneous decline in the value of gold. Be that as
it may, for upwards of twenty years subsequent to 1850, the
price of silver, as measured in gold, stood considerably above its
old value—rising from 59 3-4d per ounce to 62d, and then declining to its old value—or a fraction below it—viz., 59 1-4d in 1873.
Considering the facts of the case, this rise in the value of silver
was a very small one. As we have shown, between 1858 and
1865, the amount of silver exported to India actually absorbed

the entire contemporaneous yield of the silver mines, and £40,000,000 more. In other words, this drain of silver to the East was equivalent in its effects upon Europe and America to an entire stoppage of the silver mines, together with an actual drain and deduction of £40,000,000 from the existing currency of the Western world. But in 1873 the tables turned, and silver began to decline rapidly in value compared to gold— reaching its lowest point in 1876, the year of the Silver Panic, when the price fell to 47d. per ounce. To some extent, doubtless, this fall in the value of silver may be ascribed to the recent comparative scarcity of gold, occasioned by the decreased production of the gold mines. It has also been owing to the large increase in the supply of silver from the new Nevada mines; and also to the fact that, owing to the increase of wealth, silver has recently been gradually becoming less suitable as currency in the leading countries of the Western world, and has, to a great extent, been legislatively demonetized in some of those countries,—viz., in Germany and Scandinavia, and partially in the United States and France."

From the foregoing excellent authority I have clearly proven that both gold and silver fluctuate in value. How is it possible, then, to measure correctly when the measure itself is defective?

That gold has varied in its value, and that gold and silver have varied in their ratio to each other, I give the following carefully prepared table:

Gold, coined and uncoined, has varied greatly in value within historic times. A pound of gold in London brought:

A. D. 1344	£15	00s.	0d.	or $	75.00
" 1345	13	3	4	or	65.83
" 1347	14	00	0	or	70.00
" 1412	16	13	4	or	83.32
" 1464	20	16	8	or	104.16
" 1526	27	00	0	or	135.00
" 1549	34	00	0	or	170.00
" 1605	40	10	0	or	202.50
" 1626	44	10	0	or	222.50
" 1718	46	14	6	or	233.62

That is the value of a pound of gold, Troy weight, to-day.

The relative values of gold and silver have changed at different times, and we have collated a few of the more noteworthy variations in the subjoined table:

Herodotus recorded that 1	part gold	equaled	13			of silver
Alexander the Great's time........1	"	"	"	10		"
Rome after Punic War...........1	"	"	"	17.57		"
Rome under Julius Cæsar 1	"	"	"	18.93		"
Century after Columbus..........1	"	"	"	10	to 12	"
Following two centuries..........1	"	"	"	14	to 16	"
England under William, 1689......1	"	"	"	15		"
Berlin in 1838 1	"	"	"	15.69		"
United States laws, 1792 and 1834..1	"	"	"	15	& 15.87	"
France under and since empire.....1	"	"	"	15.50		

I have stated that value never did, and never can, measure value, any more than corn can measure corn; the idea of quantity alone determines that. Not only the quantity to be measured, but the size of the measure as well. It is no more correct to say that value shall be measured by a gold dollar than that a yard shall be measured by a gold yard-stick. We are told that a yard used to be the length of the King's arm. It increased and decreased in length with the stature of the king. So with the measure of gold or silver: it increases and decreases with the amount of it in sight or in use.

Quantity is the fundamental element that establishes value. In the attempt to evade this general law all the swindles incident to the use of money originate. As I have stated in a previous chapter, I repeat in substance again,—demonetize both gold and silver, and at the same time permit the unlimited coinage of both. Then authorize the Government to issue paper money, redeemed by taxes, to the amount of not less than fifty dollars per capita. This, in my judgment, is a complete solution of the whole currency question. With this currency there could be no variation. Gold and silver would still be worth their commodity value the same as now, with one exception. This commodity value would be a thing to sell instead of an instrument to measure values, as is now the case. Neither gold nor silver is a fair measure of value. The commercial value of one commodity can never be determined by the commercial value of another, with any degree of equity, for any length of time, because the relations existing at one time are rarely the same at another. The commercial value of the metal in the gold or silver dollar makes the size of the measure, as judged by them, with an increase or decrease corresponding to its value commercially. There is an increase or decrease in the commercial value of all commodities measured by them. If every factor in all business transactions could remain stationary this might do, but we know that at any moment changes of conditions may occur that will affect not only the material but moral world. We can no more take gold and silver at a certain ratio of value as compared with each other, and measure labor and its products, than we can take a bushel of wheat and a bushel of corn for the same purpose. The ratio of value between the two measures of value cannot be maintained with any degree of accuracy, much less the ratio of all other products. If corn should be a failure one year, there would have to be more wheat in the bushel. On the other hand, if wheat should be a failure, more corn would be put in the bushel, not to measure values by alone, but to keep the ratio exact between the two measures. This process seems burdensome and unnecessary. Some nations have one, and some another ratio by weight between the two metals. During the war the bullion in a silver dollar was worth three and a half per cent. more than the bullion in a gold dollar. It is claimed now that gold bullion, with the same ratio of weight, is worth the most. Who can tell? When the commercial value of the two measures of value is changeable and uncertain, how can their measurement be accurate?

For these and many other reasons that might be advanced I believe the time is near at hand when our circulating medium will be based on taxation. This nation could float at par fully two billions of paper money based on our present taxation. This would not only be safe but always uniform.

The difference between a treasury and a bank is, one pays out money, while the other loans it. Let the government say to the people: We will pay you this money for services and material for public use, and will receive it from you for all taxes—State as well as national. Who will doubt the success of the enterprise? The taxation for ordinary government expenses and internal improvements actually necessary for this great nation would amount to from five to eight hundred millions per annum. What a permanent and safe basis this would make for a circulating medium. In connection with an unlimited coinage of gold and silver this would give us purely an American currency for an American people.

The fatal mistake of our government was in paying one kind of money to the bondholder and another to the soldier. The war would have ended two years before it did, and the debt resulting would have been merely nothing if a full government legal-tender had been issued and kept in circulation. Besides this, there is no such thing as money value either in justice or in fact. There would be one value for gold, another for silver, another for copper. Money measures value, and therefore cannot be value itself. We want a measure that cannot fluctuate. Such a measure must be an abstract thing, of no intrinsic value, but having legal functions. That is exactly the status of the dollar. But men have coupled the abstract idea with the substance and given it a commercial value. If we should issue notes payable in wheat, the less wheat the greater the value of the notes; the more wheat the less would be the value of the notes. The same rule applies to gold and silver, because wheat and coin (bullion) are both commodities and subject to similar variations in value. For these reasons I submit that notes or currency bottomed on taxation would be stable and without any fluctuation.

"Metallic money, whilst acting as coin, is identical with paper money, in respect of being destitute of intrinsic value; with this single difference, that when it is desired to reproduce that intrinsic value, the sovereign can be instantly turned into bullion. * * * Still, whilst circulating, both make no use of intrinsic value; and this is the great point to grasp firmly."—North British Review. Nov.. 1861

CHAPTER VI.

PROTECTION TO HOME INDUSTRY AND CONTRACTION OF CURRENCY.

I am a firm believer in a protective tariff. Not an excessive tariff, but one sufficient to afford ample protection to our native industries.

Our free, intelligent, civilized labor should not be compelled to compete with foreign servile, ignorant, half-civilized labor upon our own soil.

We should not, under any circumstances, permit foreign pauper labor—made so by despotic laws—to rob our own toiling millions of their richest and most righteous inheritance, a home market for the fruits of their labor.

The products of every nation carry with them in their cost of production, the morals, civilization and intelligence of the country in which they are produced. Therefore, we should allow no foreign production to compete with its kind in our own markets, unless it represents in its cost value of production the same elements of civilization that enter into our own. If, by reason of an absence of these factors in its cost of production, its value is lessened below that with which it seeks to compete, I believe a tax should be placed upon it to make up the discrepancy. This should be done that our own laborers shall not be compelled to dispense with their civilizing and moral benefits which have placed them on a higher and happier plane of social existence than their less fortunate compet-

itors. In doing this we simply obey Nature's first great law—
self-preservation.

At the present time, with our alleged surplus, there is
much discussion about the markets of the world. Many of
our people are anxious to compete for their surmised benefits.
There is nothing to prevent such action, even now. There is
no law on our statute books against such competition. The
farmer or manufacturer, if dissatisfied with the home market,
can go to that of any other country, as there is no export duty.
But when once out from under the flag of this nation, the
rules and regulations of commerce of the nation to which they
would go must be obeyed.

The reason our exports are not larger is because some
other people sell similar products cheaper. The only question
asked by a purchaser is, "Where can I buy the product I want
cheapest?" When that condition is complied with, nothing is
easier than large sales. Wheat will serve as an example to
illustrate this fact. Russia and India compete with us in the
sale of that cereal. Our wheat goes into the market as the
product of well-paid, well-fed, intelligent, free labor. It represents in its first cost its share of the taxation that built our
highways, bridges, and improved our water ways; that pays for
our free schools, our institutions of charity and reform, our
churches, and the expense of our moral training; the enforce-
ment of laws for protection to life and property, and the general welfare of the people. These, in part, are the objects for
which, not only this product, but all others in this nation, are
compelled to contribute. The product of our competitors presents a far different example. It represents ignorance, supersti-
tion, and a want of moral culture. It brings with it no smile
of civilization, none of the higher conditions of freedom, but
instead, it comes weighted with the blight of oppression, and
brings with it the foul breath of beastly instincts. Nevertheless, these products compete with ours. If we must meet this

competition, if we must give up our home markets and go abroad, our duty is plain—we must look to the first cost of our productions, which alone will enable us to sell cheap. Every factor that enters into this first cost must be eliminated that is possible. Every endeavor must be made to render our productions cheaper than those of other countries; for by this means only can success be expected. In following out this line we must ignore public improvements, and suffer those already made to go uncared for; do away with our public school system; destroy our other institutions of learning and charity; open the doors of our penitentiaries, and close the doors of our churches. In a word, wipe out the means by which the common desire of our people to excel in all that ennobles our race can be satisfied, and we will then be on the high road toward successful industrial competition.

One of two conditions must be brought about. The civilization of other nations must be raised to the same plane as ours, or our civilization must be lowered to the level of theirs, before anything like just or fair competition can be entered into.

In order to make this argument complete, there are two other important factors to take into consideration,—first, foreign immigration, and second, domestic currency, both of which are of vital consequence to this question.

It is not right to keep the manufactured end of a piece of cloth protected from foreign competition, and at the same time permit the labor end of this piece of cloth to stand open for the labor competition of the world. If the manufacturer is permitted to go abroad for his workmen, let the laborer go also for his clothes. If the laborer is debarred from importing his coat, let the manufacturer be denied the right to import his help. Free trade in men and protection of manufactured articles builds up monopolies, and makes the rich richer, and the poor poorer. Either protect both, or make both free; that is the doctrine of common sense, and must sooner or later prevail.

For twenty-five years this Government has been guided by a protective tariff, based upon conjectured benefits, and the acknowledged purpose of bettering the condition of the laboring man—to make him more intelligent, more happy, and better fitted for a higher plane of civilization. During twenty years of that time the following law has been upon our statute books. Read it carefully, and, if possible, imagine a more gigantic fraud, a more colossal example of hypocrisy possible. The bulk of those who honestly believe in the doctrine of protection, would hardly believe such an imposition possible:

"*Be it enacted by the Senate and House of Representatives of the United States of America in Congress assembled:*

SEC. 1. That the President of the United States is hereby authorized, by and with the advice and consent of the Senate, to appoint a commissioner of immigration, who shall be subject to the direction of the Department of State, shall hold his office for four years, and shall receive a salary at the rate of two thousand five hundred dollars a year. The said commissioner may employ not more than three clerks, of such grade as the Secretary of State shall designate, to be appointed by him, with the approval of the Secretary of State, and to hold their offices at his pleasure.

SEC. 2. *And be it further enacted*, That all contracts that shall be made by emigrants to the United States in foreign countries, in conformity to regulations that may be established by the said commissioner, whereby *emigrants shall pledge the wages of their labor for a term not exceeding twelve months*, to repay the expenses of their emigration, shall be held to be valid in law, and may be enforced in the courts of the United States, or of the several States and Territories; and such advances, if so stipulated in the contract, and the contract be recorded in the recorder's office in the county where the emigrant shall settle, *shall operate as a lien upon any land thereafter acquired by the emigrant, whether under the homestead law when the title is consummated, or on property otherwise acquired until liquidated by the emigrant;* but nothing herein contained shall be deemed to authorize any contract contravening the Constitution of the United States, or creating in any way the relation of slavery or servitude.

SEC. 3. *And be it further enacted*, That no emigrant to the United States who shall arrive after the passage of this act shall be compulsively enrolled for military service during the existing insurrection, unless such emigrant shall voluntarily renounce under oath his allegiance to the country of his birth, and declare his intention to become a citizen of the United States."

Such an act as this does not tend to strengthen a belief in the integrity of those benefited through a protective tariff.

Every speaker or writer upon this subject undertakes to show that this restriction on commerce is for the entire benefit, in the ultimate, of the laborer. While at the same time another law made by the same party, and under the same administration, pours into this nation, to compete with its laborers, this stream of filthy pauper laborers from foreign countries under contract. To make absurdity absurd, in the general appropriation bill passed a few months after the one quoted above, was the following:

"For expenses under the act of Congress to carry into effect the treaty between the United States and Her Britannic Majesty for the suppression of the African slave-trade, seventeen thousand dollars.

For expenses under the act to encourage immigration, twenty-five thousand dollars."

Seventeen thousand dollars to put down black slavery, and twenty-five thousand dollars to inaugurate a system of white slavery, in order to make protection protect. This first proposition must be seriously considered.

Second. Protection of home industry and contraction of currency cannot be successful in the same country. No government can enforce both of these propositions and be prosperous for any great length of time. They are diametrically opposed to each other. To protect home industry is to increase our home business. The more successful protection is, the more these business transactions will be multiplied. The foundations on which this great doctrine stands are home markets and home consumption. The purpose of protecting our domestic industries is to increase the volume of our domestic or national business. The more it is practiced, the larger proportions will the transactions assume. On the other hand, contraction means a limitation of the currency to the smallest possible amount, thereby taking away the very means by which business transactions are made practicable. All values are measured with money, and all business transactions are leveled up with money. Consequently, the amount of business must conform to the volume of currency in circulation. " More business transactions with less currency " is pure fiction. The engineer might, with equal reason, attempt to run more machinery with less power. The ideas of protection and contraction are contradictory, and can never be successfully enforced together.

I have clearly demonstrated in the previous chapters of this book that the ability to purchase establishes the price of our products. Another proposition I desire to state is, that when we do not, for any reason, no matter what it may be, see fit to avail ourselves of the price or commercial value placed upon our products by the ability to purchase which our own people can offer, and go to some other nation to sell, we are simply exchanging the ability which that nation has to purchase, for that of our own. Many times, in that case, the price or ability to purchase of the foreign nation not only establishes the commercial value of the exports, but of all that is consumed at home. If we exported no wheat or flour, our own markets would govern their price. But now the London market rules both ; that is, the ability of England to purchase breadstuffs determines how much or how little the American consumer shall eat. We are met here with the question of overproduction. In reply I emphatically say there can be no overproduction, but instead it is always an underconsumption that gluts our markets. That underconsumption is an unsupplied demand for products, visible all over the land. The *unrequeited* demand is the result of a lack of ability to purchase. And when our products are sent abroad to be sold, in almost every case it is owing, not to a want of demand at home but to a lack of ability to purchase; and it shows conclusively that some other nation is better prepared in that respect than ours.

If every person living within the confines of our national borders was comfortably fed, clothed and housed, there could be no surplus. With our present diversified industries it would be impossible.

We exported in 1883, the last authentic report I have:

Wheat, bush..106,385,000
Flour, bbls... 9,205,000

All reduced to flour would be about 5,912,280,000 pounds. Dividing this among 60 millions of people gives 98 1-2 pounds to each, or 4 1-3 ounces each per day. That is, if as a nation we had consumed 4 1-3 ounces of flour per day, for each person, more than was consumed, no wheat or flour would have been exported.

Again, the same year there was exported:

Sheep..337,000
Cattle...104,000
Hogs... 16,000

Reduced to pounds would amount to about 71,850,000.

Hams and Bacon..340,258,000
Beef, fresh.. 81,000,000
Beef, salted.. 41,680,000
Pork... 62,116,000

Pounds total......................................596,904,000

Divide this among 60,000,000 of people and we have less than ten pounds for each person, or about one-half ounce of meat per day for each to consume, more than was consumed, in order that there would be no exportation of meats. Our whole exports amounted to only $14.00 per capita, or less than four cents each per day. Is there anyone who doubts the present demand in this nation for 4 1-3 ounces of flour and 1-2 ounce of meat per day for each person? If there is, let him make a tour of the haunts of wretchedness and starvation that exist all about us in every direction. Less than four cents per day expended by each would keep all our products at home, thereby giving our people much more labor and consequently a proportionate quantity of the comforts of life.

Why does this amount go abroad? Certainly, as I have shown, not for want of home demand, but for want of means to purchase. This want of ability to purchase their home products has been brought on the people by the contraction of our circulating medium.

For these reasons I repeat: Protection and Contraction can not prove successful. One must give way to the other.

CHAPTER VII.

CONCLUSIONS.

I have untertaken to show that price is established by an ability to purchase; that the ability to purchase depends entirely upon the volume of currency among the people; and that upon the price of labor and its products depends the prosperity of the civilized world.

I have shown clearly in the case of our own nation, and from the ablest writers and scholars of other countries, that, with an increase of currency prices advance and prosperity follows, while with a decrease of currency prices fall and adversity soon comes. Nothing is plainer than the truth of these propositions. In view of the facts, what, as intelligent men having the welfare of the whole nation at heart, ought we to do in the matter? We know the cause of our ills, and where the remedy lies. Shall we sit down and not apply the remedy—not make an effort to rectify these growing evils? If we remain inactive there should be no further complaint if trouble overtakes us in the near future.

The war between labor and capital must be settled, that is, each must have its rights as near as possible, and then continue in a state of armed neutrality to protect each other from encroachments. Capital has been the dictator for many long years; in consequence of which it has reaped a rich harvest of wealth. Labor has turned now, with the desperation of long continued spoliation, and unless given at least a portion of its just dues may soon break loose and no one can tell the destruction that may follow. There is at the present time a most bitter hatred existing among the poorer classes of our people toward the law-pampered aristocrat and millionaire. This hatred will find vent at no distant day if not prohibited ¦by just counsels and fair legislation.

Our laws are oppressive towards the poor, and generally operate in favor of capital. There can be no denial of that fact; and until they are changed it is useless to theorize upon the matter. We have had a dear dollar and a cheap day's work long enough. The people are getting tired of it. They demand a cheaper dollar and a dearer day's work. Who can blame them, and why should their demand be denied after having given the contraction and "hard pan" policies of the government a fair trial?

When the services of a skillful physician are required he first makes a careful diagnosis of the case in order that he may locate the disease. He compares the patient in health with his present condition. The difference between the two conditions is the malady. Now, if he should locate the disorder in the head, would he prescribe for the feet? or if in the lungs, would he give remedies for the brain? Under such treatment the patient would die, and the physician would be disgraced. The true practice would be a thorough treatment of the parts afflicted, to the end that they might be restored to their normal condition, in which they could, with the other members of the body, perform the usual functions necessary to health and life.

In applying the same rule to our body politic, we find, in 1866, health and vigor in every part of the system. Business was good, wages were high, and money plenty. People were out of debt and all were contented, prosperous and happy. In 1886, twenty years after, we find the debts of all kinds in the nation equal to ninety per cent of its equalized valuation.

We find all business nearly at a standstill; low prices and no work; our country full of tramps; our jails and poorhouses filled with those unable to find labor. We see want and distress on every hand. Labor strikes and riots are of daily occurrence and seem to be on the increase. The body politic of our nation is sick. It is stricken with lingering disease. Where is it located, and what is its nature?

The blessings of Deity—sunshine and rain, day and night, summer and winter, seed time and harvest, health and energy—are granted us now as they were twenty years ago. Our people are as industrious, intelligent and economical now as then. The earth yields as rich harvests; the herds and flocks are as prolific. All other bounties of nature are as abundant as ever before. The reward of labor in gross production never was greater than at present. We may search in vain through our whole economic or social system and we can find but one factor in the entire range different at this time from twenty years ago. Then the people had fifty and one-half dollars per capita to do business with, while to-day, at the outside, they have but $8. This is the root of the disease, the one great factor in all this present disorder. For twenty years contraction has cursed our land until it has gradually dried up the fountains of our prosperity. The trail of this serpent can be clearly traced by the bleached bones of its bankrupt victims— 109,000 in 20 years. Can the misery and despair of these unfortunates be measured in money? No wonder Mr. Shellabarger said:

"They—the money-loaners—are seeking to coin the gains of their infamy out of the blood of their sinking country."

Mr. Kellogg said:

"Mr. Chairman: I am pained when I sit in my place in the House, and hear members talk about the sacredness of capital; that the *interests* of money must not be touched. Yes, sir; *they will vote six hundred thousand of the flower of the American youth for the army, to be sacrificed, without a blush,* but the great interests in capital must not be touched. We have summoned the youth, *and they have come.* I would summon the *capital;* and if it does not come voluntarily, before this Republic shall go down, or one star be lost, I would take every cent from the treasury of the states, from the treasury of capitalists, from the treasury of individuals, and press it into the use of the Government."

We should call a halt; demand that the conditions under which we were prosperous and happy should again be restored, and that at once.

"Money is the life-blood of business. Make it plenty, all business prospers, and working-men are employed at good wages. Make it scarce, all business languishes; merchants become bankrupt and laborers are starving. Who don't know this?"

We are encountering the same difficulties which all nations, in all ages past, have met, when the money of account has been contracted beyond the reach of the people. Its path has been strewn with wreck and ruin, until nothing written in the pages of history is more plainly seen than the black pall which has followed every attempt to wrong the people by enhancing the value of money. A proper amount of currency will regulate the equilibrium between the rich and poor, high and low, visible and invisible capital, when all class laws and regulations fail.

I quote from the report of the Silver Commission:

"During certain periods in the past, when prices have been falling by reason of a shrinkage in the volume of money, a slow and toilsome advance has been made in the accumulation of wealth. Under such conditions its just distribution is impossible. A shrinking volume of money and falling prices always have had and always must have a tendency to concentrate wealth, to enrich the few, and to impoverish and degrade the many. This tendency is subtle, active; and portentous throughout the world to-day."

Whenever a monopolist gives public expression to his ideas, he always pleads for the laborer, that a cheap dollar is his continual curse. This is only a pretext. Capital wants a dear dollar that it may compel cheap labor, while labor wants a cheap dollar that it may increase the value of its earnings. Upon this point I will give the following illustration :

"Be it remembered ever that the legal, debt-paying value of money never changes, except to exist and not exist. The legal, debt-paying properties—the property imparted by the law-making power that creates money—never fluctuates ; it is stationary, year in and out.

PROPOSITION DEMONSTRATED.

Wages per day.	Cost of living, etc.	Sum left.
$1.00	$0.75	$0.25
50	37½	12½
25	18¾	06¼
12½	09⅜	03⅛
2.00	1.50	50
4.00	3.00	1.00

Suppose a laborer had a mortgage of $1,000 on his home, which he desired to pay as fast as his earnings accumulated. Let us notice how high wages and high cost of living compares with cheap labor and cheap cost of living, in the amount of his yearly payments :

Sums left.	Iowa rate .10 per cent.	Year's work.	Yearly interest.	Days needed.
		Days.		
$0.25	$100	313	$100	400
12½	100	313	100	800
06¼	100	313	100	1,600
03⅛	100	313	100	3,200
50	100	313	100	200
1.00	100	313	100	100

Thus we see that, $1 per day and 25 cents " left," it takes 400 days to pay the interest, for interest and debt—national, State and individual—must be paid out of "sum left" after cost of living is paid. This being the case, it taking 400 days to pay the interest and there being but 313 work days in a year, the debtor finds himself "short" 87 days. This is deferred by "credit note." But the next turn of the thumbscrews of contraction finds him short 487 days, which means credit gone for a chattel-mortgage substitute.

The next turn toward "hard-pan" finds the debtor "short" 1287 days. This means a mortgage on everything, as well present as future.

The next turn reaches out to "specie basis" and "resumption," and the court of last resort—the high sheriff (?)—bids the debtor go! in the name of law, good order, and the Christian teachings of the nineteenth century, out into God's land, if he can find any that monopolists have not gobbled ; or go, as the tramp, branded by law.

But of the up-turn to $2 per day, the "sum left" at this price, he pays his interest with 200 days' work, and has 113 left to work for wife, babies, home, improvement, with something to spare to pay the principal of debt.

But of the up-turn to $4 per day he pays his interest with 100 days' work, and has 213 left to apply for God, home, and humanity.

This means the debt honestly paid, the mortgage canceled, hopes realized, wife cheerful, children gay, hearthstone loves brightened, family educated, society built up—a better citizen—a man."

I quote the above from a speech by the Hon. L. H. Weller of Iowa.   Comment is unnecessary.

Again, when low prices are paid for labor, the prices of products are proportionally low.   It is, therefore, generally supposed that the laborer can as readily procure all needful supplies when labor is at a low price, as when it is at a high one.   But the articles whose price is diminished by the lowering of labor, are the productions of labor ; and the producing classes suffer great injury from this depression of both their labor and products.

The following illustration will exhibit the advantage of high prices for labor.   A man raises a hundred bales of cotton, sends them to market, and receives three and a half cents per pound.   A laborer in New York receives fifty cents a day for his labor; with a days work he can purchase fourteen pounds of cotton.   If labor be at a dollar per day, and cotton at seven cents per pound, with a day's labor he can purchase the same quantity.   If labor rise to a dollar and fifty cents a day, and cotton to ten and a half cents per pound, a day's labor will still purchase fourteen pounds of cotton.   Thus far we do not observe the difference of price to have any influence upon the ability of the laborer to purchase ; but we have yet to notice the condition of that class of producers who raise the cotton at the first price, three and a half cents per pound. After paying for the use or rent of the plantation one-half the price at which a loan of money can be obtained, say three or four per cent. interest on the cost of the plantation, they do not earn fifty cents a day, but, in fact, receive little or no compensation for their labor. The same labor and land are required to produce cotton when it brings three and a half cents, as when it brings fourteen cents per pound. Suppose a workman in New York to buy cotton at fourteen cents per pound; a barrel of flour at $8; wheat at $1.50 per bushel; potatoes at 40 cents; brown sugar at 10 cents; boots at $3 a pair; brown sheeting at 10 cents per yard; and good calico at 12 cents per yard. If labor falls to 50 cents per day, and he have full employment, to be as well off as when labor was at $2 per day he must buy flour at $2 per barrel; wheat at 37 1-2 cents per bushel; potatoes at 10 cents; brown sugar at 2 1-2 cents per pound; boots at 75 cents per pair; brown sheeting at 2 1-2 cents per yard; calico at 3 cents, and everything else in proportion. Traveling expenses, rents and taxes must be diminished three quarters. All the necessaries of life must be reduced in price three quarters, or the laborer who is out of debt will not be as well off when labor is fifty cents per day, as when it is at $2 per day. But suppose one class of the laborers to buy at these low prices, what will the producers of wheat, etc., receive for their labor? The reason that the laborer can buy as much cotton when labor is at fifty cents per day, as when it is at $2, is, that he buys a fellow-laborer's products at a price which will not pay a cent a day for the toil of producing them. So, when the prices of labor are reduced in this ratio, laborers, as a body, are unable to provide themselves with the necessaries of life, and sparingly live upon the meager fruits of each others toil. The reduction of the prices of labor and products, consequent upon a scarcity of money and a rise of interest, forces producers and merchants to suffer great losses, because the diminution of the prices of products does not diminish the amount of their debts, nor their legal obligations to pay them; while the capitalists who own these debts will compel laborers and owners of land and products to sell double, treble, and quadruple the quantity of these, to obtain money to satisfy the debts. Thus wealth passes with great rapidity into the hands of a few capitalists. If the merchant has bought goods at as low a price as they can be afforded by the manufacturer, it is no safeguard against loss by the fall of goods in the market, because the market-price of the goods does not depend upon the labor necessary to their production, but upon the ever-varying value of the dollar. Our laws make the dollar the real value, or standard of payment, and producers and all kinds of property are controlled by its power.

The objection is often urged, that to make money plenty would destroy the value of products. But how would or could it destroy their value to allow the needy to earn the means to purchase them? Will not a starving people buy products? Does anyone suppose that the people of Ireland would live upon their present scanty food, if their labor would afford them the means of purchasing more and better? Was there ever a bad market for products when labor was receiving what are called high prices, or a good market when labor was at a low price? The market is made poor by the inability of the laboring community to earn enough to make purchases. If labor were well paid, the market would always be good, and the laborer, assured of a just reward, would work cheerfully.

Large production, at a fair price, gives a better compensation to producers than half production at a double price. The families of producers require as many products for their own consumption when the crops are diminished one-half, and their price is doubled, as when products are abundant. The producers cannot then spare a sufficient quantity to sell for their usual profits, even at the increased price, and capital makes the same requisition upon their labor for rent or interest as if their crops were abundant.

It is a solemn truth that hard times fill up alike our poor-houses and jails; that these periods of financial depression not only bring more poverty, but increase crime. It is plain enough when understood.

When hard times begin to press upon an individual, and retrenchment of expenses are commenced, the moral luxuries go first. Next follow his intellectual luxuries; lastly he cuts off personal luxuries, and gradually little comforts of life are dropped one by one, until the struggle for the bare necessities of life takes the place of all. The moral, social and intellectual conditions are sacrificed to the physical.

From this condition come poverty, helplessness and crime from despair. When, for any reason this condition is bettered, the same route is traveled back, starting through individual comforts, then to intellectual luxuries, and finally to moral obligations and a higher life.

"Talk to the winds and reason with despair,
But tell not Misery's sons that life is fair."

History proves these propositions true, and the experiences of an ordinary lifetime confirm them.

I would not be understood that the poor are wanting in these virtues, or that they are debarred from acquiring them; but I do say that poverty and deprivations are not promoters of moral and social advancement—that the over-worked, ill-fed, distressed individual, whose whole time is occupied in "bread winning" is in no condition to discuss, much less to participate in the higher moral and social attainments. Life, to them, is but a continual fight to supply the demands of nature, with no place for elevating or refining sentiments. But in direct ratio as the battle for life is lessened, and physical energies are relieved from the constant strain of production, the

molding influences of civilization are seen to find lodgment.
We are all creatures of circumstances. Our welfare depends
upon the rules of society, or rather the customs of our associates, the regulations and restrictions of law, and our own
ability to interpret them. The importance, therefore, of salutary laws, and their proper adaptation to the circumstances and
conditions of those whose conduct is sought to be directed, is
of the first consideration. While Governments do not point
out to each individual the course he shall pursue, they should
make such general restrictions that all might fully and equally
act within their limits. These restrictions, in a government
like our own especially, are for the greatest good to the greatest number.

The great bulk of our people are producers. Almost sixty
per cent. are wage-workers. The proportion of rich to poor is
as 6 to 94. This being true, then our laws should be so framed
as to benefit the poor as against the rich, to protect the weak
against the strong. That this is not the case, that our laws are
not so constructed, we have but to glance about us for proof.
We can discern at once that something is at fault with our
economic system. That fault, in my opinion, is due to a misap-
prehension of money functions, or to a willful mismanagement
of our circulating medium. The great difference between the
extremes of poverty and prosperity in this country is wholly
due to the condition of our currency. What is commonly
called "good times" are periods when the quantity of money
is rapidly increasing. Bad times come when the quantity is
diminished or at a standstill, or not increasing as fast as the
population and needs of business require.

The history of civilization shows that the fall of Rome
and the subsequent elimination of nearly all the civilizing influences were due almost entirely to the failure of the mines
from which it derived its currency, paper substitutes being
then unknown ; that the first glimmer of returning hope was

co-incident with the discovery of paper money, which, after several evolutions, was put in the form of bank paper for the first time in Sweden, in 1658. From that day to the present, the nation using the cheapest unit as a standard of payment, has prospered the greatest.

A standard of value is like the money of the world, an impossible something, which is made use of by demagogues to frighten or mislead the people. If we are to have either silver or gold as the standard of payment, let us by all means take silver. All countries prosper where debts must be paid in the cheapest standard of payment. This means dear labor, dear productions, and cheap payments.

The curse of all monetary systems, at the present time, is caste. There is in every nation a money unit for the rich, and a money unit for the poor. We have it. England, France, Germany and other Nations have it. Why is copper, nickel, and all subsidiary coin not a full legal tender? Not for the reason advanced by many, that in payment of debts men might misuse the privilege and load down the creditor with large amounts of this coin. No; far from that being the true answer. It is because a large majority of the people are poor and can use but small amounts at best. Why is silver used in India? Because no gold coin could be made of small enough value to even pay for labor; it is so cheap. Gold is found in use with diamonds, silks, satins, palatial residences, etc., while the use of silver is discovered among rags, hovels, want and wretchedness. The United States is one of the greatest silver producing nations in the world. As one of our precious metals, it should be used as money to a much greater extent than gold. By our laws, but two million dollars each month is permitted to be coined. Silver, being one of our staple products, if not wanted at home, goes abroad like wheat or meat, but with a far different purpose. Other products of export are sent abroad to be consumed, while silver is bought from us to be used principally as money. This silver goes to those nations where silver is used as the circulating medium, and assists in building up industries to compete with our own. Large amounts of our silver has found its way to India. By the use of it, India has so improved her condition in regard to production, that to-day wheat can be laid down, duty paid, in New York, from that country, cheaper than from Dakota. A continuance of this will not only deprive us of our wheat market, but wool as well; and the solemn fact presents itself to the minds of every one that the silver using countries do now, and will in the future, compete successfully with any and all nations using gold.

When we attempt to cry down the value of silver, we are injuring one of the large factors employed in the accumulation of our own wealth. Besides this, it is a downright injury to all other forms of wealth below it, and a benefit to all forms above it. Thus we see that the depreciation of silver depreciates every other product but gold, as gold is the only production more valuable than silver intrinsically.

Just so long as we undertake to put into practice that worst of all ideas, a standard of values, just so long will the higher valued products measure the lower. The large pocket book governs the smaller, and the rich will rule the poor.

At the present time there is much said and written about the shrinkage of values. There has been really no shrinkage of values, but there has been an increase in the measure by which values were estimated. Some well-disposed, but extremely ignorant persons have introduced a bill in Congress to establish a uniform standard of value, hoping thereby to avoid these fluctuations. The Pope's bull against the comet was sound logic compared to this. In doing so, legislation seeks to establish an utter impossibility. As I have said repeatedly before, there can be no such thing as a standard of value. That, with the markets of the world, the money of the world, and the philosopher's stone, all belong in the same category of ancient fables. Coins are not standards of value, but standards of payment. The only measure of value is the money of account, that abstract thing, the dollar, of which we talk so much. Value is an abstract, intangible something that can not be measured by a concrete tangible something any more than an idea can be measured by a quart cup, or a sentiment by a foot rule. The difference between a standard of payment and a standard of value is this:

A standard of payment is a certain legally authorized amount of specified commodities which are the basis of all debts or agreements, and are received in liquidation of the same. The standard of payment in this nation is a specified number of grains of gold or silver.

A standard of value is a commodity value, ascertained by the relation which the standard of payments bear to it and all other things. It is an assumption, having no existence either in logic or fact. The only manner in which value is ascertained is by a comparison with the standard of payment. The word, standard, means stable, solid, unchanging. There never was a commodity of value in the world that was not constantly changing as its conditions to other commodities changed. The standard of payment cannot be a standard of value, because the value of that standard has always been, is, and always will be, fluctuating. The value depends upon its amount and the demand.

Value is an abstract idea, like goodness, idleness, labor and the dollar. Who ever saw a day's work or handled a dollar? Who ever bought a pound of goodness, or a foot of idleness? To have a standard of value it would be necessary to find some product that never varies in value. Where can it be found? We have a standard of length in the twelve inches to the foot; of weight, in the sixteen ounces to the pound; of time, in the sixty seconds in a minute. Who ever purchased either of these? and yet, they are real products as compared to the idea of a standard of value. We have a standard for length in the foot. It will measure distance, it will measure timber, cloth, etc. The pound weight will measure gold as well as wheat. The gallon will measure water as well as wine.

But in the standard of the measure of value there must be something found that can be applied, at any and all times, to any and all substances to determine their value with unvarying minuteness. Will a certain number of grains of gold or silver determine the value of the cargo of lumber, the cargo of wheat, or the cargo of molasses? How can 23 22-100 grains of gold do all this? How is it applied? If this amount of gold should become more valuable from scarcity, as it is now, the measure would be too large. If it should shrink in value, the measure would be too small. In fact, as before stated, there is no standard of value. Money is simply a standard of payment. Value itself cannot be measured; it can only be determined approximately by comparison. Quality cannot be measured by quantity. The abstract cannot be obtained by applying the concrete. There may be different degrees of quality, but not an increase or decrease of amount.

After all, the two great objects of law are the protection of life and the proper distribution of wealth. In fact, a just distribution of wealth itself would be one great factor in the protection of life and the prevention of crime. The lust for money is the foundation of and incentive to much of the crime committed, for which the human family is guilty. One potent agent in the equalization of wealth is taxation. A graduated income tax, increasing with the wealth of the individual, would not only be just, but would do much toward bringing about this result. When a man becomes able to command the power of one hundred thousand dollars in wealth, he at once becomes a menace to the state and the just application of law. This is true in the nature of things. His influence, in so far as his money goes, is equal to, and by virtue of its concentration, much greater than that of the 325 pauper neighbors that his accumulation of wealth necessarily brings into existence. Very few men are punished for crime who are worth this sum of money.

Now, if we should abolish all internal revenues; limit duties or customs to an amount that would protect labor and the products of labor from unfavorable competition on our own soil; then put such an income tax on the production of wealth as would make it unprofitable to be worth more than $100,000, I think the question of the just distribution of wealth would be much less difficult of solution. Let the income tax be so arranged that all the profit of business above the legitimate earnings of $100,000, be paid over to the national Treasury. Then millionaires would soon cease to curse our land.

There is nothing more disastrous to the nation than large accumulations of wealth. I do not wish to be understood as making war on capital, or not upholding a just emulation in the acquirement of wealth, but I do wish to convey this—that the laws of distribution should take from money its power of attraction to other forms of wealth; that is, I would eliminate the idea from the minds of men that "it takes money to make money," as they now express it. I would substitute instead the plain fact that it takes *labor* to make money. And I would so frame our economic laws that when men labor—no matter if they are foolish and ignorant—the result would show that labor *did* bring a reward. If after the reward was earned men squandered it, the assumption should not follow that by reason of this they should not be permitted to earn it. I would not bring in the fact of a man's incapacity to hoard money as the reason for not giving him the opportunity to earn it.

When one man goes to his grave worth ten million dollars, and his neighbor, who has been equally industrious, is buried at the public expense, it shows on its face an unjust distribution of the fruits of labor. I do not subscribe to the doctrine that what one man gains another loses, because we are producing wealth all the time through the medium of invisible capital. This would be true, however, if wealth was stationary. But I do claim when a man produces wealth through his own labor, the economic laws of the land should be so framed that he may retain peaceable possession of it. As Thomas Paine says in his Rights of Man: "When the old men go to the poorhouse, and the young men to prison, something is wrong with the economic system of the nation."

At the present time there is a general desire among all nations, to find some remedy for the increasing dissatisfaction so manifest with the laboring classes. Opinions upon this subject are widely at variance. Neither employer nor employé can answer the question satisfactorily, even to themselves. The Knights of Labor, that grand organization for good, are not quite a unit as to the real difficulty. This Brotherhood, so well disciplined, so powerful, backed up as it is with a sense of justice and right in its cause, will fall to pieces, and that soon, if it does not at once state to the world some one great remedy for the complaints made. The long list of demands shown in their platform, will require years to legislate upon singly. If these charges are true, they are simply ulcers upon our body politic. To treat them one at a time would be not only bad practice, but doubtless prove fatal. The proper course points to a thorough cleansing of the body, a powerful, searching purifier, that in its operation would rid the system of all this poison, and drive out all extraneous matter. Is there not one great panacea that will, in the proper course of its action, remedy the larger part of these evils? I think there is. Let us make the search. In previous chapters I have pointed out the causes for all these troubles. I have shown the attitude of Capital and Labor. I have endeavored to treat the matter fairly, to give facts and figures, as well as the opinions of others to sustain my position.

The remedy, in my judgment, does not lie in labor laws, tariffs, arbitration, poor laws, or anything of like character. I believe they will simply act as an irritant, and in the end do more harm than good. But I do believe that relief can be found in a proper regulation of our domestic currency. The point in the whole matter is money; the point on which it all turns is money; and the object of all this strife is money. This being true, why not use that one factor to correct what it has misplaced? Its possession or non-possession is the difference between rich and poor—between starvation and plenty. Every proposition in this book, every quotation and every argument, points out the one complete and final remedy—*an increase in the domestic currency of our country.* I have proven it by statistics, by the writings of the most eminent economists from the time of Aristotle to the present; by the condition of our own country now, as compared with other dates; in every manner and by all means by which a proposition of this character can be substantiated, that a decreasing volume of money is a curse, while an increasing volume is a blessing. While it may not be true that the greater the amount of currency, the less earnest will be the demand, it is a fact that the less the amount the more eager each one is to obtain their full share or more.

When the amount of any commodity is small or diminishing, every one interested in its use becomes at once anxious for present and future wants. If a prime article of necessity, it shows this anxiety in its higher commercial value. But if the same is in abundance, it becomes cheap, because consumers, aware of its abundance, are not in the least worried about present or future supplies. Just so with the volume of money. The one primal function of money which measures value, and the other bestowed function which pays debts, are both governed by the same rule. They can both be increased or decreased in their activity and power. The same conditions that affect the price of commodities, govern the action of money. Thus, measures of value do not of themselves perform the function of measurement, but are bought with the products of labor, or labor itself, for the purpose of being held to measure the value of some other product more desirable to the holder than the product which he sold to obtain the measures. For example, the farmer buys these measures with wheat, in order to sell them for a carriage. Of themselves, they are incapable of action, but are sought for in order that this particular function may be used, when occasion may require. Just so with the debt-paying power; it is only put in force when debts are to be paid, and as every business transaction necessitates an obligation, this function is continually being used. Now, with plenty of these measures of value in sight, people would not be anxious about their ability to obtain them when wanted. Equally true with the debt paying function; with an abundance on hand which could be had in exchange for a reasonable amount of labor, no one would be troubled.

The more products to measure, the more measures would be necessary. Also, the more business transactions to complete, the more debt-paying factors would be needed. An increase of production or of business not only calls for more money for the above reasons, but urgently demands it. A less amount of products or business transactions would require less currency. It is a settled fact among economists of all nations that money becomes more valuable at some times than at others, that it increases and decreases in value under certain conditions. This change in value is only obtained by comparing it with labor and its products. This comparison has brought out the fact that money is more valuable when its quantity is decreasing or remaining stationary, while the demand for it is increasing.

Also, this rule invariably shows labor and its products in conjunction to bring lower prices. The history of the financial world proves this to be true. Continuing to make money less in amount, would as steadily make it more valuable, and, following out the rule, would lower the price of labor and all its products. Eliminate all money, and commercial values would cease altogether. Labor value or barter would then take its place. On the other hand, increase the amount of domestic currency, and this measure will decrease in value and at the same time increase the money value of all labor and production. Continue this increase indefinitely, and in the end money value will become an absurdity and cease, which would bring about the same result, a resort to barter or labor exchange. Here we find an example of arriving at the same point from opposite directions. This would seem to imply a middle ground, alike honorable and just to both contestants.

It is evident that the quantity of domestic currency alone is master of the situation, and is the only remedy that can be applied. This never can be accomplished by granting the power to issue currency to corporations, or trust to the judgment of men in high positions. It must be a per capita amount, increasing with population. Make the amount sufficient to place capital and labor on the same footing. In other words, make dollars as plenty as days' work, and confine them to the same power of accumulation.

There is but one way to bring about this result, and that is through the increase of our domestic currency to that extent that its very abundance will make it less valuable. If, by accident or design, the laborer fails to perform the days' toil, it is lost to him forever. I would have money so constituted that it would bring in no remuneration unless actively engaged in exchanges. That can be done by making it so plenty that the surplus beyond that actually in use will be the same as so much produce unsold. I do not concur in the idea of eliminating interest in financial matters. Men do not object to the payment of fair interest, but they do rebel against returning a more valuable dollar than they borrowed.

Increase the volume of domestic currency to such an extent that a dollar will sell for a just and reasonable amount of labor or its products, and that point in our economic affairs will have been reached where tramps will be seen no more, labor strikes will cease, and the smile of happiness will once more be seen on the face of the toiler. We shall then be standing on that honorable middle ground which is so necessary to the prosperity and comfort of all nations.

Make this amount, as I have said before, mandatory, so much per capita, and to increase each year with the increase of population; then prices would fluctuate only from the effect of supply and demand, which would soon regulate itself.

With this arrangement banks of issue would be abolished, and our domestic currency come to us direct from the Government.

Finally, in conclusion, repeal the internal revenue tax. Enact a vigorous income-tax law, increasing with the amount of income. Reduce the tariff to a revenue basis, and give labor all the protection which that would afford. At the same time issue gold and silver certificates, to which add greenback paper money, each and all a full legal tender for all debts, public and private, to the full amount of $50 per capita of population, that amount to increase as population increases. This would, in my judgment, put labor and capital on nearly an equal footing, and bring prosperity and happiness to the people of this nation.

APPENDIX.

———o———

LABOR.

A LECTURE DELIVERED BY N. A. DUNNING AT THE FARMER'S INSTITUTE, HELD AT MASON, MICH., FEB, 11, 1887.

The question of Labor which I shall attempt to discuss at this time, is older than the universe, as far-reaching as humanity, and as little understood as the most marvelous works of God. It has occupied the mind of man since man was created, and will continue to demand recognition until heaven and earth shall pass away. The idea of labor at the present time is associated with but a portion or class of our people—those who are compelled to work for the necessities and comforts of life, and those who, for other reasons, choose to do so. It represents an undesirable condition of existence from which all humanity seeks to be freed—either at once, or when some cherished purpose has been accomplished. The man or woman does not live who desires to labor every day, in every year, of their whole sojourn on earth. Such desire would be unnatural, a sin against the future and a libel upon the past. Nine-tenths of the labor performed at the present time is done with the idea that *this* hard labor and toil will bring about future ease and comfort. Those who can live without labor, or, who can labor when they so elect, are envied these privileges by their less fortunate associates. This envy, this desire for like situation, has led to war, bloodshed, riot and ruin. It has been the fruitful source of the greater part of the misery and woe which have overtaken mankind since the beginning of the race.

If the present differences in the human family, regarding this question, were intended in the plan of creation, if a portion were to toil at pain and sorrow that others might live in idleness and pleasure, then it is the will of God, and we should submit. But, if these differences were *not* considered in the great scheme of humanity, they are among us through the perversion of natural laws, and our duty to each other, as well as the obligation we owe our Creator, demands, alike, they should be eliminated.

"In the sweat of thy face shalt thou eat bread," declared an outraged Jehovah! Did that apply to only a portion of the human beings who were destined to people this earth? Or, was not the entire human family, from Adam to the babe born but yesterday, included in this declaration? Common sense and a fair interpretation of the intent of Providence would answer that it was a condition put upon the race without exception— that none bearing the human form was exempt from its obligations. This fiat demanded that all should support their bodily natures through Nature's own exertion—Labor.

This was the primitive condition of labor; it knew no class, it recognized no exceptions, it made no distinction. Labor and humanity started out together, hand in hand, to fight the great battle of life, each being dependent on the other and both conscious of the will of its creator. Since that time, who can mark the changes, who can portray the vicissitudes through which both have passed? Noah and the deluge; Abram and his offering; Solomon and his wisdom; Christ and Mount Calvary; the splendor of Rome; the horrors of the Dark Ages; Martin Luther and the Reformation; King John and the Magna Charter; Columbus and the Discovery of America; the war of the Revolution, and the founding of our own great nation—through all these human nature remains the same, dependent now upon labor as in the primal hour of its existence. But the conditions under which this relationship exists have undergone a wonderful change. Then it was a companion of labor, a sharer in its joys and sorrows; now it commands, it coerces, in a word it has become the master. What has produced this change, and how to better the situation, is the Alpha and Omega of the labor question.

In the primitive state of our race, men labored, simply for personal or family wants; there was neither commerce nor exchanges. Each produced what would satisfy, and each enjoyed the full benefits of his labor. We style these people barbarians, and shudder at the thought. Why? Because they could not read or write? or, wear diamonds and silks? or, get drunk and swear in five or six different languages? Are these among the reasons? If not, what are they? A few things were true, however, of *barbarism*. If a man made a coat, it was his; he was not obliged to sell it to pay interest, or hide it from the tax-collector. If he planted a field, he was not compelled to eat the refuse and sell the best to pay rent, or make a payment on the mortgage. If they were without schools, churches, and railroads, it is no less a fact they were wanting in prisons, poor-houses and tramps. They are called cruel, blood-thirsty, and possessing none of the finer sensibilities which mark the progress of civilization—that their hopes in a future life were blasted by their condition.

How long since this great nation, the most civilized on

earth, was plunged in fraternal strife, where brother sought the blood of brother, and friend the life of friend?

Even to-day the whole earth is bristling with bayonets and rumors of war are heard at every turn. Beside, who would not rather stand in the place of an ignorant barbarian in the Day of Judgment, than a civilized hypocrite? Pope says, "All nature's difference makes all nature's peace." That may be true in nature; I doubt if it is in man. If civilization could be, as no doubt it was intended, a blessing to all alike, it would be pleasant to contemplate, but when we see its advantages granted to the few and witheld from the many, there *do* come up feelings of doubt and disappointment. It must be remembered, that a people can not be better taught than fed; that constant physical exertion in production, is not only a hindrance but, in a majority of cases, a positive check to moral and social culture. The laborer, by reason of his being a laborer, is denied by the logic of events to share in this higher civilization.

The condition of the laborer not being bettered, must as a natural sequence become worse; and society to-day presents the melancholy spectacle of a small portion of our people climbing higher and the greater portion going lower on the social ladder. This is not all; the whole fabric of civilization, all its advantages, all its various adjuncts, all things that in any manner contribute toward progress and higher life, are the direct results of labor. Nothing but its constant efforts produced it, and nothing but its continued efforts will maintain it. Labor and that alone can support what it has brought into existence. It can not be ignored; the time has come when it must and will be heard. It stands to-day on the threshold of future progress and further advancement, and sternly demands of us, of you and me, "Shall my efforts in time to come be free or enforced?" The fate of the civilized world depends upon the answer. The people of this generation must decide, and the

Nineteenth Century must declare it. We who enjoy great privileges are no less burdened with great responsibilities. Let us consider well how we discharge them. Labor must be free or enforced. The usual picture of enforced labor shows a fierce looking white man driving forward in their work a number of miserable looking black men. Happy, indeed, the world would be if it ended here. It does not. It represents the fairest part. The reverse of the picture presents to our view the great struggling mass of humanity, urged on by some unseen power, working, slaving, toiling day by day, bringing into existence untold treasures of wealth, but are permitted to enjoy but a mere per cent.

Economists all agree that labor is the sole producer of wealth. If this proposition is true, why does not the producer of this wealth possess it after production? What intervening cause steps in between the producer and this wealth and prevents his owning and enjoying what his brain and brawn have created? No one seems to question the right or justice of each individual enjoying the fruits of his own labor. But to recognize this right, however, does not explain the reason why production and possession are separated, or what line of action would remedy the evil. At this point all labor discussion must begin, and thus far all theories have had their end. I believe that labor is being enslaved, being spoiled of its reward through the laws governing land and currency. " Whoever owns the land owns the people" said John Locke ; and "whoever controls the currency of the nation rules the people" said President Garfield. All production is from the earth, and all business is through the medium of currency ; therefore make one cheap and the other plenty in order to bring prosperity.

Let us return again to barbarism. Then nothing but labor value was considered. How much warmth will it secure? or, how many of the life-giving principles will it yield? were the great questions. Soon barter and exchange of commodities began to take place between individuals and tribes. The fish of one section were exchanged for the fur of another section. It often became difficult to make these exchanges exactly balance. One class of products would possess more labor value than the other. For example, ten pieces of fur would have more labor value than ten fish, but not enough for eleven. This made the bargain unequal and entailed a loss. After a time they began to use shells and beads to represent this difference in labor value. These shells and beads had no value of themselves, but by common consent represented labor value. By and by some one hoarded up enough of these representatives of value to exchange entire for some of the fish or fur. Then the war between capital and labor began and has continued until the present time. The man with the beads and shells wanted all the fur and fish he could obtain for them, while the hunters and fishermen wanted to give him as little as possible. The self-same struggle is with us to-day. The shells and beads of barbarism are the prototypes of the gold and silver of civilization. The owners of these shells and beads of barbarism are identical with the banker and bond owner of civilization. The form and material have changed. The conditions and circumstances of exchanges have differed since that time. But the old idea of barbarism, the relationship which these representatives of value bear to each other and to all created wealth has remained the same—has obeyed, all these years, the same general laws, and has been guided by the same unvarying rules. The same general laws govern the production and distribution of wealth to-day that did when production and distribution began. With an increase of these representatives of value products are more justly distributed, labor is paid better, and prosperity makes its appearance. With a decrease, exactly the reverse of this is effected. This has proven true in all ages of the world, and is proving true at the present time. Our land laws are the worst of any age or any nation. Other countries have been robbed of their possessions by force and arms; but to the American government alone belongs the disgrace, of knowingly, recklessly, and wantonly confiscating the rightful heritage of future generations, and passing them over gratuitously to heartless corporations. No other nation would permit so vast an amount of its public domain to be owned and controlled by aliens. With our present population, land is becoming scarce; what will be the situation at the next Centennial, with four or five times the number of people? No wonder the doctrine of Henry George is being thoroughly considered. No wonder the idea is beginning to obtain that no man has the right to own one acre more land than he cultivates. The total area of the United States is given at 1,814,000,000 acres. Of this amount 831 million acres have been disposed of. Sixty-five million acres of this large amount *only* has been taken under the homestead and timber-culture act. Prior to 1860 less than 28 million acres had been granted to railroads, canals, etc. Since that time there has been over 143 million acres given to these corporations, making a total of 171 million acres in all. Hundreds of millions of acres have been patented to individuals under Spanish and other foreign claims. In one instance 2,714,765 acres was patented under one of these Spanish claims. In 1880 there were private land claims of this character, amounting to 567 millions of acres on file in the land office at Washington. It has been discovered that more than ten million acres of land have been stolen by the railroad companies by false measurement alone, and that more than 15 million acres of government land have been fenced in by herders and used as their own. Thirty-four alien land-owning syndicates own 29 million acres of American soil. Let me give you the figures. The number of acres remaining unsold is 983 millions. Take from this the area of Alaska, 370 million acres, and we have 613 million acres on hand. In this amount is included all the waste land of the nation—the swamps, the mountains, deserts etc.—which in the opinion of well posted men will reduce this amount by 400 million acres more. This leaves but 213 million acres for future generations to enjoy. Who can contemplate these facts without alarm, or consider the statesmanship which has permitted this wholesale appropriation, without disgust? Every acre of land taken in this manner makes it more difficult to obtain free homes, which of itself increases the value of the land already bought, and consequently lowers the price of labor. I believe no alien should own a single foot of American soil. I believe every railroad grant should be forfeited. All these vast tracts should be bought back by the government, and every acre given to actual settlers alone. No man has the right in justice or in fact to more land than he can cultivate, while his neighbor has none.

Land, labor and currency are the three controlling factors of every government. With proper relations between each, prosperity always follows. With lack of harmony, adversity is sure to come. Labor is dependent upon land and currency; therefore, whatever affects either is certain to be felt by labor.

A stationary, inadequate, or shrinking volume of currency is productive of greater loss to labor than all other conditions. The invention of money has corrupted the labor value of exchanges, the same as Satan corrupted the morals of Heaven. It took Michael and the hosts of Paradise to chain that monster; what will it require to bind the other? Money in its primitive and beneficial condition was the instrument, the incident, of exchange, but not the object. So long as it continued the instrument, the aid and friend, it benefited all conditions of men in a proper degree; but when it became the object, the aim and prize, that moment it ceased to do good and began to do evil. Then differences in condition began to appear, master and servant began to be seen, rich and poor broke in upon our vision. All classes of men, and all the various kinds of business, are interested in this question.

The farmers are *vitally* interested in this question. In 1866, the ten principal crops—wheat, corn, oats, barley, rye, buckwheat, potatoes, hay, cotton and tobacco—sold for $2,007,-462,231. In 1884, after a lapse of 18 years, these same crops sold for $2,043,500,481 ; only 36 millions more after 18 years of labor and improvement—a gain of less than 2 per cent in production in 18 years. The number of acres cultivated was nearly doubled, the number of farms and farm hands were doubled, agricultural machinery was greatly improved, and yet the products of 1884 brought the farmer less than 2 per cent more than the production of 1866.

The annual income of the fourteen principal States of the Union is about five thousand seven hundred millions. This is the estimated value of agricultural products and manufactured goods together. Of this total estimate, only nine hundred and forty-one millions is allowed for the products of the farmer and grazier and fruit-grower! That means that the most absolutely necessary of all the industries receives for its annual share of the common increase of the land *one-sixth* of the entire home-made income of the nation.

In 1870, the number engaged in agriculture was about seven millions. Those engaged in manufactures were about two millions. Since then the population of the country has increased from thirty-eight to fifty-two millions. The increase has been larger in the first class than in the second. The proportion of agriculturists to the other class is therefore not far from eight to two. Four times as many farmers as artisans, and these receive only one-sixth of the national income from the two branches of industry. If four times six are twenty-four, then the farmer has one twenty-fourth of the annual benefits of industry and civilization, and the factory mechanic or artisan, or *somebody else* has the rest!

Some farmer will say we can buy more with a dollar than ever before. Can you pay any more debts? Can you pay any more interest? What will it purchase more of? Nothing but the fruits of someone's else labor.

One common error which the world has fallen into, and which leads to many other mistakes, is that money buys products. Products always buys money instead of money purchasing products. The application of low wages proves this conclusively. Low wages or prices, in most cases are the result of competition among laborers or producers for money. The one who will pay the most for it, that is will part with the greatest amount of labor or its products for the smallest amount, gets the money. With money for any length of time the object and not the instrument of this competition, commerce or exchange becomes a species of confiscation as it now is. It means the products of one set of laborers competing with the products of another set of laborers; and money feasting and enriching itself on their disasters.

It is a doubtful advantage for the farmer to buy cotton cloth for five cents per yard that is really worth ten, when in consequence of the low prices of this and other products he is compelled to part with his wheat at a beggarly price to enable the producers of these products to purchase it. In this exchange money is the object because of its scarcity, and not the incident or instrument as it would be if it were sufficiently abundant. The great majority of ideas we hear regarding money comes from the owners of money. This of itself has fastened upon the people a line of thought in some instances absolutely fatal to their own best interests. They say a day's work will buy as much as it ever would. That may be true, but there are three millions of our people, at the present time unable to find the day's work. They tell us a dollar will purchase as much of the necessities of life as ever before, yet the great difficulty lies in getting the dollar. The true way to examine this great question is, how many *dollars* will a day's work purchase, or how many dollars will the products of labor buy? This is the correct test, and when labor or its products will purchase less dollars to-day than a year ago, the proof is positive that money is dearer and consequently everything else cheaper. Compare interest on money now and a few years ago with the price received for products. It will not only prove that money has increased in value but that it must be included in all "other things" that are cheapened, in order to bring about anything like fair play. Fifteen years ago money rented at ten per cent and wheat sold for two dollars per bushel; fifty bushels paid the interest on one thousand dollars. Now money loans at seven per cent and wheat sells at seventy cents per bushel; instead of taking fifty bushels to pay the interest it requires one hundred. If the use of money had lessened in value with wheat, interest would be to-day three and one-half per cent. Nothing in the end is cheap to one producer that is made so at the loss of another producer.

Let us examine carefully the wage statement of the last 40 years from the census reports. I will take up the manufactures, only:

In 1850, there were 957,000 hands employed. They produced, less raw material and wear of machinery, nett, $437,-000,000. Average wages, each, $248. Multiplying the number of employes by the average wages received gives us the following solution: The laborers received 54 per cent of this increased value as wages; the employers received 46 per cent of the same for profits. Or, each laborer received $248, and each employer received from the same laborer's profit on his labor $209.

During 1860, 1,300,000 hands produced $805,000,000; wages, $292; labor received 47 per cent, capital 53 per cent; each laborer received $292; gave capital $327.50.

During 1870, 2,000,000 hands produced $1,310,000,-000; wages, $310; labor received 47 per cent, capital

53 per cent; each laborer received $310; gave capital $345.

During 1880, 2,739,000 hands produced $1,834,000,000; wages, $346; labor received 51 2-3 per cent, capital 48 1-3; each laborer received $346; gave capital $323.50.

Of course, this vast amount of profit does not go into the pockets of manufacturers, wholly. A portion pays rent, taxes, interest—pays for lawyers, directors, etc., etc. The fact I desire to impress is, that fully one-half of the wealth produced by the laborer goes from him and into the pockets of those whose interest it is to take with each year more and more of labor's products, with no return whatever. In this difference between wages paid and the proceeds of labor lies hidden the germ of all profit, interest and rent, of all pauperism, all want, and nearly all crime. How true the poet:

"The seed ye sow another reaps;
The wealth ye find another keeps."

For these reasons and from these causes, laborers have been compelled to band together, and are putting into practice in all parts of the world, in one form or another, the God-given right of self-protection. For years capital has considered itself thoroughly entrenched behind the law, but to-day it is looking up the weak points. It has heard the sullen murmur.

"Do you dream," said the old Sheik Ilderim, of Medina, a thousand years ago, to certain Roman ingrates, "do you dream, because the Prophet of Allah dwells now beyond the bridge of Al Sirat, that therefore he is dumb, and deaf, and blind? I tell you, by the splendor of God! there is tempest brooding on his brow, there is lightning gathering in his soul for you!"

Men often ask what has brought about the present labor movement and the order of Knights of Labor? It began with the employer losing personal feeling toward his laborers, by looking upon them as so many beasts of burden ; regarding their efforts as so much commodity sold in the market. They were hired for the cheapest price, worked to the utmost limit of endurance, and, when used up, thrown aside like any other old and worthless machinery. The employers grew richer ; luxury and extravagance increased among them. The thinking laborer, noticing this, asked himself : "Is my condition improved?" He could but know it had not improved. His daily bread was not earned with less toil, nor was he any more certain of steady work. Being brought together in large shops with those of like condition, what was more natural than to talk over these matters, to discuss their wrongs and sufferings. A class feeling soon developed under these circumstances, which could only end in united action. Free competition imposed no restraints upon the powerful—they were at liberty to exploit the poor to their heart's content. The strength on the one side was so great and the ability to resist on the other so insignificant that there could exist no freedom of contract. As Sismondi said : "The rich man labored to increase his gains, the poor man to satisfy the cravings of his stomach. The one could wait, the demands of the other were imperative." As the knowledge of their wrongs became more apparent, the yoke of oppression began to get heavier. At last the idea of banding together for mutual protection against a common foe began to obtain and has resulted in these trade unions, Knights of Labor and—don't start—Grangers. Let me say at this point : United Labor, to-day, does not seek charity, does not ask for alms, is not begging bread. Instead of this it stands before the world demanding justice, asking for its God-given rights, and seeking for those privileges that were born with the human family—that of earning honorably the food it eats and the clothes it wears. These demands must be granted, these wrongs must be righted, or the whole fabric of our civilization will crumble as has others. The interests of the farmer and the Knights of

Labor are identical. Both are at war with a common enemy—monopolies or corporations.

Did you ever think what a corporation is, and its use ? It is an artificial agency of man destined to countervail certain great natural and salutary laws. It is a natural law that the man who acquires capital shall administer it ; his administration of it and his responsibility for such administration being of the essence of his proprietorship, such use of it should cease with his death. In other words, the natural law which operates to prevent the irresponsible use of capital and the undue accumulation of wealth is the law of personal responsibility for what a man has, and that it shall be distributed at his death. Corporations never die ; they keep on accumulating capital and power, defying the law of death, which arrests all human enterprises. The enormous advantages of corporations over individuals is noticed at a glance. This is one of the vested rights we read so much about.

When you hear of the next labor strike, don't get cross don't say that these Knights are disturbing business, but send them some wheat, or pork or beef—something that will sustain them in this fight. They are contending for living wages, that will enable them to pay you good prices for your products, that in the end you can pay that mortgage or that note or account without quite so much hard labor. The people are not blind to their wants, neither are they oblivious to the danger, that threatens not only them but our whole social condition. They know a permanent laboring class is being formed ; they realize the full import of that situation, because they know the conditions under which it is possible to exist. A permanent laboring class is a certain number of our people doomed to perpetual servitude ; without hope, with nothing better in prospect than the everyday drudgery of the slave. Any change for them would be better ; they could be no worse ; from this fact comes the great danger. John Stuart Mill says: "If the bulk of the human race are always to remain as at present, slaves to toil in which they have no interest and therefore feel no interest, drudging from early morning till late at night for bare necessaries, and with all the intellectual and moral deficiencies which that implies—without resources either in mind or feeling—untaught, for they cannot be better taught than fed ; selfish, for their thoughts are all required for themselves ; without interest or sentiments as citizens and members of society, and with a sense of injustice rankling in their minds, equally for what they have not and what others have, I know not what there is which should make a person of any capacity of reason concern himself about the destinies of the human race." What a fearful picture, and yet how true ! It shows us vividly the condition of this permanent laboring class which, under our present financial laws, is rapidly forming.

O luxury ! thou curst by Heaven's decree
How ill exchanged are things like these for thee !
How do thy potions, with insidious joy,
Diffuse their pleasure only to destroy !
Kingdoms by thee, to sickly greatness grown,
Boast of a florid vigor not their own.
At every draught more large and large they grow,
A bloated mass of rank unwieldy woe ;
Till sapped their strength, and every part unsound,
Down, down they sink, and spread a ruin round.

"The iron law of wages," says Ricardo, "is the natural price of labor which is necessary to enable the laborers, one with another, to subsist and to perpetuate their race without increase or decrease."

"Labor," says Karl Marx, "is bought at its exchange value and sold at its use value." Exchange value is the least amount that will permit the laborer and his family to live, while the use value is all the employer can squeeze out of it."

"You believe, perhaps, fellow laborers and citizens," said Lassalle, "that you are human beings, that you are men. Speaking from the stand-point of political economy, you make a terrible mistake. You are nothing but a commodity, a high price for which increases your numbers, just the same as a high price for stockings increases the number of stockings, if there are not enough of them—and you are swept away. Your number is diminished by smaller wages, by what Malthus calls the preventative and positive checks to population. Just as if you were vermin, against which society wages war."

> "Ill fares the land, to hastening ills a prey,
> Where wealth accumulates, and men decay;
> Princes and lords may flourish, or may fade:
> A breath can make them, as a breath has made;
> But a bold peasantry, their country's pride,
> When once destroyed, can never be supplied."
> —*Goldsmith.*

This condition must be bettered; but how? Labor laws have proven no good, as they are easily evaded. Arbitration only weakens labor, and strengthens its oppressors. Lectures upon the duties and relations of labor and capital is but idle wind. Some factor must be brought to bear upon this question that of itself will bring about the desired change. That factor, in my judgment, is money. Through its scarcity all these evils overtake us, and by its abundance prosperity and joy return. From the earliest economic history to the present, the plain fact that an increase of money has been beneficial and a decrease disastrous to the business and prosperity of the human race has been fully recognized. In fact, the degrees between barbarism and civilization are clearly defined by the volume of the circulating medium. This is no longer a party question, it is national; its truth is appreciated by men in all parties and in all conditions of life. To the laborer, for all producers are laborers, the volume of currency is of great importance, as it fixes the price both of labor and its products. Increase the amount of currency and prices advance; decrease the amount of currency and prices fall. This rule is infallible.

Whenever prices have become adjusted to a given amount of currency, an increase of that amount, other things remaining unchanged, will cause a rise, and decrease will cause a fall, in prices. But under such conditions other things never do remain unchanged. There are powerful causes, moral and material, which invariably operate, when money is increasing in volume, to moderate the rise in prices, and to intensify their fall when it is decreasing. Hence, the fall in prices caused by a decreasing volume of money would be much greater in degree than would be the rise caused by a proportionately increasing volume.

"Whenever it becomes apparent that prices are rising and money falling in value in consequence of an increase of its volume, the greatest activity takes place in exchanges and productive enterprises. Everyone becomes anxious to share in the advantages of rising markets. The inducement to hoard money is taken away, and consequently the disposition to hoard it ceases. Its circulation becomes exceedingly active, and for the very plain reason that there could be no motive for holding or hoarding money when it is falling in value, while there would be the strongest possible motive for exchanging it for property, or the labor which creates property, when prices are rising. Under these circumstances labor comes into great demand and at remunerative wages. This results in not only increased production, but increased consumption, as the wants and expenditures of laborers increase with their earnings."

"At the Christian era the metallic money of the Roman Empire amounted to $1,800,000,000. By the end of the fifteenth century it had shrunk to less than $200,000,000. During this period a most extraordinary and baleful change took place in the condition of the world.

Population dwindled, and commerce, arts, wealth and freedom, all disappeared. The people were reduced by poverty and misery to the most degraded conditions of serfdom and slavery. The disintegration of society was almost complete. The conditions of life were so hard that individual selfishness was the only thing consistent with the instinct of self-preservation. All public spirit, all generous emotions, all the noble aspirations of man, shriveled and disappeared as the volume of money shrunk and prices fell.

History records no such disastrous transition as that from the Roman Empire to the Dark Ages. Various explanations

have been given of this entire breaking down of the framework of society, but it was certainly coincident with a shrinkage in the volume of money, which was also without historical
parallel. The crumbling of institutions kept even step and
pace with the shrinkage in the stock of money and the falling
of prices. All other attendant circumstances than these last
have occurred in other historical periods unaccompanied and
unfollowed by any such mighty disasters. It is a suggestive
coincidence that the first glimmer of light only came with the
invention of bills of exchange and paper substitutes, through
which the scanty stock of the precious metals was increased in
efficiency. But not less than the energizing influence of
Potosi and all the argosies of treasure from the New World
were needed to arouse the Old World from its comatose sleep,
to quicken the torpid limbs of industry, and to plume the
leaden wings of commerce. It needed the heroic treatment of
rising prices to enable society to reunite its shattered links, to
shake off the shackles of feudalism, to relight and uplift the
almost extinguished torch of civilization. That the disasters of
the Dark Ages were caused by decreasing money and falling
prices, and that the recovery therefrom and the comparative
prosperity which followed the discovery of America were due
to an increasing supply of the precious metals and rising
prices, will not seem surprising or unreasonable when the noble
functions of money are considered.

Money is the great instrument of association, the very
fibre of social organism, the vitalizing force of industry, the
protoplasm of civilization, and as essential to its existence as
oxygen is to animal life. Without money civilization could not
have had a beginning ; with a diminishing supply it must languish, and, unless relieved, finally perish."

"It is in a volume of money keeping even pace with advancing population and commerce, and in the resulting steadiness of prices, that the wholesome nutriment of a healthy
vitality is to be found. The highest moral, intellectual and
material development of nations is promoted by the use of
money unchanging in its value. That kind of money, instead
of being the oppressor, is one of the great instrumentalities
of commerce and industry. It is as profitless as idle machinery
when it is idle; differing from all other agencies, it cannot
benefit its owner except when he parts with it. It is only
under steady prices that the production of wealth can reach its
permanent maximum, and that its equitable distribution is possible. Steadiness in prices insures labor to all and exacts labor

from all. It gives security to credit and stability and prosperity to business. It encourages large enterprises, requiring time for their development, and crowns with success well matured and carefully executed plans. It discourages purely speculative ventures, and especially those based upon disaster. It encourages actual transactions rather than gambling on future prices. It metes out justice to both debtor and creditor, and secures credit to those who deserve it. It prevents capital from oppressing labor and labor from oppressing capital, and secures to each the just share of the fruits of industry and enterprise. It secures a reasonable interest for its use to the lenders of money, and a just share in the profits of production to the borrower. It keeps up the distinction between a mortgage and a deed. It insures a moderate competence to the many rather than colossal fortunes to the few at the expense of the many."

When the stock of money is shrinking and prices are falling, this conversion can only be made at rates continually growing more unfavorable, while at the same time the products of the laborer for whose wages sacrifices have been made are also undergoing a shrinking of money-value. Thus loss and sacrifice are encountered at every turn, and the owners of other capital than money shrink from the friction of exchange, withdraw from productive enterprises, and only exchange as much of their property for money as will suffice to meet the necessary expenditures of living, which are reduced to the most economical level, as it is principal and not income that is being consumed. Little more labor will be employed under these circumstances than is sufficient to support the owners of capital on this parsimonious basis, and as a consequence the labor market will be overstocked, and the competition between laborers will reduce wages to a starvation level. But during this period, when property is being sacrificed to meet current necessities, and laborers are being remitted to idleness and destitution, money fattens on the general disaster.

The worst effect, however, economically considered, of falling prices, is not upon existing property nor upon debtors, evil as it is, but upon laborers whom it deprives of employment and consigns to poverty, and upon society, which it deprives of that vast sum of wealth which resides potentially in the vigorous arms of the idle workman. A shrinking volume of money transfers existing property unjustly, and causes a concentration and diminution of wealth. It also impairs the value of existing property by eliminating from it that important element of value conferred upon it by the skill, energy and care of the debtors from whom it is wrested. But it does not destroy any existing property, while it does absolutely annihilate all the values producible by the labor which it condemns to idleness. The estimate is not an extravagant one that there are now in the United States four million persons willing to work, but who are idle because they cannot obtain employment. This vast poverty-stricken army is increasing, and will continue to increase, as long as falling prices shall continue to separate money-capital, the fund out of which wages are paid, from labor, and to discourage its investment in other forms of property.

Labor, unlike money, cannot be hoarded. The day's labor unperformed is so much capital lost forever to the laborer, and to society. It being his only capital, his only means of existence, the laborer cannot wait on better times for better wages. Absolute necessity forces him to dispose of it on any terms which the owners of money dictate.

These are the conditions which surround the laborer throughout the commercial world to-day. The labor of the past is enslaving the labor of the present. At least that portion of the labor of the past which has been crystallized into money is enabled through a shrinkage of its volume and while lying idle in the hands of its owners to increase its command over present labor and over all forms of property and to transform vast numbers of honest and industrious workmen into tramps and beggars. These laborers must make their wants conform to their diminished earnings. They must content themselves with such things as are absolutely essential to their existence. Consumption is therefore constantly shrinking toward such limits as urgent necessity requires. Production, which must be confined to the limits indicated by consumption, is constantly tending toward its minimum, whereas its appliances, built up under more favorable conditions, are sufficient to supply the maximum of consumption. Thus idle labor, idle money, idle machinery, and idle capital stand facing each other, and the stagnation spreads wider and wider. The future affords no hope or prospect of improvement, except through a change in financial policies.

This is my version of the cause and remedy for the present distressing condition of labor. It may not please you; it may not meet with your approval; yet it is honestly given, with the hope that it or some other theory may be applied to wipe out this misery and wretchedness.

I sincerely believe our present civilization is in danger by reason of this labor question; that our further advancement depends upon its proper solution.

When the Great Augustus was transforming a Rome of brick to a Rome of marble; when its wealth seemed rapidly increasing; when its victorious legions were extending its borders in every direction; when in its manners and customs it was becoming more and more refined; when Art and Litera‐ ture were making rapid advances, who would have prophesied then that Rome had reached its zenith, that its bright sun would go down in black midnight, that the bat and the owl would soon inhabit the palaces of the Cæsars? Yet that was true; it went down amid the gathering gloom of the Dark Ages, never to reappear. Greece also followed,

"That land of scholars and nurse of arms."

Soon we find Socrates drinking the deadly hemlock, and Demosthenes slaughtered in the sanctuary of the gods. We learn that the Huns and Vandals, together with other vast hordes from the North, swept over these nations with the besom of destruction, leaving nothing but ruins and barbarism behind.

We read of the great law-giver, Lycurgus; of the wisdom of Solon; the heroism of Leonidas; the patriotism of Cincinnatus, and the statesmanship of Græcus; of the wars of Cæsar, Trojan and Constantine. We are made acquainted with their great acts and deeds, but look in vain for the benefits or results. Why were their ideas of government, social life, and the best interests of mankind, permitted to sink into the unknown of the Dark Ages, from the Fourth to the Fifteenth centuries, a period of more than one thousand years? The broad empire of Augustus Cæsar was made bright noonday by the birth of the Son of God. Why did that star at Bethlehem sink below the horizon of human vision only to reappear at the reformation after a period of more than fourteen hundred years? Why, I ask, was a civilization begun so auspiciously, allowed to sink back into oblivion? We can only answer by saying it was true.

Was their civilization of a low order? Let us examine. What position in poetry does the Iliad of Homer, or the Æneid of Virgil occupy? Where shall we place the Phillipics of Demosthenes, or the orations of Cicero, the philosophy of Plato, or the massive intellect of Euclid or Aristotle?

Would Hannibal, Alexander or Cæsar lose by comparison with the great military commanders of the present day? No. The world never saw men in their several spheres who were their superiors. Yet, notwithstanding all this, the present generation can only look with wonder upon the ruins of their greatness, and speculate as to the means in which this wholesale destruction was brought about. Our present civilization has been made possible by fire and blood, and must be watched closely and protected carefully.

The fire which burned the body of John Huss in the early

part of the fifteenth century burns even now. A torch was lighted then which to-day brightens the universe. Belted knights led by a mitered bishop curbed the proud spirit of haughty King John, and wrested from him the first great bill of human rights—the Magna Charter.

The pride of Charles I was broken by the honest piety and unsheathed sword of Oliver Cromwell. Our own nation was carved out of an unbroken wilderness. Deeds of heroism, loyalty of purpose, and judgments unbiased by prejudice, have given us the grandest nation on the face of the earth. But amid all this greatness, and with all this prosperity, are we occupying safe grounds? Has not our civilization reached its zenith? We look about us and find poverty and distress in the midst of plenty; hunger and nakedness amid bursting granaries and crowded warehouses. The wail of the starving is wafted into the banquet halls of the wealthy. The cry of the unemployed comes up from every part of our land, and the miseries and wretchedness of poverty are seen at every turn.

Our situation is almost analogous to that of Rome and Greece. Will it end as did they? Who can tell? Then, the legions, the army, whose aid and friendship enabled any one to govern, was bought and sold and the people, the oppressed, paid the tribute-money. Now, our public offices are put up at public auction, and those who have the longest purse and the most elastic conscience are usually the successful bidders.

It is claimed that we could not go back to barbarism, as there is no barbarism to conquer us. Go into the by-ways and hedges of civilization, the slums of our cities and the yards of our penitentiaries and jails. What do you find there? Worse foes to the elevating sentiments of civilization than ever were the Huns and Vandals of old. The whole world has gone mad for gain. Money seems to be the only incentive for activity. Everything is swallowed up in that one blind rage. Present joys, future prospects, kindly hopes and even the future world is valued in dollars and cents. When John sent his messenger to Christ, he directed him to ask, "Art thou he that should come, or do we look for another?" Christ said, "Go, show John those things which ye now hear and see. The blind receive their sight, and the lame walk; the lepers are cleansed and the deaf hear; the dead are raised up." Was that all? No, that which by being last was witnessed as the climax of all his deeds, more important than either: "The poor have the gospel preached unto them." Going into our churches of the present day, knowing the poverty and distress among the people, knowing the many ragged coats and threadbare garments which necessity compels to be worn, may we not ask, upon beholding the rich clothing and costly apparel seen on every side: Is this the religion of Christ, or are we to look for another?

This state of things can not endure.

Something must be done to break down the barrier between rich and poor; between those who have and those who have not. A right to live comfortably, work honorably, and act independently, must in some manner and through some medium be granted to all. For six thousand years Capital in various forms has oppressed Labor. For six thousand years the cries of the victims and the shouts of the victors have mingled together. For six thousand years the wild shrieks of the vanquished and the hoarse laugh of their persecutors have together ascended to the throne of God.

Well might we exclaim: "How long, oh, Lord, how long!" During all these years this black midnight has enveloped labor. During all these years labor has struggled manfully to dispel this gloom. Some have prayed earnestly to see the morning, but went down to their graves in the gloaming. Others have worked earnestly and well, but died in the even ing. Some fought on and hoped on, but went over to the wide beyond before the meridian of midnight. Again, others, believing the time almost at hand, plunged into the thickest of the fight, only to perish in the small hours of the waning night. But to us, here in the last quarter of the nineteenth century, are given, if we wisely improve our time, the long-looked-for privilege of beholding the gray in the east which betokens the sure rising of the orb of day. And unless these signs fail, unless we are recreant to our most solemn duties, we shall see, before the beginning of a new century, the sun, that great prototype of creative power, riding majestically high in the blue dome of heaven, sending down to earth its life-giving rays, upon Labor, protected in its rights, free in its action, and permitted to mark out its own destiny.

INDEX.

——o——

THE

PHILOSOPHY OF PRICE,

AND ITS

RELATION TO DOMESTIC CURRENCY.

SECOND EDITION.

By N. A. DUNNING.

"Ill fares the land to hastening ills a prey,
Where wealth accumulates and men decay."—*Goldsmith.*

Price · · · 25 Cents.

WASHINGTON, D. C.:
THE NATIONAL ECONOMIST PUBLISHING CO.
1890.

The National Economist

HAND-BOOK

—: OF :—

FACTS

—: AND :—

ALLIANCE INFORMATION.

A useful volume of general and statistical information, accurately prepared and carefully arranged, with a complete index, which makes it a treasury for reference. It gives every desirable kind of information in regard to the great farmers' movement, including many persons prominent in that work. It is profusely illustrated with portraits of prominent Alliance men. It is published annually, and keeps abreast of the very latest information and thought in politics, statistics, and economics Considering its intrinsic value, it is the cheapest book published of this character in the world.

SUBSCRIPTION PRICE, 25 CENTS.

Address publishers,

The National Economist,

WASHINGTON, D. C.

THE NATIONAL ECONOMIST.

OFFICIAL ORGAN

OF THE

NATIONAL FARMERS ALLIANCE

AND

INDUSTRIAL UNION.

PUBLISHED WEEKLY AT WASHINGTON, D. C.

SUBSCRIPTION PRICE, $1.00 PER YEAR.

———TESTIMONIAL.———

From the minutes of the National Farmers Alliance and Industrial Union, St. Louis meeting.

WHEREAS, THE NATIONAL ECONOMIST, our adopted National Official Organ, has so boldly and fearlessly advocated our cause and defended our principles; Therefore, be it

Resolved by this National Body, That we heartily approve of the course it has pursued, and recommend that every member of the Order should subscribe for and read the paper as one of the best means of education in the way of industrial freedom.

www.ingramcontent.com/pod-product-compliance
Lightning Source LLC
Chambersburg PA
CBHW060607030726
47498CB00005B/1585